Corporate Dreams

Corporate Dreams

Big Business in American Democracy from the Great Depression to the Great Recession

James Hoopes

Rutgers University Press

New Brunswick, New Jersey, and London

LIBRARY OF CONGRESS CATALOGING-IN-PUBLICATION DATA

Hoopes, James, 1944–
   Corporate dreams : big business in American democracy from the
Great Depression to the great recession / James Hoopes.
      p. cm.
   Includes bibliographical references and index.
   ISBN 978–0–8135–5130–2 (hardcover : alk. paper)
   1. Corporate culture—United States—History.   2. Business and politics—
United States—Case studies.   3. Political ethics—United States.   4. United
States—Politics and government—2001–2009.   5. Leadership—United States—
History.   6. United States—Moral conditions.   I. Title.
   HD58.7.H646   2011
   338.0973—dc22   2010052501

A British Cataloging-in-Publication record for this book is available
from the British Library.

Visit our Web site: http://rutgerspress.rutgers.edu

Manufactured in the United States of America

For George Cotkin, faith keeper

CONTENTS

Acknowledgments   *ix*

Introduction   I

PART I   THE CORPORATE AMERICAN DREAM AT ITS HEIGHT AND IN ITS ORIGINS

I   *The Corporate American Dream*   9
2   *Corporate and National Character*   15
3   *From Public Purpose to Private Profit*   22
4   *Corporations as Enemies of the Free Market*   27

PART II   CORPORATE FAILURE AND GOVERNMENT FIX

5   *Corporate Crashes*   35
6   *Managers versus Markets*   40
7   *Corporations Blow Their Chance to End the Depression*   45
8   *Roosevelt's Confused Anticorporatism*   51

PART III   THE CORPORATION STRIKES BACK

9   *The Right to Manage*   61
10   *Corporations Recover Their Moral Authority*   67
11   *Killing the Unions Softly*   72
12   *Creating Reagan and His Voters*   76

Part IV WHAT MANNER OF MAN(AGER)?

13 *Masking the Arrogance of Power*   87
14 *Responsibility versus Profit at General Motors*   93
15 *Critics of Managerial Character*   100
16 *JFK's Pyrrhic Victory over U.S. Steel*   106

Part V   THE CORPORATION IN THE
         WILDERNESS AGAIN

17 *McNamara and the Staffers*   115
18 *The False Confidence of the Anticorporatists*   122
19 *Corporate America Loses World Supremacy*   130
20 *Laying the Groundwork for the Corporation's
    Cultural Comeback*   137

Part VI LEADERSHIP

21 *Managing by Values*   145
22 *Creating the Concept of Corporate Culture*   152
23 *Inventing the Leadership Development Industry*   156
24 *Reagan Aids Corporations by Bashing Government*   163

Part VII ENTREPRENEURSHIP

25 *Supply-Siders versus the Big Corporation*   173
26 *Reengineering the Corporation*   180
27 *George W. Bush, Enron, and the Great Recession*   189
28 *Can the Corporate American Dream Be Saved?*   198

Notes   209
Index   219

Corporate Dreams

Introduction

LUNCHING ALONE in a business restaurant in Shanghai, I received a conversational gambit from the waiter. I was different, she said, from her usual clientele of "corporate types," a phrase she had probably learned from the corporate types themselves. They had, according to her, "cold hearts." "They're busy," I answered, "and far from home. Many have warm hearts." "No," she said with unusual assertiveness for the waiter types I had met in China. "People with warm hearts work in restaurants and bars."

Like the Shanghai waiter, we all define the moral world by antitheses such as warm hearts and cold hearts, corporate types and tavern types. Without evil, there would be no idea of good; without oppression, no freedom; without wrong, no right. Moral realists, unable to conceive of the elimination of evil, oppression, or cold hearts, aim instead to minimize them, to contain them, or to use them against themselves. The eighteenth-century American founders believed that liberty required authority. "If men were angels," James Madison wrote in the Federalist Papers, "no government would be necessary." Not an end to power but separation of power was the basis of American freedom.

Into this attempt to restrain power, this *novo ordo seclorum* or new order for the ages, as the founders called it, was soon to intrude the business corporation, bringing with it a new moral antinomy—corporate management versus the free market. The corporation created vast wealth and, with it, undemocratic managerial power to govern Americans at work. Second only to our democratic political system, the unelected power of business corporations is the modern world's most important social innovation, and it gave rise to the mid-twentieth-century American Dream. Yet it did not do so on its own but rather because it was forced to do so by a democratic society. Getting the relation right between society and the corporation will be central to any possible revival of the American Dream.

The American Dream is only one of the corporate dreams explained in this book. It came to fruition, at least for a time, whereas other corporate dreams have remained fantasies. Mainly figments of the managerial imagination, they are aimed at making corporate life seem more consistent with democracy than it can really be. These managerial fancies are harmless enough, perhaps, in corporate life, but they should now be scrapped, when corporate culture is becoming more and more our mainstream culture.

Yet in the popular mind and media, the business corporation gets scant attention as a social or cultural institution. News outlets report the ups and downs of the stock market, but comparatively little is said about the general question of the business corporation's ambiguous relation to a free society or about the particular danger that has arisen in recent years: that corporate culture could insidiously corrupt democratic values. In today's America, for example, there is almost no recognition that the corporate world's naive and unwittingly arrogant cult of moral leadership is a threat to democratic culture. The popular but mistaken idea of values-based leadership has seeped from the corporate sphere into American culture at large, where it endangers the old democratic recognition that power corrupts. Even CEOs, if they are wise and generous, will guard themselves against such conceit. Running the company well is the goal. Claiming the mantle of moral leadership is the first step in taking one's eye off the ball.

Awareness of the danger of corporate culture is the only safeguard against it. Otherwise, the "furnishings" of the mind may be "little by little changed" as a great historian wrote of the evolving ideas of seventeenth-century New England Puritans as they encountered unexpected economic opportunities and temptations in the New World. Through a process "hardly perceptible to the actors themselves," they eventually came to look "upon themselves with amazement, hardly capable of understanding how they had come to be what they were."[1]

This book aims to keep in place the democratic furnishings of the mind through a viewpoint that, for want of a better term, I call moderate anticorporatism. The goal is not to attack those who live the corporate life, let alone the wealth they create, but only to reveal some dangerous corporate confusions and illusions. Too much of what is written on the subject of business management denies the reality of the tension between democracy and corporate life—or succeeds merely in covering it up. We are most likely to balance a corporate economy and a democratic polity, however, by recognizing the tension between them and maintaining it.

My intention here is to maintain the friction between corporate life and democracy by revealing the little-known political, social, and intellectual history of corporate America. For example, the role of the corporation in the English colonization of North America is frequently forgotten. Colonies were often corporations, such as the Virginia Company and the Massachusetts Bay Company. Even after the English monarchy revoked those charters and took direct control over the colonies, the crown still relied on the service of corporations like the East India Company, which the colonists came to loathe as a symbol of monopoly and oppression. After the American Revolution, the new nation was understandably suspicious of corporate power. Why and how this early anticorporatism was subdued is one of the major themes of the early parts of this book. Only gradually did early Americans' anticorporatism give way to today's situation, where the corporation is accepted as a more or less natural part of the free market.

A renewed anticorporatism was manifest, of course, in the antitrust laws of the late nineteenth century and in the government regulations of the early-twentieth-century Progressive Era. But only in the Great Depression of the 1930s did antipathy to corporations re-enter the political mainstream with something like the intense suspicion with which eighteenth-century Americans had viewed the East India Company. And that Depression-era anticorporatism did not easily come to pass. Only after the failure of the First New Deal, with its mistaken confidence that corporate leaders would lead the way to renewed prosperity, did the Roosevelt administration create, in the Second New Deal, the business regulation and labor laws that made real the 1950s American Dream.

Undoing the New Deal and identifying corporate freedom with political freedom became the work of subsequent generations of managers and conservative ideologues. They have succeeded to an extraordinary degree, despite setbacks in the late 1960s and early 1970s, when managerial arrogance in both government and business—the loss of the Vietnam War and the loss of supremacy in the automobile industry to the Japanese—shook Americans' faith in corporate leadership. It took the 1970s rise of the leadership development industry to redeem corporate management by teaching it to talk up values and to dismiss subsequent corruption and incompetence such as was revealed in the 2007 credit collapse as a matter of a few bad apples.

There is, however, a new and subtle anticorporatism abroad in the land. It takes the form of faith in entrepreneurship and small business, supposedly facilitated by the communications revolution. Although I sympathize to a significant degree with this implicitly anticorporate entrepreneurialism, I try to show in the last section of the book that it is probably overstated. Big business can be plenty entrepreneurial itself and, in many instances, can make better use of communications technology than can small enterprise.

So I conclude that the large corporation is likely to be with us for a long time to come. It is a dangerous institution, as early American victims of the East India Company understood perhaps better than we do today. But it is also a useful institution. History has turned up no better form of organization than the business corporation for enriching the world and improving humanity's material lot. Thus this book proposes moderate anticorporatism as the right approach for living with corporate power, accepting of its usefulness and wary of its danger.

Moderate anticorporatism no more seeks to destroy the business corporation than do moderate antigovernment ideologues seek to abolish government. Thomas Jefferson was moderately antigovernment in the sense that he wanted not to destroy government but to guard against its potential tyranny. So too, a moderate anticorporatism would seek not to deny the large benefits of our business economy but only to guard against corporate power that hurts rather than helps the people.

To say that we need to develop some anticorporatism may seem strange. Everyone has a grudge against one corporation or another. Isn't there already a good supply of anticorporatism on offer? Yes, but as opposed to antigovernment ideology, which is systematic and sustained, anticorporatism is reactive and episodic. In the fall of 2008, for instance, the CEOs of the American automakers flew in corporate jets to Washington to request a financial bailout from Uncle Sam. Howls of anticorporate outrage flooded the airwaves and the Internet. What hubris to ask for a helping hand from hard-pressed taxpayers while traveling in luxury! The next week the humbled CEOs returned to Washington, traveling this time by car, got their bailout, and the anticorporatism subsided.

We need a more sustained, thorough, and wise anticorporatism. Every few years there is a major corporate scandal in the United States. The aftermath, with equal regularity, features high-minded CEOs who speak of rebuilding trust, a program that the rest of us should reject. We demonstrate our democratic spirit through wariness about our freely elected political leaders. We should demonstrate our spirit of economic freedom through suspicion of our unelected corporate chiefs. If "that government is best which governs least," then corporate power, which governs much, needs watching and should be eyed with distrust.

Moderate anticorporatists will support public policies that make for a healthy business environment and entrepreneurial opportunity. Companies that do well by doing good are especially deserving of our support. We should be no less supportive of good companies than of good government. However, appreciation of virtuous firms can be heightened only by recognizing the business corporation as the moral paradox it is, an entity that improves our prosperity by subjecting us to overbearing managerial power. How the people can preserve the productivity of corporate power while protecting themselves against its abuse is a timeless problem. Madison might just as well have said that if we were not born hungry there would be no need for managers. I once heard a witty congressman acknowledge that "politicians are bozos," only to add that "the voters are no prize either." Fractious democracy can be antithetical to the social coherence on which prosperity often depends. To this organizational challenge of economic life, history has unfortunately so far turned up no better answer than corporate power.

The Shanghai waiter was partly right. Too often does ice water run in corporate veins. The danger of cold-heartedness increases in proportion to power, same as always. And she was partly wrong. Ardent corporate types are numbered in the millions. May the recognition that corporate corruption can be cultural as well as financial stir them to yet more democratic warmth.

PART I

*The Corporate
American Dream
at Its Height and
in Its Origins*

CHAPTER 1

The Corporate American Dream

CORPORATE CAPITAL AND FACTORY GRIT gave rise to the American Dream. At its 1950s zenith, the dream included suburban bungalows, stay-at-home moms, and a middle-class life for the common man. But the squeaky cleanness stopped at the workplace door. Grimy hands were the reality behind the reverie. Manufacturing jobs and heavy industry were the heart of America's mid-twentieth-century prosperity. Giant corporations invested huge sums in plant and equipment, supporting mass production, economies of scale, and low unit costs.

Despite the business corporation's central role in the American Dream, the intellectual and social history of the corporation gets little attention. Now we seem to be waking into a dreary new day. It is time to clear our heads and recognize that corporations made the shimmer solid. Not of their own free will did corporations create the American Dream. Rather, they shared their wealth at the behest of labor unions and government. The mass manufacturers who dominated the mid-twentieth-century economy needed tens and sometimes even hundreds of thousands of people to run their factories. Ponderously bureaucratic and slow to change, the mass producers made good targets for government regulation and for the labor unions those regulations often supported.

By the 1950s some corporate managers saw labor unions as a positive force, others as a bad bargain. Either way, the American Dream rested on a symbiotic relation between mass producers and organized labor. Unions extracted the high wages that in turn enabled Americans to consume the factories' output. With organized labor delivering middle-class incomes, workers gladly supported the labor movement. Thirty percent of the American workforce was unionized in the 1950s. The largest share worked in mass production. But tradesmen and journeymen—carpenters, plumbers, electricians, and others—also

benefited from union organization. The union umbrella shielded unor-
ganized workers as well. Non-union employers had to pay good wages
to compete with unionized shops for quality labor. Some anti-union
companies paid well in order to fend off unionization.

High pay for working people made the United States the world's
first middle-class society. America was a gigantic diamond, wider in the
middle than at the top or bottom. All previous societies, at least all large
ones, were pyramids with a small upper class at the apex and a vast lower
class at the base. Between the apex and base of previous societies fell
the traditional middle-class occupations of law, medicine, education,
small business, corporate management, government administration, and
religious ministry. But in 1950s America, factory workers could earn
incomes equal to some of those traditional middle-class occupations.
For the first time in history, there was a society where people earning
middle-class incomes outnumbered those at the bottom.

Not just middle-class wages for working people but a measure of
control over high incomes was part of the 1950s recipe for prosperity.
The financial sector, corporate management, lawyers, doctors, and other
top-tier earners did not claim nearly as large a portion of the national
income as they did half a century later. High earners also faced steeply
progressive tax rates left over from World War II, further curbing
moneyed pretense. With income distributed more evenly then than now,
working Americans had the purchasing power to consume the country's
industrial output. Banks were well regulated, government deficits within
reason, inflation and interest rates relatively low. Easy credit did not fuel
inordinate speculation but kept the wheels of industry turning.

Many corporate jobs carried good benefits. During World War II,
the government had ordered wage freezes to fight inflation. Employers
therefore competed for workers through non-wage benefits such as
health insurance, a corporate perk that surged after the war. In the 1950s,
as now, employers matched their employees' taxes for Social Security,
a system that had been established during the Great Depression of the
1930s. In 1961, Congress added Medicare to the Social Security program, providing health insurance for seniors. Less and less did Americans
suffer nightmares of poverty from illness and old age.

Midcentury Americans also slept well in the knowledge that their
children's futures were secure. After high school and then military

service for many men and some women, young couples had the security to start families thanks to plentiful factory jobs with ever-rising union pay. And these working parents could afford to send their kids to college. Children of the working class moved fairly easily into traditional middle-class careers in law, medicine, and education. Or a college degree might lead to a management job in industry. The ranks of corporate CEOs included children of blue-collar workers. What better proof could there be that the shiny American Dream was a rock-hard reality?

Wasn't there always an American Dream? Yes, from Jamestown and Plymouth Rock onward, many Americans have looked optimistically to the future and believed that life would be better for their children. Yet Americans have dreamt not only of prosperity but of liberty. So we have mixed top-down corporations with bottom-up politics. Democratic government has made for freedom. The corporate economy has made for prosperity. This mélange of corporate power and democratic freedom is mostly ignored, even by those who live intensely corporate lives. Americans may look to the stock market to improve their individual fortunes. But when they seek to understand the economic success of their society at large, they usually credit political and economic freedom, not the top-down hierarchy of the business corporation.

Those who do think about the fact that we are a corporate society often do not like it. They see, even if only implicitly, that the corporation is a fundamentally undemocratic institution. Only reluctantly do they accept the business corporation as a basis of the American Dream. This book supports those who recognize that business corporations endanger democracy. But even though the business corporation bears watching, it also needs nurturing. The fact that the business corporation was the basis of the American Dream means that it is worth the work it takes to balance corporate prosperity and democratic freedom.

It bears noting, however, that "the American Dream" is a mid-twentieth-century phrase. Its original meaning has been lost in popular expression. It originally connoted a vague foreboding about the corporate form of the good life in America, an unvoiced fear that all was not well in the self-proclaimed land of the free. The difficulty of balancing freedom and prosperity, democratic government and the corporate economy, was on the mind of the forgotten man who coined the term. James Truslow Adams, a once-well-known historian, wrote in his 1931 book, *The Epic of America*, that Americans dream of more than a fat paycheck. Americans, he said, dream of a society where "each man and each woman" has the freedom to attain "the fullest stature of which they are innately capable."[1]

Adams meant that Americans should have the freedom to develop their characters as well as their bank accounts. A free person should aim at more than the backyard patios and swimming pools that symbolized 1950s prosperity. Not acquisitiveness and comfort but energy and audacity—whether to fight tyranny or to launch a business—ought to characterize a free people. The American Dream, according to Adams, "is not a dream of motor cars and high wages merely."[2] The "merely" made him sound a little defensive about freedom, a little worried that liberty had been forgotten amid the 1920s boom with which his book concluded. And in the early 1950s, a generation after Adams's book was published, "freedom" did seem, in many parts of American society, a hollow mantra.

A viewer who judged by the color of the faces in 1950s television commercials would have thought that only whites and never blacks used dish detergents and aluminum foil. Gays and lesbians lived closeted lives, sometimes full of hellish self-loathing from internalized bigotry. Women were largely shut out of the well-paying factory jobs they had filled during World War II when eight million men were in the military. Wartime surveys had shown that women had wanted to stay at work.[3] But in the postwar era their corporate opportunities were largely limited to the secretarial pool. Many women had returned to their traditional occupations—teaching, nursing, and homemaking.

There was certainly no relief for any of these injustices in the corporate world. Business corporations had shown and would continue to show that when it came to social justice they followed the crowd. Only when pressed, whether by consumers or government, would the ordinary corporation support movements for justice. Nineteen-fifties Americans, preoccupied with the communist challenge, did not press corporations to create a more just society. Self-righteous notions of moral superiority governed too many citizens' view of the rest of the globe. The United States was by far the world's richest country, unscarred by the two world wars that in the first half of the twentieth century had wrecked the economies of other major nations. More than a few

Americans surrendered to the temptation to interpret their country's singular prosperity as a mark of divine favor, a reward for the ideal of freedom that they loudly professed and in the practice of which they often fell short.

Moral complacency compensated for deeper fear of undefeated devils. Priding themselves on their own liberty, Americans worried that freedom was in retreat in the rest of the world. Soviet Russia and atheistic communism held sway over puppet regimes in eastern Europe. China had fallen to the communists in 1949, a shock to American Christians for whom conversion of the Chinese had long been a missionary goal. Communists were also advancing in strength in southeast Asia. Many citizens feared that the United States would not or could not turn back the Red tide. A seeming chance to roll back communism in 1950—the Korean War—did no such thing. American troops drove back an invasion of South Korea by the communist North, only to have the Chinese communists rush to the rescue of their puppet regime. After three years of fighting and fifty thousand Americans killed, the war ended in an armistice that left the communists in their original position.

The communist challenge abroad prompted Americans' fear of enemies within. Witch hunts ferreted out those of suspect loyalty in the government, in universities, and in the news and entertainment industries. Anticommunist zealots were the actual enemies of democracy as they fell into a frightened patriotism inimical to freedom. Yet some of the 1950s American pride in freedom was productive. On racial justice, where America fell farthest from its ideals, there was increasing impetus for improvement. A decade earlier, after all, the United States had helped to defeat Nazi racism, making it increasingly difficult to deny the injustice of racial oppression at home. Cold War competition with communism for influence among newly liberated peoples of color in Asia and Africa made racial injustice increasingly untenable in America.

The civil rights movement was stirring. Bolstered by the 1954 Supreme Court decision integrating public schools, civil rights proponents would soon be registering voters, sitting in at lunch counters, and everywhere demanding equality. Endangering and sometimes sacrificing their lives in opposition to racial segregation, the nonviolent activists were true freedom fighters. The civil rights movement focused on schools rather than corporations because education represented

America's commitment to democracy. Corporations are not part of public life as that phrase is usually understood. Only after the schools were integrated did civil rights activists begin to deal with the fact that corporations were the locus of prosperity and press them to become "equal opportunity/affirmative action" employers.

The laggard movement toward racial justice in the corporate economy reveals how wrong it is to speak of ideals as if they are fantasies come true. To balance freedom and prosperity takes hard work. To combine democracy and corporate prosperity is not only a dream but a job.

CHAPTER 2

Corporate and National Character

TO LIVE IN A DREAM is to endanger one's character. The American Dream of freedom and prosperity must be understood as a goal, not a given. To assume that a dream is inherently real is to encourage indolence and, eventually, a rude awakening. Character—whether individual, corporate, or national—is a matter of integrity, not just in the sense of acting honestly but in the sense of integrating our various passions and ideals in a fairly harmonious personality. An integrated personality gives strength of character. We cannot act consistently if our passions diverge too far from our proclaimed ideals. A well-integrated personality is a matter of degree, not perfection. We all have passions that conflict with our ideals. Americans often lust after chocolate yet long for slimness.

So there is a paradox in the notion of a well-integrated character. One sign of psychological health is awareness of not being a fully integrated personality. Real integrity includes honest recognition, not denial, of one's inner conflicts. Awareness of our internal conflicts may allow us to achieve a healthy balance. It is better to indulge moderately in both chocolate and thinness than to take a bender on one or the other. Denial of internal conflict can lead to an outburst of repressed desires in a self-destructive binge.

America, with its democratic government and corporate economy, has long suffered from denial of internal psychological conflicts. Our political freedom depends on bottom-up democracy while our economic prosperity is based on top-down corporate power. Americans vote to elect a president once every four years. The rest of the time they do what the boss tells them. Exaggerated though that statement is, it contains a core truth. The American Dream is based on an unnatural alliance between corporatism and democracy. The tension between democratic freedom and corporate prosperity has too often gone unnoticed.

Yes, most people understand that corporate power is undemocratic and often unjust. Who does not have a grievance against one corporate monster or another, whether in the oil industry or in finance, in health care or in high tech? Still, many Americans accept the business corporation as if it were a natural part of a free, democratic society. After all, democracy in practice has plenty of injustice. Corporate wrongdoing can therefore easily be misread as one more flaw in our democratic system rather than as part of a different, undemocratic system. To the casual observer there is no necessary contradiction between the American political system and the American economic system.

In other words, the assumption is all too common that we live in a coherent culture. Too few see that our lives are shaped by two different systems. Our corporate economy and our democratic government are, at heart, as different as two species of animals. Watch the right-wing talking heads on television wax eloquent about capitalism and democracy as if a corporate economy and a free society were one and the same. They occasionally acknowledge corporate wrongdoing and see it as a clash with integrity and the rule of law. But they never see, or at least do not admit, that the very existence of the business corporation is a contradiction of basic democratic values. To them, corporations and democracy, capitalism and freedom, have come to seem like blood kin.

If we too often fail to see the tension between corporatism and democracy in the national character, what about the character of individual Americans? Almost no one asks anymore—though Americans used to ask, as chapter 15 shows—whether corporate life is good for the character of individual citizens. Democratic suspicion of power is weakened by today's corporate cult of moral leadership, which encourages those at the top of the heap and even some naive souls at the bottom to suppose that a high office indicates virtue in its occupant.

In the corporate world, ethics far too often begins with the assumption that one knows what is right and the only question is how to make right prevail. The great questions of moral philosophy such as the difficulty of self-knowledge and the challenge that so strategic a focus on ethics poses to one's character are utterly lost and, with them, the moral caution that a democracy needs in its citizens. The art of spin overshadows substance among too many corporate denizens, and in the end the spinners deceive themselves.

The big question of business ethics today—a question almost entirely ignored—is how corporate life affects personal integrity and renders citizens fit or unfit for democracy. Keeping one's hands off other people's money, treating stakeholders well, and sustaining the natural world are the right things to do, but they are not the fundamental issues of business ethics. To make the utmost progress on such issues requires the building of good corporate character in people and companies, character that treats leadership and values as goals in themselves rather than as instruments of corporate profit.

This book, far from urging that we chuck the corporate system, only suggests that we recognize its tension with democracy. The tension between democracy and corporatism is useful. Liberty must be balanced by order, freedom by power. Democratic societies need the economic services of undemocratic corporations. The not-so-easy trick is to ensure that corporations are the servants, not the masters. To sustain the delicate balance where corporatism and democracy can live with rather than against each other requires either skill or luck. I aim to show that the success of American political economy has involved a lot of good luck on which we would be wise not to rely too long. Corporatism and democracy are each capable of undoing the other. If we want to save the American Dream of both freedom and prosperity, we had better wake up.

One reason that many people miss the complexity of the American Dream is that it was an accident of history. All of the nation's founders dreamt of freedom, but only one of them, Alexander Hamilton, dreamt of corporations. None of them, not even Hamilton, dreamt of a middle-class society where corporate employees earned good wages. Thomas Jefferson believed that the fewer the number of wage earners in America the better: "Let us never wish to see our fellow citizens occupied at a work-bench."[1] America's foremost exponent of democracy, Jefferson warned against the danger of becoming a manufacturing nation. Manufacturers employ wage earners dependent on their bosses for their living. The result of such dependence, Jefferson thought, could only be servility, not liberty.

The sage of Monticello urged his countrymen to retain their agricultural economy in order to preserve their freedom. Independent farmers, living on their own land, would have the strength of character to face down tyranny. According to Jefferson, "Those who labor in the earth are the chosen people of God." Farmers' independence from employers gave them the "substantial and genuine virtue" necessary for a free society. Wage earners, dependent on employers, would lose the virtuous characters produced by agrarian independence. Jefferson believed that eighteenth-century England had been made despotic by its urban proletariat: "The mobs of great cities add just so much to the support of pure government, as sores do to the strength of the human body." Because "it is the manners and spirit of a people which preserve a republic in vigour," Americans could best maintain their freedom-loving characters by sticking to agriculture and shunning manufacturing.

If America remained an agricultural nation, how would it obtain whatever manufactured goods it needed? Jefferson did not know the word *outsourcing*, but it was his recipe for preserving democracy in America: "Let our workshops remain in Europe." Importation of finished products would ensure that Europe rather than America suffered the evils of a population of servile workers dependent on their employers. But Alexander Hamilton, Jefferson's great adversary, opposed out-sourcing or, as he called it, the substitution of "foreign for domestic manufacturing."[2] In 1791, as the first secretary of the treasury, Hamilton responded to a congressional request for a "Report on Manufactures." Hamilton's report rejected Jefferson's idea that agriculture should be Americans' "exclusive" occupation and asserted that they needed to develop a manufacturing sector. Without domestic manufacturing, Americans would have to exchange the "surplus of our agricultural produce" for other nations' manufactured goods. We would therefore be at the mercy of other countries' tariffs and "restrictive regulations." To protect our national independence, "a more extensive demand" for farmers' surplus must "be created at home."

Hamilton asserted that prosperity depended on productivity and productivity on technology. In the late eighteenth century, manufacturing was more amenable to machine production than was agriculture. Therefore, Hamilton believed that Jefferson's idea of importing manu-factured goods was really a program to "transfer to foreign nations" the advantages of the newest improvements in machinery and technology. One of the great boons of machine production, according to Hamilton, was that "women and children are rendered more useful by manufacturing establishments." Farmers' wives and children may have made cloth in America, but they worked at spinning wheels and house looms rather than at the spinning jennies and power looms with which English women and children clothed the world.

Hamilton scarcely had a dreamlike vision. He hoped to subject American women and children to working conditions that, on the other side of the Atlantic, would be deplored by critics as different as Charles Dickens and Karl Marx. No more than Jefferson did Hamilton foresee a manufacturing sector that would employ the great mass of Americans at middle-class wages. The coming of the American Dream was as much an accident to those who favored manufacturing as to those who opposed it.

Still, Hamilton helped to launch America's corporate economy. In 1791, he persuaded Congress to enact a corporate charter for a Bank of the United States. The bank—part of Hamilton's scheme to provide the young, cash-strapped American republic with a ready medium of exchange—worked brilliantly in expanding the money supply. That same year Hamilton got the state of New Jersey to charter a corporation to develop the falls of the Passaic River into what he hoped would be a "national manufactory." Hamilton's company, the Society for the Establishment of Useful Manufactures, was soon running in the red and got out of manufacturing. But the corporation's ownership of property abutting the Passaic's waterfalls eventually made it a profitable firm. Hamilton's company leased its lands to other mill owners and sold them water power, leading to the nineteenth-century prominence of Paterson, New Jersey, as an industrial site.

Meanwhile, the textile industry got under way in the United States without benefit of corporate charters. The earliest American textile firm was a partnership rather than a corporation. Moses Brown and Samuel Slater, the former a Providence merchant and the latter an English textile worker, built a textile mill in Pawtucket, Rhode Island, in 1789. Slater, a skilled mechanic with knowledge of textile machinery, had broken an English law forbidding such men to emigrate. Even with the benefit of Slater's technological know-how, the American textile industry developed slowly. The nation's capitalists found more attractive opportunities in international trade than in domestic manufacturing. They invested their money in ships, not machines.

Ironically, it was Jefferson, the opponent of manufacturing, who helped to divert American capitalists' attention toward machine production. In 1807, Jefferson, who was nearing the end of his presidency, imposed an embargo on American shipping as a diplomatic maneuver during the Napoleonic Wars. American capitalists had to keep their ships at home and therefore made alternative investments in textile manufacturing. By the time the embargo and then the War of 1812 were over, the United States had more than two hundred spinning mills.

And then came the power loom, thanks to industrial espionage. A wealthy Boston merchant named Francis Cabot Lowell had toured England from 1810 to 1812. Ostensibly traveling for his health, he visited Manchester mills and managed to memorize the structure of the power loom so he could build his own back home. If Lowell was an imitator in technology, he was an innovator in organization. In England, spinning and weaving were still done in separate mills, under separate owners, as in the days of hand production. Lowell integrated spinning and weaving in the factory he built at Waltham, Massachusetts, raising the efficiency of textile production and inaugurating the century and a half in which America led the world in managerial proficiency and economic productivity.

Lowell obtained a corporate charter from the state of Massachusetts, making his Boston Manufacturing Company the first successful industrial corporation in the United States. It is not clear that Lowell incorporated for economic reasons. Rather, he seems to have wanted to signal that he founded the Boston Manufacturing Company not just to make money but to serve the public good.[3] For in the early nineteenth century, American legislatures gave corporate charters mainly to businesses with a public purpose such as toll roads and bridges.

Like Jefferson, Lowell feared the development of a degenerate working class in America. Lowell staffed his factory by recruiting the readiest available supply of labor—single women from the surrounding farms. Seeking to protect their character, he housed them in decent dormitories and hired respectable matrons to safeguard their virtue. Thousands of young women soon flocked to his namesake city of Lowell, Massachusetts, to enjoy a few years of independence from fathers and brothers before taking a husband and returning to life on the farm.

But even at Lowell corporate prosperity came into conflict with freedom. By the 1830s competition had risen in the textile industry. Factory managers tried to improve their competitive position by cutting wages and raising dormitory charges. The women workers went on strike, invoking the spirit of 1776 and vowing to act in "the spirit of our Patriotic Ancestors" who "preferred privation to bondage."[4] Their strikes were sometimes successful, owing in part to the shortage of labor in America.

The Lowell manufacturers found their solution to the shortage of labor in the Irish potato blight and the resulting immigration of Celts to America. Unlike the native-born women who first staffed New England's textile mills, Irish workers could not easily return to their farms, which were famine-ridden and across the sea. They were far less likely to resist their corporate bosses. Successive waves of immigrants from disparate regions of the world would be core to American corporate prosperity. Their numbers and, therefore, relative weakness in the labor market made them a tractable workforce with which corporate America would move from textile manufacturing to heavy industries such as railroads, steel, and eventually automobiles. The challenge for workers would be to preserve the independence of character on which democracy depends.

CHAPTER 3

From Public Purpose
to Private Profit

A POORLY UNDERSTOOD but vitally important factor
in the course of American economic development was the transformation of corporations from instruments of social purpose to organizations
for individual profit. In early America corporations were created mainly
to accomplish public objectives such as the building of roads and
canals. Even early American banking corporations often had an at least
partly public purpose. The currency—the medium of exchange—that
they created was in short supply and was a desperately needed public
good.

Today, of course, the primary goal of most corporations is not to
enrich the public. Shareholders are supposed to be the corporations'
primary beneficiaries. During the nineteenth century the business corporation underwent a transformation from the people's employee to the
people's employer. *Incorporation* is a Latinate word describing the practice
of treating a group of individuals as one body (*corpus*), with a life independent of any of its members. Long before there were business corporations, there were philanthropic corporations, educational corporations,
and governmental corporations. In 1075, for example, William the
Conqueror issued a corporate charter to London, making it an entity dis-
tinct from the rest of England. His goal was to give London, the richest
city in the country, a basis for local government and, not incidentally,
taxes with which to fill the royal coffers. The English crown also issued
corporate charters to universities and charitable institutions. As opposed
to the city of London, universities and charities often received tax
exemptions. Just as important, their charters provided a legal basis for
governing these institutions through corporate boards whose members
were usually appointed.

It took five hundred more years before European imperialism led to the modern world's first business corporations, the most famous of which were the Dutch and the English East India Companies. The latter was formed in 1600 by a charter from Queen Elizabeth I granting the company monopolistic trading privileges in the East Indies. So too with the Levant Company, the Muscovy Company, the Hudson Bay Company, and many others. England established some of its American colonies through corporations such as the Virginia and the Massachusetts Bay Companies.

All of these seventeenth-century English business corporations had a public purpose, which was to enable England to compete with France and Spain for empire in the Americas and Asia. The powerful French and Spanish crowns could raise taxes and armies relatively easily, giving them a seeming advantage in the struggle for imperial expansion. The English crown lacked such power because of the ascendance of parliamentary government. English monarchs therefore relied on grants of corporate privilege to encourage their powerful subjects to invest in empire building.

Americans' experience with the East India Company, whose tea they threw into Boston Harbor in 1773, helped make them wary of corporate power. The Scottish moral philosopher and economist Adam Smith—author of the bible of free-market ideologues, *The Wealth of Nations* (1776)—won the hearts of Americans partly because he loathed business corporations in general and the East India Company in particular. Smith used the East India Company as an example to support his warning that corporations were "a great enemy to good management." What is today called the "agency problem"—the fact that managers are supposed to act as agents of stockholders but often act in their own interests instead—made Smith an opponent of business corporations in general and their managers in particular: ". . . being the managers rather of other people's money than of their own, it cannot well be expected, that they should watch over it with the same anxious vigilance. . . . Negligence and profusion, therefore, must always prevail, more or less, in the management of the affairs of such a company."[1]

Smith also cautioned that business corporations could not be trusted to exercise political power.[2] His primary example was the East India Company's 1770 monopolistic cornering of the rice market in Bengal. The result was starvation for a million or so Bengalis. Today, Smith's strictures against corporate power are mostly forgotten. Some who think of themselves as adherents of his free-market ideas unwittingly contradict him by arguing that government should not regulate business corporations. Smith was for free people and free markets, not free corporations.

After Americans won their independence from England and the East India Company, they did not quickly forget their distrust of corporations. But the United States was forced, out of necessity, to accept them. Both the federal and state governments were weak and unable to levy high taxes for public purposes. Therefore, just as England had harnessed the energy of wealthy citizens for social purposes by chartering business corporations, so—reluctantly—did the United States. For example, both the federal and state governments issued corporate charters for banks. The goal, however, was not to create rich financiers but to expand the supply of paper money in order to encourage commerce and economic development. Similarly, state governments chartered corporations for the public purpose of improved transportation, granting corporate monopolies over transportation routes and the right to charge tolls in return for building roads and bridges.

But early Americans usually drew the line at chartering business corporations strictly for private profit. In 1787, a Connecticut newspaper editorial warned against creating corporations whose sole motive was to enrich shareholders. The state legislature must not, it cautioned, "parcel out the commonwealth into little aristocracies."[3] In 1789, there were only six non-bank business corporations in the United States.[4] Throughout the 1790s, newspapers carried many letters from readers urging their state legislatures not to issue corporate charters for the purpose of private profit. Such sentiments were not marginal but were shared by many leading politicians, especially Jeffersonian Republicans. In 1809, the Virginia Supreme Court held that "[w]ith respect to articles of incorporation, they ought never to be passed, but in consideration of the services rendered to the public. . . . [I]f their object is merely private . . . , they have no adequate claim upon the legislature for privileges."[5]

As late as the 1830s, part of President Andrew Jackson's popularity could be attributed to his avowed anticorporatism. He fought a pitched battle to destroy the Second Bank of the United States, heir of the national bank for which Hamilton had persuaded Congress to issue a corporate charter in 1791. Jackson won the "Bank War," thanks partly to his charge that the Bank of the United States was a "money monopoly" and that it interfered in elections. To Jacksonians, monopoly and political corruption in a corporate behemoth were all too reminiscent of the East India Company.

Anticorporatism continues down to our own time, of course, but with far less success than in Jackson's time. Modern anticorporatism expresses not a foreboding that corporate power might become a reality but, rather, resentment that it has done so. The victory of the for-profit corporation in nineteenth-century America was clear by 1869 when Charles Francis Adams, a descendant of two presidents, lamented the fact that it was only a few years "since the existence of a corporation controlling a few millions of dollars was . . . a subject of grave apprehension." Yet by Adams's time America had corporations controlling "thousands of millions" of dollars, and he believed them powerful enough to establish "despotisms which no spasmodic popular effort will be able to shake off."[6]

In other words, by the middle of the nineteenth century, anticorporate Americans had lost their battle against the creation of for-profit corporations. For many centuries the corporation—be it a city, a university, a colony, a turnpike, or a bridge—had been understood as an organization chartered by the government for a public purpose. Then, in a relatively brief span in the nineteenth century, the corporation came to be understood as an instrument of private purpose, organized mainly for shareholder profit.

The decisive factor in the transition of the corporation from public purpose to private profit was the coming of the railroad in the second quarter of the nineteenth century. If the railroads had been built a few years earlier, they might have become state-owned enterprises, and the United States, for better or worse, might have developed a more statist, less corporate economy. But in the first quarter of the nineteenth century some state governments had lost a lot of their taxpayers' money in a rash of publicly funded canals and turnpikes. State treasuries being largely depleted, American railroads were built by business corporations.

Railroads incorporated because enormous amounts of capital had to be invested in tracks and trains before even a single dollar of revenue was earned. It took many investors to finance a railroad. Those investors feared the legal disadvantages of a traditional partnership in which one partner could be held responsible for the obligations of another. So railroads sought limited liability to reduce investors' risk. If the company went bust, investors were liable for—that is, could lose—no more than their original investment. The only way to get limited liability that could be sustained in a court of law was to have it written into the corporate charters that railroad investors were soon extracting by the hundreds from state legislatures. The coming of limited liability helped open up the corporation's use as a device for private profit rather than public purpose. Of course, the public good was served by the railroads' creation of a national transportation system. But the public good was incidental to corporate investors, who aimed to fatten their own wallets rather than those of Americans in general. The sense of the corporation as a public institution was being reduced.

Adding to early-nineteenth-century Americans' fear of corporate power had been the fact that only the rich and powerful were able to incorporate. That was because only legislatures could enact corporate charters, and it took a lot of clout to influence a legislature. Only Francis Cabot Lowell's social standing as part of Boston's merchant elite had enabled him to get a corporate charter for his Boston Manufacturing Company in 1813. If Americans could not stop the transformation of the corporation into an engine of private profit, they could at least try to create more democratic access to corporate charters. Over the course of the nineteenth century, state legislatures passed "general incorporation" laws that delegated the ability to create corporations to state agencies and bureaus. Any citizen could file an application at the state bureau of corporations, pay a nominal fee, and obtain a corporate charter. General incorporation laws were supposedly democratic in that they made it possible for ordinary citizens to enjoy the privileges of incorporation. But only a small minority of Americans exercised their newfound ability to incorporate. It turned out that the best economic decision for many people was not to start a corporation but to go to work for one.

Railroads, as the first big businesses, exemplified the difficulty of democratizing the corporation in an industrializing society. It took many millions of dollars to build a railroad and many thousands of people to operate it. If nineteenth-century Americans were to enjoy the benefit of mass transportation, some of them would have to work for railroads, sacrificing some of their personal independence by obeying the dictates not of the free market but of corporate managers.

CHAPTER 4

Corporations as Enemies of the Free Market

UNTIL THE COMING OF THE TEXTILE and railroad industries, large-scale capitalism was a mercantile phenomenon. Great merchants, investing in ships and precious cargo in order to engage in long-distance trade, were the business world's great capitalists. But in the late eighteenth and early nineteenth centuries mercantile capitalism was surpassed by a new kind of capitalism, industrial capitalism, which was to make some of Adam Smith's ideas outmoded almost before they were published.

Railroads provided the best example of why Smith's laissez-faire ideas would not always be the right prescription for economic efficiency in an economy of large industrial corporations. Over the long term, railroad corporations proved as economically inept as governments in planning and building infrastructure. Just as the states had overinvested in canals, corporations built too many railroads. The overbuilding of railroads led to a new kind of competition, "capital-intensive" competition. A large part of railroads' expenses were for interest on the borrowed capital with which they had been built. That capital was invested in trains and tracks, which were pretty hard to put out of business, no matter how intense the competition. For example, an efficient railroad company might drive an inefficient competitor into bankruptcy. That was a seeming vindication of the free-market ideology. The most efficient competitor had apparently won out.

But from there the story diverged from the way it was supposed to go according to Adam Smith. He wrote during the labor-intensive economy of the eighteenth century, when most of a business's expenses were for wages and materials, not interest payments on capital equipment. In Smith's economy, if a baker drove a competitor out of business, the losing baker and his employees might go to work for a harness maker. However, tracks and trains were only good for moving people and freight. Tracks and trains could not be diverted away from transportation the way that a failed baker might go to work for a harness maker. When a railroad corporation went bust, a bankruptcy court would sell its property to new owners who put the equipment back to work hauling passengers and freight.

The new owners of the formerly bankrupt railroad would not have been very smart if they paid as much for the railroad as had its original builders. After all, the railroad had lost money at its original cost. So the new owners who bought the railroad in bankruptcy court paid much less for it. They therefore borrowed less money and paid less interest, giving the railroad lower operating costs than it had incurred before it went bankrupt. With its newly reduced operating costs, the formerly bankrupt railroad might now be a tough competitor. Even if it remained inefficient and poorly managed, it might be able to triumph over better-managed railroads that were saddled with higher debt and higher costs. In fact, the formerly bankrupt railroad might be able to bankrupt the very competitor that, in the earlier round of competition, had bankrupted it!

A nineteenth-century railroad executive is supposed to have quipped that he believed in survival of the fittest, but you couldn't kill a railroad. Adam Smith's free market was supposed to lead to the victory of the efficient, not the inefficient. Smith, having no crystal ball, had not foreseen such capital-intensive businesses as railroads. So he did not predict that a railroad might be driven out of business only to emerge from bankruptcy court as a tougher competitor thanks to lower capital costs. Not surprisingly, railroads were soon placing less emphasis on competing than on cooperating with each other. They understandably aimed to find a way to prevent the "ruinous competition" that made losers into winners and winners into losers. First, they tried price fixing, which was not yet illegal. But price-fixing agreements often did not work. If a railroad saw a chance to gain more traffic, it would break the promise it had made to its competitors not to lower prices. Competing corporations could not rely on each others' word—again no surprise.

Because price fixing was not effective, the railroads sometimes agreed to share or pool traffic rather than to compete for it. For example, in 1877, the four main trunk lines in the eastern United States—the

Baltimore & Ohio, the Pennsylvania, the Erie, and the New York Central—signed an agreement aimed at ending their competition by sharing traffic.[1] But their agreement soon collapsed, as such traffic pools usually did. When railroad companies saw a chance to get an advantage, they broke their promises to pool traffic just as they had earlier broken their word to fix prices.

If price fixing and traffic pools were going to work, there had to be a way of enforcing them. Some of the railroads tried to get Congress to pass a law that would have made price fixing agreements and traffic pools into legal contracts that could be enforced in court. In other words, the railroads wanted the government's help in creating anticompetitive cartels. But consumers and voters believed there was too little competition among railroads, not too much. The popular mind did not understand the complexities of capital-intensive competition. And in any case, the railroads had made themselves unloved by charging, in areas where there was no competition, "all the traffic would bear." So in 1887, when Congress created the Interstate Commerce Commission (ICC) to regulate the railroads, it gave the agency authority to set maximum but not minimum rates. Thus, the ICC did not protect railroads against price competition. It only protected consumers against monopolistic price gouging.

The investment banker J. P. Morgan finally solved the problem of cutthroat competition among the railroads. During the depression of the 1890s, railroad traffic naturally fell, leading to massive bankruptcies of railroad corporations. More than half of the track in the United States passed through the bankruptcy courts, where Morgan bought and reorganized numerous railroads. As a banker, Morgan worked with other people's money. He wanted all his clients to earn profits. So he sought to end competition by organizing railroads into large "communities of interest" where the companies held stock in each other. Because one railroad held stock in another and vice versa, it was self-defeating for them to compete.

In other industries, too, corporations attempted to prevent competition. As the railroad and the telegraph knit the American economy into a huge, unified market, new corporate giants arose to take advantage of opportunities for mass distribution and mass production in basic industries from food to steel. As with the railroads earlier, the new mass distributors and mass producers helped to enrich the American people as a whole, but that was no part of their goal. Rather, they aimed to end competition in order to charge Americans high prices.

First and most famous of the nineteenth-century mass producers was the oil tycoon John D. Rockefeller. Taking advantage of new technology—mainly steam-driven pumps and long-distance pipelines—he achieved unprecedented economies of speed and scale in refining kerosene, a product in high demand for oil lamps. Later, as electric lighting replaced kerosene lamps, Rockefeller's oil business found a new source of profit in the advent of gas-guzzling automobiles.

Rockefeller's Standard Oil Trust was actually a combination of many separate corporations. Owners of these other companies allowed Rockefeller to manage their property "in trust." The companies Rockefeller held in trust were often former competitors who made more money not just for him but for themselves by letting him serve as their "trustee," a role that enabled him to avoid competition and set high prices. Oil companies that insisted on competing soon found themselves driven out of business by Rockefeller. But he destroyed his competitors reluctantly, as it was cheaper to take over their businesses "in trust" than it was to drive down prices in order to kill them. But either way, Rockefeller's Standard Oil Trust achieved monopolistic power over prices, saving him and the owners of the companies he held in trust the expense of competing. It was win–win for everyone but consumers.

Congress tried to rein in trust agreements like Rockefeller's by passing the Sherman Anti-Trust Act in 1890. The Sherman Act made it illegal to "conspire" to restrain trade. In other words, it was illegal for other oil companies to agree to make Rockefeller their trustee in order to achieve a monopoly. But Rockefeller believed he could get around the Sherman Anti-Trust Act thanks to New Jersey's compliant state legislature. The 1889, New Jersey Holding Company Act authorized corporations chartered in the Garden State to own the stock of corporations chartered in other states. So Rockefeller created a new corporation, Standard Oil of New Jersey, and used it instead of the Standard Oil Trust to own and manage his diverse companies. Rockefeller now had what his lawyers called "legal unity." Because he had combined all his companies into one, he did not have to break the law by "conspiring" to raise prices. Instead of conspiring with anyone else, he could simply order that prices be raised.

Rockefeller soon had corporate imitators in other industries. During the 1890s, it seemed that the Sherman Anti-Trust Act had backfired. Instead of supporting small business and free markets, it encouraged hundreds of mergers aimed at creating big, monopolistic corporations like Rockefeller's. Relatively small firms merged into giant companies, often chartered in New Jersey or the equally amenable state of Delaware. Some of these mergers resulted in corporate powerhouses such as DuPont and General Electric that have lasted down to the present.

But many of the mergers of the 1890s failed in their goal of establishing corporate monopolies because their industries had no expensive new technologies, no barriers to entry that would prevent the rise of new competitors. For example, in 1890, the main American rope manufacturers merged into the National Cordage Association (chartered, of course, in New Jersey). But whereas Rockefeller's monopoly worked, the rope makers' attempt at monopoly failed because of a fundamental difference between the oil and rope industries. In the oil industry, expensive new pumps and pipelines gave Rockefeller his initial advantage and made it hard for new competitors to arise. To compete with Rockefeller, a new entrant into the market would have to acquire all at once the expensive technology that he had acquired over time. But there was no expensive new technology in rope making. So when the National Cordage Association tried to raise prices, new rope makers easily entered the market.[2]

The 1890s mergers succeeded only in industries where expensive new technology created barriers to entry. In explosives and in electric street lighting, mergers created DuPont and General Electric, which are still economic giants more than a century later. These companies had monopolistic or at least oligopolistic power to fix prices, restrict supply, or otherwise interfere with the free market. Just as with Standard Oil of New Jersey, other successful monopolies of the period believed that their operations were legal. Their mergers into a single company meant that they no longer had to "conspire" to fix prices. Like Standard Oil, they had "legal unity," so the top executive could simply order a price increase instead of engaging with others in "conspiracies in restraint of trade."

But Theodore Roosevelt, who was president from 1901 to 1909, did not buy Rockefeller's legal argument. He insisted that the act of merging was itself sometimes a conspiracy in restraint of trade and therefore a violation of the Sherman Anti-Trust Act. Roosevelt won a reputation as a "trust buster" by successfully prosecuting a number of large corporate monopolies, including Rockefeller's. In 1911, the Supreme Court ordered Rockefeller's Standard Oil of New Jersey to break up into competing companies. Yet Roosevelt did not aim to bust all trusts. He believed that many large corporations fostered efficiency and benefited society as a whole. The DuPont and General Electric mergers, along with many others, were allowed to stand.

For all of Roosevelt's popularity as a trust buster, the sophistication of his approach did not take hold in the popular mind. Just as free-market ideologues had forgotten Adam Smith's contempt for corporations, they soon forgot how Roosevelt had tried to limit corporate power in order to balance freedom and prosperity. Many Americans cling to the old, simplistic notion that the best medicine for any economic problem is more of the free market and that the enemy of the free market is always government, not business corporations.

As a result, we get political tracts today premised on the idea that "the fight between free enterprise and big government will shape America's future."[3] Big business is mentioned, but barely. The possibility is largely ignored that when government fights business corporations it may be fighting *for* free enterprise. The reason the free-enterprise system makes people happiest, we are told, is because it gives people control of their own fate.[4] On the basis of personal and historical experience, I could not agree more. The happiest period of American history in living memory, the era of the mid-twentieth-century American Dream, resulted from the use of government power in the 1930s to partly free Americans from corporate control.

To turn the early-twentieth-century corporate economy into the American Dream required some combination of good luck and intellectual awakening. The degree to which human beings drive events or events drive them is a matter of how large a role fortune plays versus human understanding. Having failed to understand the corporate economy in which they had unexpectedly come to live, Americans would create a dreamlike society out of good luck and, in the 1930s, the government's ad hoc, unsystematic response to the Great Depression.

PART II

Corporate Failure and Government Fix

CHAPTER 5

Corporate Crashes

PROPONENTS OF BUSINESS are fond of calling government ineffective. But in many ways the business corporation has proven far less effective than government. The corporate economy that took shape in the United States in the late nineteenth and early twentieth centuries sometimes failed the most basic test of a good society. During the Great Depression of the 1930s and in some earlier financial crises as well, corporate America failed to supply industrious citizens with the work they needed to live a decent life.

The corporate economy was central to mid-twentieth-century American prosperity, yet it was also central to the 1930s economic collapse. In the final analysis it was government, not the corporate economy, that took the decisive steps to lift ordinary citizens out of the Depression and into the postwar American Dream. The corporate economy came into being during the Second Industrial Revolution—the seventy-five years of heavy industry between the Civil War and World War II—a period in which there was little that was dreamlike in the lives of many corporate employees. As the railroads and then other capital-intensive industries such as steel and automobiles took shape, they created immense wealth but also huge disparities of income. Gaps between rich and poor were no new thing in history, but in America the poor were supposed to be able to become rich. As long as America had been a land of farmers with new land for settlement reaching almost infinitely west, there had seemed to be equal opportunity for all, or at least for free white males.

In the new era of heavy industry, however, most of those who labored in a factory or on a railroad seemed likely to remain there. There could be no factory owners without factory workers. The old Jeffersonian dream of free men living independently on their own land was replaced by the mundane reality of wage earners dependent on corporations for their livelihoods. By substituting dependency on employers for the independent life of the yeoman farmer, Americans won the material benefits of industrialism. Working people's incomes rose overall. But the corporate economy was subject to dramatic downturns, with the greatest hardships falling on workers.

Workers faced international competition. Corporations did not. The industrialized North, led by a corporate lawyer named Abraham Lincoln, had won the Civil War and raised protective tariffs. Having protected industrial corporations against competition from abroad, Congress ensured them a supply of cheap labor by keeping the door open to immigrants—just the reverse of today's policy of free trade in goods, as information technology allows corporations to exploit cheap labor overseas, without bringing the workers to America. But in the nineteenth century, corporations were best served by an influx of cheap labor, a fact that resulted in an unrestrictive immigration policy.

Workers' mobility was more geographic than economic. Some moved into skilled trades or at least made it possible for their sons to do so. But many others moved desperately from city to city in search of jobs and livable wages. For example, 36 percent of the men who lived in Boston at the start of the 1880s were not there at the end of that decade.[1] These men had evidently moved on, hoping for better prospects in another city. Women were not included in many of the official records, but it is a reasonable inference that their mobility bore some connection to men's. Still more remarkably, in that same decade of the 1880s, twelve times more men moved into Boston than the city gained in male population.[2] That statistic can only mean that men were rotating in and out of Boston at a remarkably high turnover. As new men arrived, others were leaving. Of course some men left Boston not for another city but for a cemetery. Still, it is clear that a sizable percentage of the men who came to Boston in the 1880s quickly moved on to another town. They seem not to have found sustenance in the home of the bean and the cod.

The demographics of other cities have not been studied so closely, but there is reason to think that Bostonians' extraordinary mobility was representative of other urban populations in nineteenth-century America.[3] To some degree, probably a large one, that high mobility was driven by Americans' unsuccessful search for economic opportunity. Many moved to a new city, failed to make economic headway, and moved again. For a lot of these itinerants, corporate America was not the land of plenty. Some of the restless job seekers did eventually find places where they could improve their lives and their children's. But success for some does not contradict what a careful historian calls the possibility—certainty in my view—that "many, perhaps even most, of the men who were moving about . . . drifted helplessly from place to place for a lifetime, forming a permanent and ever moving but largely invisible proletariat."[4]

Rags-to-riches stories were the exception, not the rule. Andrew Carnegie came penniless from Scotland to the United States, went into steel, and became the richest man in the world. But many thousands of other immigrants spent their lives shoveling coal into Carnegie's blast furnaces. Carnegie symbolized the tension between democratic freedom and corporate profit. Back in Scotland his family had been Chartists, fighting for rights such as universal male suffrage that the United States already had. As Carnegie grew rich in America, he prided himself on maintaining his democratic spirit and announced that he would never employ strikebreakers. Yet in 1892, when Carnegie faced cost pressures at his Homestead Mill near Pittsburgh, his company provoked a strike by lowering its wage scale. And then his company did what Carnegie had vowed he would not. It imported three hundred Pinkerton "detectives"—strikebreakers. The Homestead workers fought the Pinkertons into a humiliating surrender but not before people were killed on both sides. The governor, who was beholden to Carnegie interests, ordered out the state militia. The troops enforced the peace and let strikebreakers into the mill.

Such government support for employers rather than employees was the common pattern in dozens of late-nineteenth- and early-twentieth-century labor disputes. For example, in 1894 workers who built Pullman sleeping cars for the railroads went on strike against atrocious working conditions. Railroad workers, supporting the Pullman strikers, refused to move any train containing a Pullman car. President Grover Cleveland jailed the leaders of the railroad union. His reason? The boycott of Pullman cars was a conspiracy to restrain trade, putting the leaders of a labor union in violation of the Sherman Anti-Trust Act!

Only once in this period did the national government act impartially in a labor dispute. In the autumn of 1902, during the Anthracite

Strike by the United Mine Workers, President Theodore Roosevelt brokered a "square deal," giving both sides some of what they wanted. Roosevelt's main concern seems to have been avoiding a national coal shortage during the approach of both the cold season and congressional elections. The lesson was clear. Only when the government sided with workers would there be a chance for the corporate economy to create the American Dream, a society in which workers earned middle-class wages. The government would not side significantly with workers until there was a clear failure of the corporate economy.

During the nineteenth and early twentieth centuries, the corporate economy periodically put large numbers of Americans out of work. Business recessions caused steep increases in unemployment in 1819, 1837, 1857, 1873, 1893, 1907, and 1918. Most of these recessions lasted several years. Irresponsible banks helped bring on the suffering. They overextended credit during good times and then, in downturns, were caught with dubious loans on their books. The loans might not yield the cash the banks needed to cover withdrawals, especially if depositors panicked and there was a run on the banks. Therefore, the banks guarded their liquidity by tightening their lending at just the time when the economy needed a cash infusion. The banks, in short, made hard times harder.

Still, many citizens weathered these recessions relatively unscathed. As long as the suffering was restricted to a small part of the population, there was little pressure on government to create far-reaching change in the corporate economy. Reforms were piecemeal responses to specific problems rather than broad attempts to make the corporate economy work better for all the people. State and local governments began to limit child labor, to set minimum wages, and to establish public utility companies. The federal government regulated railroad rates (Interstate Commerce Act, 1887), prevented the sale of adulterated food and medicine (Pure Food and Drug Act, 1906), and took control of the money supply away from banks (Federal Reserve Act, 1913). But while these measures healthily asserted democratic authority, they did not fundamentally change the nature of the corporate economy.

Government's refusal to alter the economic power structure and the place of the corporation in it changed with the coming of the Great Depression of the 1930s. When President Franklin Roosevelt took office in March 1933, three and a half years after the stock market crash of 1929, the corporate economy had suffered the most catastrophic decline in American history. Something close to a third of the country's economic capacity was going unused as factories stood still, as banks went bust, as farms were foreclosed, as small businesses folded, and as workers lost their jobs. The unemployment rate reached 25 percent in 1932. Homelessness and hunger surged. The writer Edmund Wilson witnessed hundreds of people scavenging daily for food at a Chicago garbage dump. He reported that one woman took off her glasses in order not to see the maggots.

Beneath the misery and destitution of the Depression, many Americans were deeply puzzled by what had happened to them. Perhaps Wilson best captured their bewilderment in his word picture of "A Man in the Street." Like millions of others, his face bore "a curious dazed expression, as if he were not really a part of the world in which he is walking, as if his life had come under a shadow from which he can see no way of escaping and for which he has no means of accounting. . . . You cannot tell whether he is a skilled mechanic or a former auto-dealer or a department store manager or a bank cashier."[5] Confused as he was, the man in the street at least had the power to vote. In 1932, Americans elected a new president, Franklin Roosevelt, who aimed to use the powers of government to help them. He inspired courage with the phrase that the only thing they had to fear was fear itself. It would have been even better if he had also inspired some understanding of how the corporate economy worked.

CHAPTER 6

Managers versus Markets

BENEATH THE PRACTICAL AND MORAL FAILURES of the corporate economy in the Great Depression lay a failure of intellect. Many Americans did not see that the corporate economy had shown that the laissez-faire ideology was not the whole truth. They did not see that the success of the large business corporation proved that, in some circumstances, a free market is inefficient.

If the market were always the most efficient system, there should have been no corporations employing large numbers of people. All Americans should have been self-employed, selling their autonomously produced goods and services. But the United States had developed into the world's richest nation by going in exactly the opposite direction. Instead of working freely in the marketplace, an ever-larger number of citizens were employed by large corporations where they did what the boss said. In other words, America grew rich not just because of the free market but also because many citizens surrendered some of their economic freedom to corporate employers. Corporations might answer to the law of supply and demand. But employees answered to corporate managers. Managers, not markets, became the primary force in the working lives of many Americans. Markets still mattered to business, because even corporate titans sometimes had to compete. Yet the main force in the lives of most corporate employees was not the market but the company, not the customer but the boss.

What explains the fact that managers, not markets, increasingly drove the actions of Americans at work during the late nineteenth and early twentieth centuries? Why did many Americans, even if they still espoused Jeffersonian independence on the Fourth of July, subordinate themselves to managers the rest of the year? Why were more and more citizens able to increase their economic well-being by giving up their freedom to work on their own in favor of doing what a corporate boss told them to do?

An English economist attempted to answer that question, not just for the United States but for the entire industrial world. Ronald Coase's answer was so good that his 1937 essay, "On the Nature of the Firm," won him a Nobel Prize. Coase's answer to the question of why business firms exist—the question of why everyone does not work for himself or herself—was that top-down managerial power is sometimes more efficient than the free market. Coase still exerts considerable influence today, and his ideas underlie much of what follows in this chapter.

In the nineteenth century, new technology in many industries raised managers' efficiency more than it raised the efficiency of the market. The railroad and telegraph often made it cheaper for managers than for the market to coordinate the flow of goods in the American economy. The result was that many Americans could make more money working for those managers and corporations than they could if they worked freely in the market. The old saying that there is no free lunch applies to markets. Markets have operating costs, especially transaction costs. To buy and sell takes time and money. The railroad and the telegraph saved time and money by enabling corporate managers to reduce the number of market transactions involved in moving goods from one place to another.

In the early nineteenth century, for example, it took several costly market transactions to move manufactured goods such as cotton cloth from the east coast to the Midwest. Transportation and communication, often by river, were slow and risky. It was hard for eastern merchants to know what was happening to their goods on the other side of the Appalachians and hard to know what price they might command when they got there. Therefore, eastern merchants and manufacturers sold their goods to middlemen. These middlemen or "jobbers" specialized in the risky business of moving manufactured goods from the east coast into the Midwest and selling them, again, to the region's general stores.[1] These transactions raised the price that farmers paid when they shopped at the general store. After all, the middlemen had to eat.

By the end of the nineteenth century the middlemen and their market transactions were gone, replaced by corporate managers in large retailers. For example, Marshall Fields, a big department store in Chicago, had managers or "buyers" in the eastern United States and in Europe. Once the Marshall Fields buyer purchased goods in New York or London, the goods were shipped to the Windy City with no more market transactions. Only when Chicagoans came in off the street to buy the goods in Marshall Fields's department store did the market again play a role in the distribution process. The Marshall Fields managers who coordinated the flow of goods from east to west did not work for nothing. But they were still cheaper than the old middlemen with their costly market transactions. Thanks to the railroad and telegraph, Marshall Fields buyers in New York could know prices in Chicago and could move goods there quickly, before prices changed.

The same dynamic—coordination by managers rather than markets—was also at work in manufacturing. Distilling, refining, food processing, metal making, and the assembly of machinery all came to be dominated by large corporations because their managers were more efficient than the market. The market still mattered, because the companies bought raw materials and sold finished products. But within the corporations, managers, not the market, coordinated the flow of goods. Corporate managers made America rich by reducing transaction costs, thus lowering unit costs to a level that the free market alone could never have achieved.

The coming of the automobile assembly line in the early twentieth century epitomized this triumph of managers over markets. An assembly line building Model T Fords could have operated on market principles, at least in theory. One assembly-line worker might have bought the chassis from a previous worker, added axles, and sold the car to the next worker, who would put on the wheels. But the workers would have lost time and money negotiating prices and making all those transactions. Cars would have cost more, and the nation would have been poorer if the market rather than corporate managers had coordinated automobile assembly. Instead of relying on the free market, it was more efficient for managers to just tell workers what to do, which is why the managerial corporation made America rich.

The trade-off of freedom for wealth in the managerial corporation was clearly demonstrated by the increase in efficiency on the Ford assembly line. When workers did what their managers told them—as opposed to working on their own in the free market—their standard of living rose. After Ford introduced the assembly line, some workers could earn five dollars a day, several times the pay of ordinary laborers at the time. Yet the Ford Company was scarcely a beneficent employer. To the contrary, it early gained a reputation for ruthless tyranny. As in other capital-intensive industries, so too on the assembly line, the secret of profitability was return on invested capital. Ford, like the railroads, aimed to "run fast, run full." The company had a Service Department that was originally in charge of security, but it became famous for bullying assembly-line workers to step up the pace.

Top-down corporate power did not always lead to the heightened standard of living for the masses that was its only chance at justification. Americans may have escaped the vicissitudes of rain and drought by abandoning the farm for the factory. But they faced a new existential risk, the danger of unemployment from business slumps, which corporate managers often made worse. In the 1920s, the new big businesses such as General Electric and General Motors began to engage in economic forecasting. Their goal was to "calibrate supply with demand."[2] With immense sums of capital invested in plant and equipment, they ran the risk of vast losses if they produced either more or less than the market would buy. They tried to prevent such losses by forecasting demand and then raising or lowering production to meet that anticipated demand.

But economic forecasts that improved a company's bottom line might make things worse for everyone else, especially in hard times. During the early years of the Depression, General Motors and General Electric both forecast falling markets. They therefore cut production, reduced personnel, and curtailed purchasing. Such actions further reduced consumers' purchasing power and lowered aggregate demand in the already depressed economy. In short, "[t]he very ability to effectively coordinate supply with demand intensified the economic decline."[3] In 1931, GM and GE forecast demand for 1932 that would only justify their operating at 25 percent of capacity. They laid off still more workers, who were then unable to purchase manufacturers' products, thereby throwing still more people out of work and further worsening the Depression.

By 1933, the business corporation had proven not its efficiency but its inefficiency at delivering a good life to the American people. Yet as is often true of historical change, many people at the time, especially many business people, did not understand what was happening. They still clung to faith in pure laissez-faire and a conviction that somehow the government—not business—must have bungled things. Everything would be all right, such people thought, if only the government would get out of the way.

Still, a few business people understood that it was the corporate economy and the managerial class, not the government, that had failed. These discerning businessmen joined the mass of ordinary Americans who elected Franklin Roosevelt president in 1932. Progressive business people, like the majority of Americans, looked to the government to clean up the mess that business corporations had made. Yet even progressive business people did not aim to reduce corporate power. Their idea of how to fix the economy was to give big business more power, not less. And indeed, the initial economic program of the Roosevelt administration, the First New Deal, enlarged corporate power. The failure of the First New Deal showed—though many citizens failed to learn the lesson—that even when the government gave corporations enhanced power, they were incapable of creating a good society, let alone a dreamlike one.

CHAPTER 7

Corporations Blow Their Chance to End the Depression

THE FIRST NEW DEAL was famously influenced by what newspapers at the time called the "Brains Trust," a group of Columbia University professors who served as close advisers to President Roosevelt. Less widely appreciated is the fact that corporate executives were often as influential as the professors in shaping the economic policy of the First New Deal. Many people today understand that Roosevelt failed to revive the economy with the First New Deal. But few understand that he failed because he followed the advice of businessmen to give corporations more power, not less.

There were exceptions to the failure of the First New Deal and its general tendency to enhance corporate power. The Glass-Steagall Act of 1933 created more responsible banking practices by denying commercial banks the right to practice investment banking—that is, investment in the market for corporate securities. The Securities Exchange Act of 1934 set up the Securities and Exchange Commission (SEC) to regulate the securities markets and to protect investors against fraudulent accounting and unfair trading practices. (The repeal of Glass-Steagall during the Clinton administration and lax regulation by the SEC during the George W. Bush administration were important factors in causing the Great Recession that began in December 2007.) But these long-lasting, successful, and therefore well-remembered measures of the First New Deal depended on restricting corporate power. The primary thrust of the First New Deal was in the opposite direction, toward enhancing corporate power. The idea was to give corporations more power so that they could run the corporate economy for the benefit of the country as a whole.

There were a fair number of prominent businessmen who saw that the Depression amounted to a failure of the corporate economy—men like Henry Dennison, head of a large paper manufacturer; Edward Filene, a department store magnate; Henry Harriman, the president of the U.S. Chamber of Commerce; Joseph Kennedy, a financier and commodities investor; George Peek, a manufacturer of farm implements; and Gerard Swope, president of General Electric. But the most influential of all such figures was the famous Wall Street speculator who was also considered an elder statesman of American politics—Bernard Baruch.

Baruch had headed the War Industries Board during World War I. Partly by personal charm, partly by tolerating large corporate profits even while soldiers sacrificed their lives, and partly by involuntary methods such as quotas and government takeovers, he had built a system of industrial cooperation aimed at ensuring victory in the war by maximizing production. Some critics believed that Baruch actually did not understand production and had therefore failed to expand it as fully as possible during the war. They thought that war production could have been much higher if it had been managed by an engineer rather than a financier. But the degree of Baruch's relative success or failure was masked—and to some degree remains masked—by his immense talent for self-promotion. Whether rightly or wrongly, Americans believed that during World War I Baruch had offered an example of corporate cooperation in the national interest.

So it was scarcely surprising that fifteen years later, during the Great Depression, many people looked to Baruch for answers. He and a fair number of other progressive businessmen believed that some of the capitalist system's worst evils resulted from cutthroat competition among corporations. Obviously they were at least partly right. Competition intensified the pressure on corporations to hire children, to create wretched working conditions, and to pay low wages. Unreasonable competitive pressures, according to progressive businessmen like Baruch, caused the Depression and explained corporations' failure to provide workers with enough economic security and purchasing power to support aggregate demand. With low incomes even for those who had jobs, Americans could not purchase industry's output, let alone spend their way out of the Depression.

To progressive businessmen who thought in this way, the question was what to do about ruthless competition. Their answer was cooperation. Corporations should agree on industrywide standards in working conditions and wages in order to raise workers' purchasing power. Only then would the ordinary citizen be able to buy and consume enough goods to lift the country out of the Depression. But those who favored cooperation faced legal obstacles. Corporate cooperation was an illegal "restraint of trade" under the Sherman Act of 1890 and subsequent antitrust legislation as well. Progressive businessmen such as Baruch supported Roosevelt in the campaign of 1932 because they hoped he would give them a way around the antitrust laws. And Roosevelt did just that.

The president had a bit of experience that made him sympathetic to the idea of corporate cooperation aimed at raising pay and working conditions. During his brief legal career, FDR had represented the Building Trades Council, the sort of workers' group that might stand to gain from Baruch's promise of enlightened corporate cooperation if only the antitrust laws were lifted. Also, as assistant secretary of the navy during World War I, Roosevelt had had a fairly close look at corporate cooperation under Baruch's War Industries Board. The depth of the Depression had left conservative business interests paralyzed with fear and unable to obstruct the efforts of their more liberal colleagues. Nearly everyone recognized that something had to be done. Because Baruch and other progressive businessmen at least had an idea for action, they found the government receptive. The Brains Trust—the professors who were Roosevelt's close advisers during this time—were sympathetic to progressive businessmen's idea that cutthroat competition was responsible for the Depression. So they cooperated with key members of Congress and with a Baruch ally named Hugh Johnson in drafting legislation to give corporations relief from the antitrust laws.

The result was the National Industrial Recovery Act (NIRA), which Roosevelt signed into law in June 1933. The idea was to provide for cooperative self-government by American industry. Corporations, cooperating with each other, would be able to stop using low wages to enhance their competitive advantage. Incomes of ordinary people would rise—at least that was the idea—and they would use their increased purchasing power to end the Depression. The NIRA brought some reforms that were not directly related to the goal of corporate cooperation. It outlawed child labor and, in its famous section 7(a), gave workers the right to bargain collectively, that is, to organize unions. It also authorized spending on public works to help stimulate recovery. All these measures were considered secondary parts of the legislation and were aimed at consoling Roosevelt's more leftist supporters for the fact that the president had officially committed America to a corporate economy. The central feature of the act was the setting aside of the antitrust laws. Corporations were to be allowed to draft industrywide codes of conduct and register them with a new federal agency, the National Recovery Administration. The idea was to undo the aggressive competition that had supposedly caused the Depression by encouraging corporations to hold down workers' wages and purchasing power.

In the National Industrial Recovery Act, Congress tacitly admitted the centrality of corporations to the American economy. Business corporations had a respite from the antitrust laws so that they could supposedly manage their affairs for the benefit of all Americans. In short, the NIRA was based on a naive belief that corporate executives could set aside their natural tendency to work for the benefit of themselves and, instead, cooperate for the benefit of the American people. Was it really surprising that NIRA was a failure?

To implement the new law, Roosevelt put Baruch's ally, Hugh Johnson, in charge of the National Recovery Administration (NRA). A man of immense energy but psychologically unstable and prone to drunken benders, Johnson was a West Point graduate who had distinguished himself as a logistics officer during World War I. After the war he went into business and ended up running the Moline Implement Company, a plow manufacturer. After taking command of the NRA in the summer of 1933, Johnson became one of the most famous people in America as he tried to lead the country out of the Depression.

Johnson worked furiously, pushing companies into writing cooperative codes for their industries. Textile, automobile, steel, newspaper, coal, oil, and lumber companies quickly fell into line. They drafted codes setting prices, wages, and working conditions in their industries. Johnson ran the National Recovery Administration in about the way that Baruch had run the War Industries Board during World War I. He kept labor and public interest groups out of the code negotiations and dealt mainly with businessmen. By keeping everyone but corporations out of the code negotiations, Johnson ensured the failure of his attempt to cure the Depression.

Many business executives wanted only to stem the flood of red ink in their company income statements. They were far more eager to cooperate in charging higher prices than in paying higher wages. The NRA allowed them to do so. How useful, then, could corporate cooperation be in fighting the Depression? If Johnson's agency allowed corporate prices to rise faster than wages, the industrial codes would decrease rather than raise Americans' aggregate purchasing power and would hinder economic recovery rather than help it. Johnson understood the problem but was unable to prevent price hikes that outstripped wage increases.[1]

The National Industrial Recovery Act had given corporate executives the opportunity to cooperate for the good of the country. Not surprisingly—for after all, profit remained their primary goal—the business leaders chose to put their self-interest ahead of the public interest. The First New Deal's experiment in corporate cooperation was a failure. Yet in a perverse way, the NRA did help the economy recover a bit in the spring and summer of 1933. Businesses rushed to purchase materials before their suppliers could write industrial codes and raise prices. Businessmen's very knowledge that the NRA was en route to long-term failure helped make it a short-term success.

But what small success the National Recovery Administration enjoyed was not the result of corporations cooperating for the common good. Many companies signed an NRA code only for the sake of public relations and then cheated on it as quickly as possible. Often, corporations failed to raise wages to the level stipulated in the NRA code or else sold below the code price, thus restoring the cutthroat competition that their newfound freedom from the antitrust laws was supposed to end. It was not long before ordinary citizens began to lose faith in the agency. The public saw that business corporations cheated and that price hikes outstripped wage increases. Millions of American consumers had signed personal pledges to shop at businesses that displayed the NRA logo—a blue eagle over the slogan "We Do Our Part." But when Johnson took blue eagles away from stores that had cheated on their codes, some consumers rushed to shop there to display their contempt for the NRA.

As the economy improved somewhat in 1933, conservative business people regained confidence and began to denounce the New Deal in general and the National Recovery Administration in particular. One of Roosevelt's aides described the business world's resurgent and fatuous self-congratulation (a still too prominent and ugly quality of corporate life): "It was not unusual for Chamber of Commerce meetings, trade conventions, and similar gatherings even then to break down at some point into soggy, almost tearful self-praise. . . . [T]here had been a rapidly spreading public hostility to the business establishment for a time . . . ; but the rehabilitation was proceeding in Washington with sickening success."[2]

Progressive businessmen now tempered their enthusiasm for corporate cooperation. President Roosevelt eased off his support of the National Recovery Administration by manipulating Johnson into resigning in 1934. In 1935, the Supreme Court brought the NRA to an end by declaring it unconstitutional. The Court ruled that the NRA's code-making authority was an unconstitutional delegation of legislative power to the executive branch of the government as well as a misapplication of the Constitution's interstate commerce clause.

President Roosevelt was famously indignant at the Supreme Court decision and charged the justices with living in the "horse and buggy" era. He launched an effort to enlarge the Supreme Court and to pack it with justices friendly to his program, a scheme that Congress and the public rejected and that was one of the Roosevelt administration's worst gaffes. But Roosevelt's real mistake had been in thinking that business corporations could work together in good will to end the Depression. He was politically fortunate that the Court brought his program to an end.

Unfortunately, the Supreme Court's decision spared corporate executives from having to recognize their moral failure and, still worse, from having their moral failure recognized by Americans at large. The corporations had sought relief from the antitrust laws and had promised in return to serve the public good. Thanks to the Court's abrupt ending of the NRA, business corporations' broken promise was not widely recognized.

CHAPTER 8

Roosevelt's Confused Anticorporatism

SO BEGAN THE SECOND NEW DEAL, which would fight the Depression not by enhancing corporate power but by reducing it. Unfortunately, there was no widely shared understanding within the administration or among the American people as to the reasons for the shift in policy. Many knew then and know now that the Second New Deal weakened business corporations. Too few knew then or now that business corporations had it coming.

Foremost among those who failed to understand what was happening was the president himself. During the campaign of 1932, Roosevelt had given a speech at the Commonwealth Club in San Francisco that has often been taken as marking the spirit of the New Deal. And the speech does correspond to the some of what happened in the Second New Deal, with its weakening of corporate power. In his speech, FDR argued that big government was not necessarily the enemy of individualism. In modern production with its economies of scale, big government had to protect individual freedom against the depredations of big business. In American history, Roosevelt declared, "the victory of the central Government" has often created a "refuge to the individual."[1]

But the Commonwealth Club speech was the exception rather than the rule of Roosevelt's 1932 campaign, which was mainly conservative in its thrust. The Commonwealth address was the work of a member of FDR's Brains Trust, Columbia University Professor Adolf Berle, who with a coauthor named Gardiner Means, had recently written a still-influential book called *The Modern Corporation and Private Property* (1932). Berle and Means argued that owners' supposed control was actually dissipated among thousands of shareholders while real power was concentrated in corporate management. Corporate management was therefore

free from shareholder control. According to Berle, that meant that traditional theories of property rights and free markets should not apply to
corporate behavior: "The translation of perhaps two-thirds of the industrial wealth of the country from individual ownership to ownership by
the large, publicly financed corporations vitally changes the lives of property owners, the lives of workers, and the methods of property tenure.
The divorce of ownership from control consequent on that process almost
necessarily involves a new form of economic organization of society."[2]

Berle's argument retains some influence in academic circles but
never gained popular traction as it might have done if Roosevelt had
consistently spoken for such views. Roosevelt was so open to new ideas
that he no sooner picked one up than he dropped it in favor of another.
It was the force of events, not Berle's analysis, that drove Roosevelt
toward the implicitly anticorporate policies of the Second New Deal.
Americans' understanding of their economic lives suffered because of
Roosevelt's consistent failure to articulate the fact that the real issues had
nothing to do with abstractions such as socialism and free markets. FDR
lambasted "economic royalists," but such vague expressions could easily
be taken to mean simply the rich. Perhaps because he did not adequately
understand it himself, the president never made clear to the American
people that the real issue was the use and abuse of corporate power.

After the 1935 Supreme Court decision invalidating NRA, Roosevelt
had to try something else to fight the Depression. In July of that year
he signed legislation sponsored by New York Senator Robert Wagner,
legislation toward which the president had previously been ambivalent.
The Wagner Act reduced corporate power by strengthening labor
unions. Officially titled the National Labor Relations Act, the new law
would succeed where the National Industrial Recovery Act had failed.
The Wagner Act would lift purchasing power through wage increases
secured by cooperation among workers rather than corporations. More
than any other single piece of legislation in the first half of the twentieth
century, the Wagner Act would raise the standard of living and, after
World War II, would create the American Dream.

Where section 7(a) of the 1933 National Industrial Recovery Act
had simply *announced* the right of workers to unionize, the Wagner Act
created government machinery to *enforce* the right to unionize. The
Wagner Act created a National Labor Relations Board, which workers

could petition to conduct union elections. If a majority of workers in a factory voted for it, the union became the official bargaining agent for all the workers. The Wagner Act scarcely gave unions absolute power, but it greatly strengthened their hand vis-à-vis management. If employees went on strike, employers could not hire replacements but had to shut down until an agreement was reached with the union. This increase in power for organized labor was central to its ability to win higher wages and better working conditions.

Business interests such as the National Association of Manufacturers and the Liberty League—the latter founded in 1934 for the explicit purpose of fighting the New Deal—were predictably outraged. Seeing the Wagner Act as a violation of traditional property rights and individual freedom, they comforted themselves with the assumption that the Supreme Court would declare the new law unconstitutional, just as it had done with the National Industrial Recovery Act. That assumption turned out to be wrong. The Court upheld the Wagner Act in 1937. Nevertheless, for two years after the act's passage in 1935, business owners and corporate executives believed that the objectionable law would soon be gone courtesy of the Supreme Court. So why should they obey it in the meantime? Rather, they believed that constitutional law and sound economics justified them in defying the Wagner Act.

Foremost among the Wagner Act's flouters was the country's largest carmaker, General Motors. GM's brilliant president, Alfred Sloan, possessed a masterly understanding of corporate strategy and organization. Sloan was to become recognized as the greatest manager of the twentieth century by building GM into the world's largest and most successful corporation. But he proved far less insightful in handling the Second New Deal's challenge to corporate power. An engineer with a cold, hard intellect and a charmless physiognomy, Sloan was nevertheless a master of public relations. Whether out of personal decency or concern for GM's corporate image, he never engaged in the violent suppression practiced by his competitor Ford, whose beatings of workers and union leaders led some Americans to refuse to buy Ford cars. Still, Sloan's understanding of GM's relationship with its employees was bound by traditional concepts of property rights and free markets.

Section 7(a) of the 1933 National Industrial Relations Act had said that in the negotiation of collective bargaining agreements workers were entitled to "representatives of their own choosing." Sloan and GM claimed this meant that no worker could be forced to join any particular union. They held to this view even after the 1935 Wagner Act said that if a majority of workers at a plant voted for a union, it represented all employees. What was at stake was power or, as Sloan put it, "the prerogatives of management," which had come under pressure even before the Wagner Act.[3] In 1934, for example, GM had headed off a strike by agreeing that in laying off employees or in rehiring them "such human relationships as married men with families come first and then seniority, individual skill and efficient service."[4] That was exactly the opposite order of priorities GM management would have preferred in deciding who to lay off or rehire. Still greater loss of GM's management power was certain to follow if the autoworkers succeeded in establishing one industrywide union. This principle of "industrial unionism"—one large union for each of the basic industries—dominated the 1930s drive to organize workers in the automobile, rubber, steel, and electrical industries. Sloan aimed, but failed, to stop industrial unionism at GM.

The Committee for Industrial Organization (CIO), a new national labor organization, arose to organize mass production workers. In 1936, the CIO won a victory for rubber workers over Goodyear tire, launched a committee to organize steel workers, and in November helped reelect Roosevelt, whom Sloan opposed. The next step was for the CIO—or rather, its affiliate, the United Auto Workers—to organize the automobile industry. In late December 1936, several hundred GM workers at two key plants in Flint, Michigan, launched a sit-down strike. The "sit-down" was a radical measure for fighting management's traditional use of strike breakers. Instead of leaving the plant, strikers occupied it.

Sloan was well known for his careful handling of his managers, but he had never shown any interest in GM's workers. He believed, rightly, that GM paid good wages by the standard of the time and, wrongly, that that was good enough. Sloan seemed oblivious to the fact that workers could be dissatisfied by their powerlessness in the face of hard-driving foremen's demands for ever more effort and by the threat that if they could not work ever harder there were plenty of unemployed workers eager to replace them.

Sloan reacted to the sit-down strike with a five-page letter that summed up his idea of the fundamental question: "Will a labor organization run the plants of General Motors Corporation or will the management continue to do so?" Warning the workers that the union would force them to pay "tribute" to it, he called on GM workers to trust "the management of General Motors Corporation to make the business a good business, not only for the workers and for the stockholders, but . . . [for] the prosperity of the country."[5] But Sloan's appeal to the workers was futile, as it really was not up to them to decide. The sit-down strikers were only a tiny fraction of GM employees. Most workers watched warily, fearful that defiance of GM might cost them their jobs. But even though relatively few workers participated in the sit-down strike, it captured national attention.

The real question was whether Michigan Governor Frank Murphy would order out the National Guard to break the strike. The local Flint police had proven unequal to the strikers, who beat back a police assault on the plant in the "Battle of the Running Bulls." The newly elected Governor Murphy was a Roosevelt Democrat and less likely to be influenced by Sloan's view than by general public opinion. Although Sloan was used to winning the struggle for public opinion, he lost it this time. Secretary of Labor Frances Perkins believed that she had gotten a commitment from Sloan to meet with leaders of the United Auto Workers. But according to her, Sloan reneged. The newspapers printed Perkins's claim that she had denounced him to his face, or rather over the phone, as a "scoundrel and a skunk." And Sloan, she claimed, had angrily answered: "You can't talk to me like that! I'm worth seventy million dollars. . . . I'm Alfred Sloan."[6]

Meanwhile, the sit-down strikers in the plants were giving polite interviews to reporters and making it clear that they were not damaging GM's property. Some of the workers claimed that they slept on the uncovered springs of car seats so as not to soil any upholstery. In the face of the strikers' avowed peacefulness and respectful treatment of the plants, there was no chance that the sympathetic Governor Murphy would intervene on behalf of GM. Sloan had no choice but to give in. As he wrote in his memoirs, "President Franklin D. Roosevelt, Secretary of Labor Frances Perkins, and Governor Frank Murphy of Michigan exerted steady pressure upon the corporation, and upon me personally, to negotiate with the strikers who had seized our property, until finally we felt obliged to do so."[7] The six-week strike ended in February 1937 with a humiliating surrender by General Motors, which recognized the United Automobile Workers as the official union of its employees. Later in 1937, one of GM's competitors, Chrysler, signed an agreement with the United Auto Workers after a shorter sit-down strike at some of its plants. That same year, US Steel negotiated a deal with the steelworkers without a strike. Even Ford signed a contract with the United Auto Workers in 1940.

In the new industrial unions the nation had found a countervailing power structure to ensure wider sharing of corporate bounty, but the workers would have to wait a while to enjoy the fruits of their victory. The coming of World War II restored full employment but prevented rapid wage gains. The government held wages in check to fight wartime inflation. But the road had been opened for the high-wage, post–World War II American Dream. Yet many corporate executives would not accept that the new social order was either intellectually or morally justified. Charles Stewart Mott, a member of the GM board and beloved in Michigan for his philanthropy, bitterly said that Governor Murphy "didn't do his job. He didn't enforce the law. . . . He didn't protect our property."[8]

The largest complaint of the corporate class, however, as always with elites who lose some of their power, was moral rather than legal. They claimed that power had shifted to a morally inferior group— workers—whose new economic clout would only further reduce their character. The new power of labor, according to Bernard Baruch, was a victory for laziness and sloth in the working class: ". . . people were losing their initiative."[9] Baruch, one of the originators of the First New Deal, had been all for the government's helping corporations to cooperate with each other. But he thought that ordinary Americans should stand on their own two feet rather than cooperate in labor unions thanks to government legislation. Government, Baruch said, had become "a great mother to whom we could run whenever we were in trouble. . . . The thing that bothered me most about certain aspects of the New Deal was its tendency to dampen initiative and incentive in our people."[10]

In short, the power shift that took place during the Second New Deal was not accompanied by an intellectual shift, not accompanied by any broad understanding that the old concepts of rugged individualism and the free market needed modifying if Americans' ideas were to reflect corporate reality with a reasonable degree of accuracy. Everyone understood that the Second New Deal had strengthened union power at the expense of corporate management. But few understood that organized labor had to somewhat displace management because management had somewhat displaced the free market.

The lack of intellectual clarity as to the reasons for the reining in of corporate power that had taken place in the Second New Deal would have important consequences. Half a century later, when some of the achievements of the New Deal had outlived their usefulness, conservatives would not contest them on the healthy basis of new understandings of new economic realities. Rather, the work of the New Deal would be undone in the name of outworn shibboleths about the market versus collectivism that had had little relevance even in the 1930s and still less in the 1980s, let alone in our own time when, again, foolish cries of "socialism!" have been raised against sensible initiatives such as corporate health insurance reform beneficial to the overall economy.

The practical success and intellectual failure of Americans in the New Deal era leaves us with a hard question today. How long can a nation that has poorly understood its own economic history build new institutions capable of sustaining a good life for its people in a global economy? It was an unfortunate thing that the nation's recovery from the Depression occurred with little understanding among its business people and its citizens in general that they lived and worked in an economy that was run by power as well as freedom, run by corporate managers as well as the market.

PART III

The Corporation Strikes Back

CHAPTER 9

The Right to Manage

CORPORATE LEADERS RECOVERED their moxie in the late 1930s. Since the early days of the Roosevelt administration, many of them had lived in unrealistic fear that the survival of the business system was in doubt. The depth of the Depression had rendered more than a few of them passive, even cowed. But as the economic crisis waned, they found the will to fight for what they considered the essence of the business system, their "right to manage."

In the election of 1938, for the first time in a decade, Republicans gained rather than lost seats in both houses of Congress. Republican congressmen and senators found allies among conservative Democrats whom Roosevelt had tried, unsuccessfully, to purge from his party. This alliance of Republicans and anti-Roosevelt Democrats ended the New Deal. Corporate profits rose in 1938, thanks partly to a surge in government spending to fight an economic dip the year before. The 1939 outbreak of war in Europe further stimulated the American economy. Orders for war materiel poured in from England. The United States adopted a policy of "preparedness" for war, lifting both military spending and the financial prospects of American manufacturers. After the U.S. entrance into World War II in 1941, businessmen could also take heart from relative quiet in the labor movement. With young Americans fighting abroad, the public had no patience for labor conflicts at home. Most national unions, including the United Auto Workers, issued a no-strike pledge and held to it, despite occasional wildcat strikes by local affiliates.

Even though business had begun to regain some of its former profit and power, many corporate executives still feared that they were on the verge of losing control of their firms. During the war it was not easy to see that the labor movement was approaching high tide and would eventually begin to ebb. Despite the unions' no-strike pledge during the war, their membership had risen and their leaders had spoken militantly. The wartime shortage of labor emboldened the rank and file. From management's perspective, shop floor discipline was lax.

Equally distressing to corporate executives was the new militancy of foremen, caught between workers and managers, the former eager to assert their new power and the latter insistent on ever more production. Foremen began to organize and move toward unionization themselves. The movement to unionize foremen had begun among distressed supervisors at Ford, where brutal top-down oppression was still the order of the day. As the foremen's drive for union protection spread to other companies, frightened executives feared the onset of a new threat to managerial control.

Managers saw a foremen's union as de facto socialism. C. C. Carlton, president of the Automobile Manufacturers Association, said that if management lost control of foremen, "then you have taken over our company. . . . [W]e will have nobody to represent us and our stockholders and the owners of the business."[1] Unionization of foremen was a threat to the right to manage. Executives believed that the "right" to manage was a corollary of traditional property rights. Managers, as agents of shareholders, exercised the property rights of the company's owners. Limitation on managerial authority was therefore tantamount to socialism. Thomas Roy Jones, a prominent member of the National Association of Manufacturers, said that loss of the right to manage would amount to "relinquishment of the stockholders' last right—the ownership of the corporate stock."[2]

By tying themselves so closely to stockholders' property rights, corporate executives were in effect answering—or more accurately ignoring—Adolf Berle's and Gardiner Means's ideas described in the previous chapter. In *The Modern Corporation and Private Property* (1932) Berle and Means had argued that with corporate ownership divided among many shareholders, companies were often controlled by managers, not owners. Therefore, corporations, and especially their managers, could not legitimately cite traditional property rights in defense of the privileges and prerogatives they sought to preserve. But few corporate officers had ever heard of Berle and Means. Even if they had, they would have given short shrift to their idea that managers had control. Whether or not corporate managers had more power than shareholders, the executives' time in the political wilderness of the New Deal had convinced them that unions and government had the ultimate upper hand.

Breaking union and government control became corporate leaders' primary political objective. They would be largely successful over the next two decades. Business executives would convince many Americans that they still lived in a society where the basic division was between government power and individual liberty, with business corporations entitled to the same freedoms as individual property holders. Ordinary Americans would lose sight of their eighteenth-century forebears' view of corporations as "little aristocracies." Anticorporatism would of course survive, but it was mainly expressed as an ad hoc resentment of some particular corporate outrage. The popular mind came to accept the corporate economy in general the way it accepted, say, the weather or the landscape. Public forgetfulness that corporations had once been considered un-American eased the task of executives in their pursuit of social status and moral standing.

It would eventually become credible to many citizens that corporations were fighting for liberty, not against it. Corporations were protecting freedom against oppression, just as Americans always had. While business corporations supposedly spoke for freedom, labor unions became, for many conservatives, one more form of the anti-American tyranny previously embodied in the England of George III or in Nazi Germany's Third Reich. The fact that Communist Russia was then America's principal external opponent only added to the idea that unions, with their threat to the "right to manage," were forerunners of socialist oppression.

Corporate executives' fears of tyranny were fueled by what they saw as government abandonment of the free market during World War II. The public had been on guard against war profiteering and corporate gouging, so the Roosevelt administration had created the Office of Price Administration to set prices and prevent inflation. In this wartime atmosphere of governmental control it was easy for corporate folk to believe that free enterprise was in jeopardy.

Corporate leaders also believed that government favored labor unions during the war. FDR had established the National War Labor Board and given it the job of preventing strikes by arbitrating labor disputes, which seemed pro-union to many businessmen. Alfred Sloan of General Motors believed at the end of the war, as he had at the beginning, that unions were "able to enlist the support of the government in any great crisis."[3] Actually, the War Labor Board worked to keep unions from meddling with management. Washington's wartime agencies were laden with corporate dollar-a-year men who believed in the right to manage.[4] Despite the politically necessary facade of government control, the war drove the Roosevelt administration into an accommodation with business corporations.

Secretary of War Henry Stimson reflected the administration's point of view in a private diary entry. To make "war in a capitalist country, you have got to let business make money out of the process."[5] The nation needed weapons, and corporations owned the means of production. Many corporations were fearful of building new production facilities for the war effort. If the war were short, they would have sunk large, unrecoverable sums into factories that would never return a profit. So even as the government controlled prices, it rallied corporate America with generous contracts for weapons, grants for new factories, and tax write-offs for business investments.

Corporations' improving profits heightened business executives' self-esteem, making them all the more resentful of the low regard in which the public had held them since the Great Crash. Businessmen fought not just to make money but to recover the social status and prestige they had enjoyed before the Depression. The best historian of the business mind during this period observed that managers and executives were fighting not just for power and profit but for "moral authority."[6]

Business faced an uphill struggle to regain the stature it had once enjoyed. It was widely believed that the business system was incapable of offering full employment in peacetime and that the Depression would resume once the Germans and the Japanese were defeated. The government was expected to reduce weapons purchases once peace came, and many believed that civilian consumer spending would not be sufficient to maintain the full employment brought by the war. For example, the nation's largest industry—automobiles—was thought to have no growth potential. Everyone who needed a car supposedly had one. The postwar auto market was expected to be limited to replacements, as old cars wore out. With a static market in America's most vital industry, how could the country not return to a Depression when the war ended?

Many in the labor movement shared these views and believed that unions, not corporations, had to lead the way to postwar prosperity. Donald Montgomery—economics adviser to Walter Reuther, who headed the United Auto Workers—wrote that industry "can produce at half or three-quarters of production and break even. . . . It does not intend to adopt a new pattern just because we have passed through a war which has demonstrated—to its embarrassment—the tremendous, but strenuous, profit potential of capacity operations."[7]

Fortunately, Montgomery was mistaken, at least if his assertion was meant to include the most important auto executive. Alfred Sloan of General Motors saw massive growth potential in the American automobile market. He cited Americans' huge personal savings thanks to the combined effect of wartime full employment and consumer rationing. It seemed a certainty to Sloan that Americans would spend those savings after the war. The only obstacle to a postwar boom that Sloan could see was government interference in the economy. But he was confident that the government would get out of the way: " . . . the rabbit-out-of-the-hat business, the something for nothing . . . and a lot of other panaceas . . . of the New Deal in the 1930s, are finished, and will not be carried into the postwar period."[8]

Sloan planned not only to use all of GM's factories but to expand them after the war. He maintained that such a policy would benefit all Americans. For all his reactionary corporatism, Sloan nevertheless envisioned a postwar American Dream. In a wartime speech, Sloan had pointed to pent-up purchasing power as a basis for a postwar vision that many must have thought was a castle in the sky but became a reality: "Would it be possible if American industry stepped forward . . . and expanded its operations, . . . to capitalize this purchasing power? Would it be possible to raise . . . the standard of living to an amount far in excess of what we have ever had before?"[9] Under Sloan's leadership, General Motors invested $500 million in new plants and equipment to manufacture cars for the postwar boom he expected. By September 1945, only a month after the end of the war, GM was again producing civilian automobiles, and consumers were lining up to buy them. Aided by suburbanization, the two-car family, and the new youth market for used cars, Sloan led the nation toward prosperity and full employment in the postwar period.

Sloan also led the nation toward a postwar resurgence not only of corporate power but of the corporation's moral standing with the American people. The corporation's sudden rise in social prestige was explained in part by Sloan's adroit handling of a 1946 strike against GM, but it also resulted from the self-fulfilling quality of his prophecy of prosperity. Just as GM's forecast of abysmal demand in the early years of the Depression helped make bad times worse, the automobile corporation's optimistic investment in postwar production facilities helped make good times better. As GM hired and geared up for postwar production, workers gained purchasing power to fuel a postwar boom. Corporate power meets far fewer objections from the public when it contributes to a boom rather than a bust.

CHAPTER 10

Corporations Recover Their
Moral Authority

FOR ALL OF ALFRED SLOAN's tough-minded contributions to the postwar American Dream, he nevertheless shared in some of the corporate world's most popular fantasies about freedom. In one of his wartime speeches he described the $500 million investment that GM was about to make in postwar production as "the contribution we are prepared to make to help preserve the free competitive enterprise system as the keystone of the American economy."[1] It was scarcely Sloan's fault that $500 million was the price of admission to the "free competitive enterprise system." But he might at least have recognized that ordinary citizens could not compete in this "free" market. Rather than start their own auto companies, citizens had to go to work for them.

Sloan bore responsibility, along with his fellow corporate executives, for the fact that the postwar American Dream era would be not only a fantastically prosperous time but also a time of inaccurate fictions about how corporations were fighting for freedom. It was true, of course, that corporate executives resisted government power. But they did so for the sake of corporate power, not individual liberty, or at least not the liberty of any individuals other than themselves. Corporate executives would succeed to an impressive degree in imposing on citizens at large the idea that the corporate economy expressed Americans' traditional democratic values. They clung to Adam Smith's original laissez-faire ideology as if heavy industry, economies of scale, and managerial power had not arisen in the two intervening centuries. Despite the New Deal or, more accurately, because of the failure of the Roosevelt administration to offer a consistent philosophy for its actions, liberals would be dealt a weak ideological hand for the rest of the twentieth century and into the twenty-first.

The issue of how to shift to a peacetime economy had not seemed pressing even as late as the summer of 1945. Although Germany had surrendered in May of that year, the war against Japan was expected to last until 1946 and possibly beyond. But the surprise dropping of atomic bombs on Hiroshima and Nagasaki ended the war in August 1945. With unexpected suddenness, the race was on between management and labor for postwar moral authority. Labor was first out of the gate. In September 1945, Walter Reuther, who had led the movement to unionize GM in 1937 and who would soon head the United Auto Workers, said that the war had shown that consumption drove employment and prosperity. To maintain full employment after the war, civilian consumption would have to replace military consumption.[2]

One of the main barriers that Reuther saw to civilian consumption was an expected inflationary surge as President Harry Truman (Roosevelt had died in the spring of 1945) moved to end wartime economic controls. Rising prices, Reuther thought, could easily plunge the postwar economy back into economic depression. If prices rose faster than wages, workers would slowly lose their ability to consume industry's products. As demand fell, industry would lay off workers, further lowering demand and depressing the economy. So Reuther attempted to make prices as well as wages the business of the United Auto Workers. He announced two major goals for the union's next contract with General Motors. The union wanted a 30 percent pay raise and, just as important, a GM commitment not to raise car prices.

With his call for GM to raise wages but not prices, Reuther hoped to prevent a postwar depression. If wages rose 30 percent while prices stayed the same, workers could buy 30 percent more of manufacturers' products. The increased demand would promote full employment. Essentially, Reuther aimed to fuel a postwar boom by reducing corporate profit margins in order to raise wages. Higher wages, he reasoned, would lead to greater demand for corporate products and the creation of ever more jobs.

Alfred Sloan, having suffered through government constraints during the Depression and then World War II, was not about to be hamstrung now by the United Auto Workers. Predictably, he saw Reuther's attempt to control GM's prices as interference with shareholders' property rights, which they had delegated to management. As the shareholders' agent, Sloan and only Sloan had the "right to manage." To Sloan, the issue was not just prices but principle. Even though GM had a new president—Charles Wilson or, as he became known, "Engine Charlie"—Sloan still had a large hand in the company's management. When Sloan recoiled from the auto workers' demands that car prices not rise, Reuther proposed that a board of impartial auditors examine the company's books. The goal of the audit would be to see if GM could afford to raise wages and not prices. GM refused, and UAW workers voted to strike in late November 1945.

Reuther believed that his demand for no price increase was not only good policy but good public relations. By trying to get GM to hold the line on prices, the union could claim it was representing the interests not only of workers but also of consumers. "Labor is not fighting for a larger share of the national pie," Reuther declared. "Labor is fighting for a larger pie."[3] Unfortunately for Reuther, his opponent Alfred Sloan was a master of public relations. Sloan, too, could claim he had the public interest at heart. And unlike the UAW, GM could afford to tell its story to the public in a national advertising campaign. In newspaper ads all over the country, GM argued that wages should be governed by the "going rate" in the labor market. In other words, the issue was economic freedom: "America is at the crossroads! It must preserve the freedom . . . of American business to determine its own destiny."[4] The issue, as GM presented it to the public, was free enterprise. GM executives Sloan and Wilson objected to Reuther's emphasis on the company's ability to pay. The effect of auto workers' demand for a pay raise and no price increase would be to lower GM's profits.

GM and the UAW both settled in for a long strike. But unfortunately for the UAW, there were many other strikes to attract public attention in late 1945 and early 1946. Workers in many industries were done with their wartime no-strike pledge and were eager to push for higher wages. Railroad workers, lumbermen, teamsters, machinists, meat packers, oil company employees, and countless others went on strike. The nation was soon in the greatest labor turmoil of the twentieth century. Late 1945 and early 1946 brought thousands of strikes. On any given day there were somewhere between 3 million and 6 million workers off the job, causing massive production losses.

The vast labor unrest grabbed the headlines. Reuther's claim that the auto workers were seeking a bigger pie for everyone was drowned out by less skillful labor leaders in other industries. These other labor leaders ignored Reuther's drive to hold the line on prices. They demanded higher wages, pure and simple, depriving workers of the claim that they were looking out for the public's interest as well as their own. GM was able to portray the UAW as just one more union in the national labor turmoil that was threatening social order and frightening middle-class citizens.

In March 1946, after a strike of five months, the United Auto Workers surrendered. The union accepted a raise of 15 percent, about half the size it had sought. The auto workers could probably have had the same settlement the previous November, without a strike and without the lost wages their strike had cost them. Adding to the UAW's humiliation, GM not only made no promise on prices but soon raised them. Inflation surged 14 percent between March and November 1946, consuming the gains GM workers had gotten in their March settlement. Not only had their strike been unnecessary to what gains they had achieved, but the gains were gone. The UAW had fought for absolutely nothing.

From the perspective of Sloan, GM, the auto industry, and the corporate world in general, the strike had ended in an immense victory for the "right to manage." The 1946 GM strike was the effective endpoint for consideration of ability to pay in American labor relations (except when financially troubled corporations sought union "give backs"). Sloan had defeated Reuther's attempt to claim that the labor movement represented the people's interests and therefore should have a say in management decisions such as pricing.

Sloan, like Reuther, wanted full employment, but he believed that both principle and prosperity required the preservation of management prerogatives. Sloan later recalled his years of struggle against the United Auto Workers as a "grim" time. Freedom itself, he believed, had been on the line. But once victory was his, Sloan spoke with characteristic understatement: "we were fairly successful. . . . There is no longer any doubt that pricing is a management, not a union, function."[5]

Neither government nor labor unions but, instead, business corporations—their sales fueled by Americans' wartime savings—would lead the way to full employment. Rather than the policy of no price increases that Reuther had envisioned to generate consumption and full employment, 1950s American Dream prosperity would be built on a cycle of alternately rising wages and prices that boosted aggregate demand, brought full employment, and lifted the standard of living. It was a far less systematic approach to the issue of full employment than Reuther and the UAW had imagined. Unions would negotiate pay raises only to have their employers announce price increases.

As inflation became part of life during the American Dream era, conservatives spoke of the "wage–price spiral," with the emphasis on wages. Thanks to Sloan, and contrary to Reuther's hopes, a large portion of Americans came to view labor unions as the cause of rising prices. Inflation was what happened when unions demanded higher pay rather than what happened when corporations charged higher prices. Sloan, GM, and the business system in general defeated the labor movement in the postwar struggle for moral authority.

CHAPTER 11

Killing the Unions Softly

CORPORATE EXECUTIVES NOW SET ABOUT converting their newly recovered moral authority into political power. Here, too, they were successful. The anti-union legislation they persuaded Congress to enact would, in the long run, help to diminish the American Dream. Corporations used their postwar moral victory over the unions to shape Americans' understanding of freedom. To many, freedom came to mean weak government, weak unions, and minimal interference with the supposedly free market. The issue of corporate power as a threat to freedom slipped off the radar.

The Democrats' identification with the unions, which had once been a political asset, would increasingly become a liability. Truman had tried to escape the labor incubus by opposing some of the postwar strikes. He had even threatened to draft railroad workers into the army before they settled their 1946 strike on his terms. Nevertheless, voters blamed the Democrats for inflation and for the postwar strike wave. For the first time in a generation, voters saw Republicans as better equipped than Democrats to manage the economy. In the midterm election of 1946, Republicans gained control of both houses of Congress, a feat they had last achieved in 1928. The election results amounted to a rebuke of the labor movement by the American public. By contrast, corporations enjoyed more status, prestige, and political power than since the days of Calvin Coolidge.

Should newly empowered corporate interests try to repeal the Wagner Act of 1935? That law had given a majority of a plant's workers the right to elect a union that spoke for all. The Wagner Act had made possible the new industrial unions such as the United Auto Workers, the United Steelworkers, and the United Rubber Workers. Many businessmen, their heads swelled by their new political power, were tempted to try for a knock-out punch, a complete repeal of the Wagner Act. Cooler heads prevailed in corporate groups such as the National Association of Manufacturers. They saw that President Truman would almost surely veto a Wagner Act repeal. Even with Republican majorities in both houses of Congress, it might not be possible to get the two-thirds vote needed to override a presidential veto. If corporate interests overreached, they might end up with no legislative gains at all.

Anyway, the industrial unions were well established and would have some staying power even if the Wagner Act were repealed. A frontal attack on the unions might only make them more militant while sacrificing business leaders' new moral authority. Having succeeded in convincing the public that they were more reasonable and public-spirited than labor leaders, corporate chiefs wanted to hang on to their advantage. Corporate managers had made gains in public favor by positioning themselves as defenders of freedom. They would lose their hard-won moral weight if they appeared to oppose workers' freedom to organize unions. Business had to be *for* freedom, including workers' freedom. The National Association of Manufacturers therefore argued that "[t]he right of employees to organize in unions . . . should continue to be protected by law." But workers should also have the "right not to organize" and "should be protected against coercion from any source" including unions.[1] Corporate America would protect employees from union tyranny. Let freedom ring!

The great civil right to which corporate interests committed themselves in the late 1940s was workers' freedom *not* to unionize. For many business leaders this approach was not cynical. They often spoke warmly of workers as "*our* men" who shared management's conservative American values but could not say so, owing to union oppression. The idea of protecting workers against union tyranny sold well in the new Congress that took office in 1947. The Republican majority shared the anti-union sentiments of citizens frightened by the great postwar strike wave of 1945 and 1946. On the first day of the new Congress, legislators introduced seventeen anti-labor bills.[2] There was a real chance that congressional conservatives might try for a stronger anti-union law than was favored by corporate interest groups, thereby forfeiting the reputation for moderation that business now enjoyed with the public.

The decisive figure in the congressional negotiations over a new labor law was Republican Senator Robert A. Taft. A skillful parliamentarian, he brought in a bill that reflected the shrewdly restrained goals of corporate interest groups. Rather than attempting to kill the unions with one blow, the Taft-Hartley Act only lamed them, setting them on a gradual, long-term path toward near-extinction.

Ostensibly, the Taft-Hartley Act enlarged employees' freedom, especially their "right to work." The new law outlawed "closed shops," where workers had to belong to a union before they could be hired. It also allowed individual states to outlaw "union shops" in which an employee, once hired, had to join the union. Referendums on such "right-to-work" laws were some of the most bitterly fought state elections of the 1950s. Taft-Hartley also enacted "free speech" for employers. Corporate managers could express opposition to the formation of a union. Firms that already had unions could petition the National Labor Relations Board for an election to see if the union still had majority support. And some Taft-Hartley measures directly reduced union power. Foremen were not allowed to unionize. Strikes to obtain jurisdiction over a particular set of workers were outlawed. So were secondary boycotts of firms doing business with a company being struck. The president of the United States could order strikers back to work for a "cooling off" period.

The shrewdness of conservative businessmen in refusing to go for all-out repeal of the Wagner Act now bore fruit. Truman did veto the Taft-Hartley Act, just as expected. But because of the law's supposed moderation, the Republicans had enough Democratic allies to override the president's veto. The most important immediate effect of the Taft-Hartley law was symbolic. Corporate executives could take heart from the fact that the pendulum had swung. Business, not labor, now enjoyed the political support of middle America. If corporations were heartened, labor was bitter. The unions damned Taft-Hartley as a "slave labor law" and launched a movement to repeal it. Truman's support of repeal brought labor support that was probably decisive in his 1948 reelection. But the president and the unions failed in their 1949 bid for Congress to repeal Taft-Hartley. The law is still on the books.

Taft-Hartley is seldom mentioned in the popular media today, but that may attest to its long-run effectiveness. In the 1950s, twenty-two states exercised their option under Taft-Hartley to pass "right-to-work" laws. In those right-to-work states, a union, even if supported by a majority of employees, could not bargain collectively on behalf of all. In effect, twenty-two states repealed the Wagner Act. The right-to-work states were located entirely in the South and West. Northern and midwestern states refused to follow suit. In other words, northern and midwestern states had strong labor laws and a strong labor movement, whereas the South and West did not. From the corporate perspective, the location of right-to-work states in the South and West was fortunate. These regions would enjoy far greater economic growth in the second half of the twentieth century than would the Midwest and Northeast. The right-to-work laws contained the union movement within the slowest growing regions of the country. At the end of World War II, 30 percent of the American workforce was unionized. Today it is 7 percent.

The cautious goal set by the National Association of Manufacturers and other corporate interests—not to kill the labor movement but only to cripple it—paid large dividends in the form of favorable public opinion. For many Americans, corporations, even corporate giants, had confirmed their moral superiority to labor unions. Many people accepted the corporate system's self-identification with freedom. Still, the established unions remained in place. They would continue throughout the 1950s and into the 1960s to create the American Dream. But despite their role in the new economic prosperity, the unions were losing the culture war on which their moral authority and standing depended.

Corporate interests would not wait passively for Taft-Hartley to slowly kill the labor movement but would try to assist in that process and speed it up a bit. From the corporate perspective, it was time to move beyond Congress and to fight the unions out on the shop floor, in workers' communities, and even in their homes. The corporate system had to be an intellectual as well as material creation. Not all citizens could be won to a corporate worldview, but it might be possible to convince some, or maybe even many, that what was good for the company was good for them. A largely forgotten executive took on this job with such energy and skill that he helped shape American politics for two generations.

CHAPTER 12

Creating Reagan and His Voters

GRADUATING STUDENTS TURNED OUT in large numbers to hear Lemuel Boulware speak at Harvard Business School (HBS) in June 1949, just a few days before commencement. The HBS class of 1949 would be renowned for its patriotism and its success. Many had fought in the war, had gone to school on the GI bill, and were destined for rich rewards in the corporate world. They listened attentively as Boulware outlined a conservative manifesto that, over the next thirty years, would spread into society at large and undo much of the New Deal.

"Boulwarism" had recently become famous in the business world and infamous in the labor movement. The graduating HBS students had already studied Boulwarism in some of their classes. As vice president for employee relations at General Electric, Boulware sought to provide workers with economic education that would fend off union proselytizing. He aimed to make workers into appreciative, manageable citizens of corporate America.

Boulware came to prominence as a result of General Electric's attempt to improve relations with employees and the public following a bitter strike in 1946. GE had bungled public relations during the strike. Police had violently suppressed picketers, some of whom were newly returned veterans carrying placards that read "GI versus GE." Although the great strike wave of 1945–1946 had alienated many middle-class Americans from the labor movement, the public made an exception for the electrical workers. Newspapers, politicians, and clergy had loudly condemned the electrical manufacturer. Americans mostly condemned GE and sided with the strikers. GE suffered a devastating defeat. To end the strike, the company had to double the wage increase it had initially offered. GE's paternalistic managers had been shocked at the "bitter conditions" in their "relationship with our people."[1]

General Electric President Charles Wilson—called "*Electric* Charlie" to distinguish him from General Motors's "*Engine* Charlie" Wilson— turned to Boulware for help. Boulware managed employee relations at a number of GE subsidiaries such as Hotpoint. Not a single one of the sixteen thousand employees that Boulware managed had gone on strike in 1946. It was only logical for Wilson to assign Boulware, in the latter's words, "to correct the ridiculous situation where . . . the company was distrusted and disapproved of by employees and neighbors."[2]

Speaking in 1949 to the Harvard Business School students, Boulware attributed the bitter feeling against GE not to its sorry 1946 treatment of workers but to general social pathologies. He listed a range of grievances on which conservatives had dwelled since the New Deal and on which they would focus until the present day. Taxes were too high, government too big, and the nation in moral decline. But Boulware's real focus in his Harvard speech was on a problem that, thanks to him, is of less concern to conservatives today. According to Boulware, too many citizens believed that corporations were "anti-social."[3] Ignoring the clear turn of public opinion in favor of corporations versus labor unions as represented in the Taft-Hartley Act of 1947, Boulware dwelt on lingering anticorporatism from the 1930s. It hurt. No matter how large the pay and perks of corporate folk, they could not be consoled for being considered enemies of society. Boulware told the Harvard students that the public's contempt for business corporations is "our greatest distress."[4]

Boulware nursed the pain of his pro-business audience with caustic and balm. Having touched their sore point, the contempt in which they were held, he inspired hope of self-cure by blaming them for the boil: "*This can only be the fault of us businessmen ourselves.*"[5] Businessmen themselves created their negative image. They "always seem to be coldly against everything." Too seldom did they "speak up warmly" about what they were for. That left the public ignorant of the fact that the business system worked for the "common good."[6] Boulware urged his Harvard audience to speak cheerfully about how they enriched the nation. "We are great physicists, chemists, engineers. We are phenomenal manufacturers. We have been fabulous financiers. We are superb in individual selling and mass marketing."[7] These same skills had to be used to tell the public that "profitable, competitive business" was a social good.

Americans suffered, Boulware said, from "economic illiteracy."[8] They did not "understand how we got this standard of living."[9] In other words, they did not understand the corporate system or, as Boulware described it, the interrelated "parts played by the customer, the worker, the manager, as well as the saver." Each would refuse to play his part "unless the incentive is there, unless he . . . get[s] what's right from the others for what he does."[10]

Some were losing incentive because of high taxes. The problem was the New Deal attitude, according to Boulware, that people could enjoy free benefits from taxes imposed on others. Sounding an idea that would remain profoundly influential down to the present day, Boulware insisted that Americans did not realize that once others were overtaxed, they had less reason to play their parts in the interrelation of customers, workers, managers, and investors on which we all depend.

Politicians knew there was no free lunch but, eager for votes, legislated gratis noonday repasts. The politicians "think the public just would not understand" the facts. Cognoscenti such as Boulware's Harvard Business School audience could only be "horrified at the way representatives, both in government and in unions" refused to speak the truth.[11] The only solution was for businessmen to get into politics. But their job was not to run for office, at least not yet. As truth tellers, they would have no chance of getting elected. Rather, the political job of businessmen was the long, slow job of educating the public. The American people had to be taught "sound economics."[12] Only after citizens knew the truth would they be ready to elect responsible officials. Boulware closed his speech—titled "Salvation Is Not Free"—with a combination of evangelism and patriotism that would become characteristic of modern conservatism. "Let us . . . covenant together" to "go at this job fearlessly" because "mightier than armies is the power of a righteous idea." Businessmen should "boldly take . . . the patriot's job of . . . speaking out."[13]

Determined that GE would lead the way, Boulware launched a marketing effort, not to sell a product, but to sell employees on the company. GE foremen became "job salesmen" who were to teach their subordinates not just to do their jobs but to appreciate them. He began his campaign to sell workers on their jobs with a survey of their attitudes, just as if he were conducting a marketing survey of potential customers.

His goal was to learn what employees wanted from their work. Predictably, he found that they wanted good pay, security, respect, and opportunity. But Boulware also found that workers had a neglected need for "information," "belief," and "satisfaction." Employees needed to be informed not only about the how but also the why of their jobs so that they could work "intelligently and voluntarily."[14] Workers needed to believe in "the great good accomplished by the final GE product." Above all, they needed to go "home to the family after a day's work" with the satisfaction "that something has been accomplished," that the accomplishment "has earned the respect" of fellow employees, "and that the job is a good one."[15]

To help meet employees' need for information, belief, and satisfaction, Boulware launched a massive publishing program. Bulletins and magazines poured from his office. Every Friday, every GE employee got a free newspaper, *Works News*, with information on happenings at the local plant and an insert from GE headquarters on companywide matters. Boulware's publications aimed to educate workers economically and politically. One article might teach that the business system worked for the good of all: "Corporate Profits Help Increase Flow of Income to All Classes." Another might correct incipient leftists: "What Is Communism? What Is Capitalism? What Is the Difference to You?"[16] One of Boulware's favorite themes was "How Big Are General Electric Profits?—Are They Too Big?"[17] He published pie charts showing what happened to each dollar of GE's gross income. For example, out of every dollar that customers paid to GE in 1953, the company spent thirty-six cents on workers' wages. Another hefty piece of the pie—forty-three cents—went to GE's suppliers. Taxes took fifteen cents. That left only six cents for profit, of which three cents went to shareholder dividends and three cents was invested in new plant and equipment to grow the company.[18]

Boulware's focus on how GE spent its revenues actually left employees in the dark as to the company's profit as measured by financial accountants. The company's ROI (return on investment) was nowhere to be found in these publications. Did the six cents of profit from the customer's dollar amount to a 6 percent, a 60 percent, or a 600 percent return on shareholders' investment? Boulware's obvious goal was to avoid telling employees how profitable GE really was. His idea of providing economic education for workers did not include giving them the understanding of financial accounting they would have needed to measure their employer's profitability. He wanted employees to conclude that GE was accomplishing miracles for others and claiming little for itself.

In addition to his publications, Boulware created a companywide Employee Relations Department with three thousand employees spread across GE's sprawling empire of more than a hundred factories. These specialists in employee relations coached GE's supervisors on how to discuss delicate issues such as "why the company has no choice but to 'take' a strike rather than be forced beyond what is right."[19] On company time, the Employee Relations Department taught a course of four and a half hours to workers. The course was called HOBSO (How Our Business System Operates).

But it was not enough to reach employees at work. GE supported employee book clubs that met in workers' homes. There they discussed conservative economic texts such as Lewis Haney's *How You Really Earn Your Living* and Henry Hazlitt's *Economics in One Lesson*. The goal of the GE book clubs was to educate not only the workers but their wives. Boulware also aimed to win over clergy and the press, both of which had outspokenly criticized GE during the 1946 strike. His subordinates worked at getting articles favorable to GE into local newspapers in towns where the company had plants, papers such as the *Daily Gazette* in Schenectady, New York, and the *Berkshire Eagle* in Lynn, Massachusetts. Men of the cloth were given plant tours aimed at showing them how the company contributed to society.

Boulware's obvious strategy was to bypass the workers' elected representatives, the United Electrical Workers, in order to reach out directly to employees and convince them, as well as the public at large, that they shared common interests with GE. It would have been surprising if he had not spotted the potential for reaching GE's nationwide workforce with the new medium of television. The result was a popular Sunday evening program, *General Electric Theater*, hosted by an actor whose film career was on the wane, Ronald Reagan. The show aired on Sunday evenings, immediately following one of the most popular television programs of all time, *The Ed Sullivan Show*. Reagan introduced *General Electric Theater*, sometimes acted in the dramas, always followed them up with a short homily on Boulware's we're-all-in-it-together theme, and signed off by affirming, "At General Electric, progress is our most important product."

When Reagan began to host *GE Theater* in 1954, he was not only a New Deal Democrat but a labor leader, thanks to his presidency of the Screen Actors Guild. When he left GE in 1962, he was a free-market advocate about to jump to the Republican Party. Boulware and GE helped to convert Reagan from New Deal Democrat to conservative Republican and, through him, the nation as well. Reagan's GE contract called for the actor to spend a fourth of his time touring GE's plants. Boulware's idea was that workers, face to face with the famous GE spokesman, would have a new sense of identity with the company, making them more receptive to its political and economic teachings. On the plant tours, Reagan absorbed the message Boulware was delivering to employees. Personally resentful of the high tax bracket in which his film success had placed him, Reagan was receptive to Boulware's antigovernment themes. But Reagan needed a broader social ideology to justify a shift away from New Deal orthodoxy. He found it in the economics texts that Boulware was pushing on GE workers, both in the plant and in home book clubs.

Boulware's ideological bible was a book by the conservative economist Henry Hazlitt, *Economics in One Lesson* (1946). Hazlitt's one lesson was that government largesse is a devilish delusion. His book ignored the issues of frothy credit markets and insufficient demand that had dominated economics since the Depression. According to Hazlitt, government programs to smooth the credit markets or raise demand did far more harm than good. He contended that government programs are usually wasteful once their whole cost is calculated. Reagan took the lesson to heart, and by the late 1950s his standard GE speech was loaded with examples of government waste. "The annual interest on the TVA [Tennessee Valley Authority—a signature program of the New Deal]," Reagan informed GE workers, "is five times as great as flood damage it prevents."[20]

But Boulware always insisted on a positive side to every message. Therefore, Reagan associated big business with freedom, the same correlation that the corporate world had been trying to teach Americans since the New Deal. Reagan's GE speeches had titles like "Encroaching

Control" and "Our Eroding Freedoms." For Reagan, GE's support for freedom of expression seemed personal and genuine. Ralph Cordiner— the GE president who succeeded Wilson—refused to censor one of Reagan's speeches even though it alienated an important GE customer. Reagan described himself as "overwhelmed" by Cordiner's support for free speech and said he finally abandoned his "lingering boyhood ideas from the Great Depression about big business."[21]

A poorly led strike against GE in 1960 confirmed the shrewdness of Boulware's strategy. A large minority of workers, maybe even the majority, struck reluctantly, more or less forced into it by a foolishly aggressive union president.[22] After only three weeks, the union accepted GE's original offer with a few face-saving changes. Fourteen years after GE had suffered a devastating loss in the great strike wave of 1946, the company won, thanks to Boulware, a thrilling victory over its unionized workforce in the 1960 strike. The *New York Times* called it labor's worst setback since World War II. Understandably, many companies now set out to emulate Boulware's methods.[23]

Boulware's soft touch was demonstrated by GE's handling of the fact that Reagan, a few months earlier, had led the Screen Actors Guild in a strike against the movie studios. How could GE oppose a strike when the company spokesman was leading another? Easy. Newspapers, probably fed by GE's public relations department, reported Reagan's statement that the company "never said a word to me about it."[24] Corporate America, guided by Boulware, had shown it was freedom's friend. From Boulware, Reagan learned not only economics but also the political importance of message discipline. Boulware helped teach Reagan the incessant driving of his message that made him so effective a politician. From 1966, when he became governor of California, to 1989, when he left the White House, Reagan campaigned not just on election day but every day.

There had to be a conservative movement before Reagan could become its leader and use it to propel him into the White House. Boulware helped to create that movement, not only by his work at GE but in other ways as well. He personally contributed to the founding of the *National Review*, which, under the editorship of William F. Buckley, became the leading magazine of American conservatism.[25] In a sense, the *National Review* succeeded GE's weekly *Employee Relations Newsletter*, which Boulware had mailed not only to GE executives and supervisors but to opinion makers—"columnists, teachers, clergymen, politicians and other businessmen," whose numbers were "perhaps several times" the fifteen thousand GE managers who received the company publication.[26]

The resurgent conservative movement won the 1964 Republican presidential nomination for Senator Barry Goldwater by adopting Boulware's strategy of working around the establishment to reach the people directly. Just as GE had communicated directly with workers rather than going through the union, the "draft Goldwater" movement worked to reach the grass-roots voters and to outmaneuver the moderate Republican National Committee. Ralph Cordiner, by then retired from the GE presidency, oversaw Goldwater's campaign finances while Reagan contributed his celebrity and speaking skill.

Reagan gave a widely discussed, nationally televised speech in support of Goldwater in late October 1964, just a week before the presidential election. Reagan's speech, one of the high points of the Goldwater campaign, was soon celebrated by political pundits as "the most successful political debut since William Jennings Bryan's Cross of Gold speech in 1896."[27] The national broadcast of Reagan's speech had cost $60,000, funds that Boulware and another retired GE executive, J. J. Wuerthner, were instrumental in raising.[28]

In Reagan's 1964 speech for Goldwater, he outlined the eventual themes of his presidency. Both his address and its themes were directly descended from the talk Boulware had given at the Harvard Business School in 1949. Above all, government regulation was to be understood not as an antidote to corporate power but as a threat to freedom. Reagan opened his Goldwater speech by saying that he had "been talking about this subject for ten years." He left out the fact that for eight of those years GE had paid him to do so.[29] Although Goldwater was trounced in the 1964 presidential election, Reagan's brilliantly successful speech gave corporate America a candidate who would eventually attain the White House.

Like Taft-Hartley, Boulwarism succeeded so well that it is scarcely heard of today. Following the failed 1960 strike against GE, angry union leaders successfully argued to the National Labor Relations Board that the company's communication strategy amounted to a failure to negotiate in good faith.[30] By going around the union and communicating directly with employees, GE was violating its legal obligation to recognize the union as the employees' representative.

The government ruling against Boulwarism only temporarily strengthened the hand of the labor movement. For Boulwarism helped give birth to the conservative movement and its leader, Ronald Reagan. As president of the United States, Reagan would secure the late-twentieth-century triumph of business corporations over the unions. Thanks to Boulware and Reagan, the challenge to the business corporation from government and labor was met. Now it was up to the corporations to show that, left alone to practice their ideology of free enterprise, they could create a better society. Were corporate managers up to the job?

PART IV

What Manner of Man(ager)?

CHAPTER 13

Masking the Arrogance of Power

TYCOONS AND FINANCIERS had long starred in the drama of capitalism. But corporate managers took center stage during the 1930s and held the spotlight for sixty years. Were managers the heroes or the villains of the piece? Management has always had an image problem in democratic America. Before the Civil War, overseers on slave plantations had been the largest cohort of salaried managers in the country. Later, as free whites went to work for corporations and fell under managerial control, they called a hard boss a "slave driver."

In the late nineteenth century and early in the twentieth, a movement for "scientific management" arose in steel mills and machine shops. Mechanical engineers sought to speed up workers in order to raise the return on capital invested in the machines they operated. Armed with stopwatches and motion studies, they created a new profession—the "efficiency expert." Critics claimed that scientific management was ineffective. But that seems to have been wishful thinking. Serious scholars have shown that scientific management raised productivity.[1] Some high-minded reformers hoped to make scientific management an agent of social change. These reformers believed that the savings from scientific management could be used to raise wages and improve the lot of the proletariat. But shareholders and customers wanted higher profits and lower prices. In the face of such pressures, scientific management was often used not to raise wages but to sweat ever more effort out of workers for the same pay or even less.

Some of the scientific managers blamed financiers and accountants for the injustices of modern capitalism, and with some reason. The bankers and bean counters siphoned off the gains that engineers and production managers made possible. Workers, customers, and shareholders all suffered at the hands of the money men and the green eyeshades.

Later, during the Depression, some engineer-managers hoped that hard times would discredit the financiers and destroy their power. The engineer-managers leapt into the limelight by proclaiming that they should run the whole country, not just its factories. Thus rose a brief, splashy movement for a government of "technocrats," a movement that quickly fizzled out when its leader, a somewhat mysterious figure named Howard Scott, gave a loony speech with fascist overtones. At about the same time he was found to have overstated his engineering qualifications.

Many engineer-managers were more level-headed than the technocrats yet fell short of the communication skills needed to make management more respectable. The way was open for others—unskilled in operations but fluent in communication—to represent management. The new managers identified themselves not as engineers but as leaders. Leader-managers gained prestige over engineer-managers thanks partly to the New Deal. President Franklin Roosevelt symbolized the change. His predecessor, Herbert Hoover, before assuming the presidency, had succeeded brilliantly as a mining engineer, as a businessman, and as a humanitarian manager of disaster relief. Yet Hoover was a failed president whereas Roosevelt, a mere lawyer with no special technical competence, became one of the Oval Office's most successful occupants.

Roosevelt used the idea of leadership to create a managerial presidency, which his successors have imitated ever since. Acquiring a vast staff, he assumed responsibility for managing everything from the people's morale to the state of the economy. One of his advisers, the political scientist Charles Merriam, tried to assuage the concerns of Congress over Roosevelt's expansion of the executive branch by claiming that leadership rose not out of power but out of intangible qualities of character.[2]

The New Deal led to a mushrooming of government agencies controlled by leader-managers. During the next forty years, conservatives would abhor such visionary, big-government, leader-managers as foes of freedom. Liberals admired them for protecting the poor and weak against corporate power. Either way, government managers whose qualifications rested not on technical competence but on their claim of superior personal qualities, vision, and, above all, leadership became a symbol of the era. For example, the Tennessee Valley Authority, a New Deal program of rural electrification and flood control, was run by a controversial manager named David Lilienthal. A Harvard-educated lawyer, Lilienthal spent much of his life working for government. He believed that public utilities, not business corporations, should provide essential services like electricity.

To conservatives, Lilienthal symbolized government wastefulness and aversion to market discipline. To liberals, he was a heroic public servant who brought light and flood protection to the Tennessee Valley. But the real issue was two different visions, not just of government agencies but of the kind of person who should lead them. When President Truman nominated Lilienthal to head the Atomic Energy Commission in 1947, Republicans bitterly opposed his appointment, charging that he would underemphasize the development of atomic bombs with which to hold off Soviet aggression. Anti-Semitism underlay the attack on Lilienthal. But hatred of him was further inflamed by what some saw as his undemocratic, elitist arrogance with his claim to power resting not on technical competence but on soaring rhetoric and visionary leadership.

Although conservatives loathed leader-managers in government, they embraced such leaders in business. Corporate leader-managers cloaked their undemocratic power in the mantle of the free market. Their leadership, rather than being a form of elitist, unelected, un–American power, was a part of the *free* enterprise system. Business leader-managers often had a softer style, at least superficially, than the engineer-managers. Engineer-managers tended to think of the company as a piece of heavy machinery to be handled with a hammer and a wrench. Leader-managers thought of the company as an organism to be grown and nurtured. There was, according to the leader-managers, a "blind spot in scientific management" with its tyrannical bossing of workers.[3]

Mild-mannered leader-managers sold themselves to subordinates and to the public as proponents of freedom. Actually, with their well-honed communication skills and political savvy, the leader-managers could be tough and sometimes vicious bosses. But their claim that they were freedom-loving humanists made them seem more compatible with America's official democratic values. The leader-managers also won out by developing their psychological skills. They learned to control the workforce through psychological manipulation as opposed to the direct brutality of scientific management. At least superficially, the leader-managers treated subordinates with sympathetic attention, not top-down tyranny.

The key figure in the development of leader-managers' psychological skills was a Harvard Business School professor named Elton Mayo. He was the main interpreter of famous 1920s experiments on worker productivity at the Hawthorne Works in Cicero, Illinois. At this giant plant, tens of thousands of workers assembled most of America's telephones. Hawthorne's huge workforce meant that research on worker productivity might pay big dividends. So the Hawthorne managers had set up a special work room to test the effect of varied working conditions on a handful of employees. Lights were brightened, rest breaks extended, and snacks brought in. Productivity surged.

To the Hawthorne managers' surprise, when working conditions were returned to their original state, productivity kept on surging! They turned to Mayo for an explanation. Backed by his Harvard credentials, Mayo told the Hawthorne managers that improved working conditions had nothing to do with the workers' surging productivity. According to Mayo, sympathetic observation by the experimenters was the main cause of the workers' rising output.[4] The "Hawthorne effect" became a popular name for Mayo's idea that an observer's sympathetic attention will raise the performance of the people being observed. More important, Mayo's ideas became the basis for the human relations movement and for the new, softer style of leader-managers. According to human relations specialists, sympathetic leader-managers were more productive than bossy engineer-managers.

Unfortunately, subsequent scholars revealed that Mayo was a charlatan who cherry-picked the evidence for data that supported his ideas. The Hawthorne records show that the workers actually resented the experimenters. Contrary to Mayo, the workers did not raise their output thanks to sympathetic supervision. Rather, they raised productivity because they knew the piece rate (the amount they were paid per piece) would not be reduced during the experiment.[5] Subsequent revelations of Mayo's fraud did not dampen his influence. The false legend of the Hawthorne experiment and the human relations movement live on in American management—indeed in world management—until this day. Mayo's disingenuous "humanism" became the basis of much of modern management.

Mayo influenced an important executive named Chester Barnard who developed the idea that leadership is mainly about moral influence. During the 1920s and 1930s, Barnard was president of New Jersey Bell, a telephone monopoly in the Garden State and, by the standards of the time, a high-tech company. Something of a renaissance man in the humanities and social sciences, Barnard was out of his depth in technology and the hard sciences. Resenting protests against management of engineers "by those not engineers," Barnard wrote a book, *The Functions of the Executive* (1938), which aimed to show that not just technology but "operating arts"—that is, corporate management—created modern prosperity.[6]

Emphasizing the importance of leadership over bossism, Barnard claimed that even corporate power flows from the bottom up. Authority, he said, is a "fiction" that cannot "be supported to a great extent merely by coercion."[7] Managers therefore have to be leaders, not bosses, who win employees' cooperation through moral influence rather than power. If power flows from the bottom up and authority is a fiction, why do employees obey the boss's orders? Barnard argued that employees follow orders because they fear responsibility. An order builds morale by relieving workers of responsibility for action they could take on their own but for which they lack the courage.[8]

Despite Barnard's off-putting insinuation that followers are moral cowards, he was on to something profound about leadership. No leader ever has as much authority as he or she would like, so leadership does take courage. And that courage does inspire followers. But Barnard underemphasized the importance of power. He thereby opened the way toward an overestimation of the importance of morality in leadership— as opposed to hands-on competence—that has lasted to the present day. Barnard was a friend of Mayo's and of others in the human relations group at the Harvard Business School. When graduates of Harvard's doctoral program carried the human relations ideology into other business schools and into the business world at large, they carried Barnard's ideas with them. Barnard's self-righteous, self-serving emphasis on moral leadership became the conventional wisdom in business schools and in corporate, managerial ideology.

The masking of managerial power under cover of moral leadership posed a long-term danger for democracy. Corporations' false imitation

of bottom-up moral leadership was bad enough. But what if the influence began to flow the other way? What if corporate leaders' illusion
that their leadership was about morality more than power flowed out
into democratic society at large? The basic principle of democracy is the
moral danger of power, the tendency of power to corrupt. If not just
corporate managers but citizens at large began to accept the notion of
leaders' moral superiority, politicians would become even more inclined
to believe their own moral press releases. By weakening suspicion of the
powerful, ideas of corporate leadership like Barnard's ran the risk of
weakening democracy.

Self-righteous notions of moral leadership would suffer setbacks in
the Vietnam and Watergate eras of the 1960s and 1970s. So it would
take half a century for the tree planted by Mayo and Barnard to bear its
poisoned fruit. But the corporate world's self-appointed moral leaders
would eventually have their counterparts in government and in the
White House.

CHAPTER 14

Responsibility versus Profit at General Motors

IN THE 1930S, self-proclaimed moral leadership was not unique to American corporate managers with the bad luck to fall under the influence of Mayo and Barnard or their acolytes. Adolf Hitler in Germany and Benito Mussolini in Italy—der Fuhrer and il Duce—governed on the "leadership principle." In Russia, Stalin made a cult of his personality. It was easy to conclude that America would soon have a similar dictator. After all, Roosevelt claimed intangible qualities of leadership as justification for expanding his powers. Some conservatives saw the New Deal as an American version of European syndicalism.

Such was the argument of a widely read 1941 book, *The Managerial Revolution*, by James Burnham. A former communist turned conservative, Burnham had not given up the Marxist taste for vast historical generalizations. He argued that capitalism was being overthrown by a new ruling class of managers. Burnham built as so many others did, on Berle and Means's 1932 book, *The Modern Corporation and Private Property*. As explained in chapter 8, Berle and Means had argued that managers were overthrowing shareholders in a struggle for corporate control. Burnham extended their argument and held that managers were taking over not just in corporations but in government.[1] The New Dealers, according to Burnham, were unwittingly creating in the United States the same sort of dictatorship that Hitler and Stalin were intentionally building in Europe. The New Dealers claimed they were saving capitalism from itself. But Burnham believed the New Dealers were replacing capitalists with managers, just as Nazi functionaries were challenging German bankers, just as communist commissars had toppled tsarist Russia's fledgling middle class.

Burnham turned out to be wrong. Financiers were far from finished in America. Managers, rather than taking over the state, would remain subordinate to corporate financial interests, as the business history of the late twentieth and early twenty-first centuries demonstrated. Nevertheless, management and leadership became far more widely discussed topics than banking and finance.

The dominant voice in the new cacophony of management studies was an Austrian immigrant, Peter Drucker. As opposed to Burnham, who saw managers everywhere as all of a piece, Drucker believed American managers were morally superior to Nazi functionaries and Russian commissars. Burnham, with his taste for impersonal historical forces, had specifically rejected any moral judgment of the managerial revolution.[2] But Drucker insisted on "the reality of the moral issues."[3]

Born in pre–World War I Austria, Drucker would transport to America some of his European intellectual heritage, including his realistic understanding of the inevitability of power and his unrealistic belief that power could be made morally legitimate. In the 1920s, Drucker had moved from Austria to Germany, where he witnessed Hitler's rise to power. Opposing Nazi anti-Semitism, Drucker was nonetheless impressed by the Nazis' Depression-era success at not just putting Germans back to work but at restoring their morale.

In 1937, Drucker fled to the United States, where he wrote a book, *The End of Economic Man* (1939), explaining how the Nazis, despite their evil, created a measure of spiritual and psychological justice in a managerial society. By making the Nazi Party a social institution in the factories, Hitler created a sphere where the janitor might have more social status than the corporate manager. Drucker saw that American workers, like their German counterparts, suffered humiliation from their subordination to managerial power. American corporate management, unlike the U.S. Constitution, had not come into being through a conscious political process. Corporate life was an inadvertent result of economic development. Citizens had had little voice, Drucker said, in the process that placed them under corporate managers with "more power . . . than most of the political authorities proper."[4]

But Drucker believed there was a possible solution to the illegitimacy of managerial power. He saw American managers as exceptionally moral in spirit: "[T]here has never been a more efficient, a more honest, a more capable and conscientious group of rulers."[5] All that American managers needed was a way to express their morality in the corporate context. Drucker proposed that American managers adopt Nazi methods for democratic goals. Like Hitler, American managers should build auxiliary social organizations where workers could rise in status. American workers would run the cafeteria, the child-care facility, or whatever organization could contribute to employee social life. By electing the leaders of such auxiliary organizations, they would make the workplace into a democratic "self-governing community."[6]

But was Drucker right that what worked for the Nazis could have worked in America, where money and status greatly overlap? Electing the cafeteria board might ensure employees a decent meal at a fair price. But corporate control and its monetary rewards, not the lunch menu, secures dignity in America. If democratizing the factory had been the extent of Drucker's ideas, he would no more deserve to be remembered than the now-forgotten James Burnham. Drucker avoided that fate thanks at least partly to a manager at General Motors named Donaldson Brown, who had read and liked one of his books. In 1943, Brown offered Drucker a two-year job writing a study of what he called GM's "pioneering work."[7]

GM had followed the lead of the DuPont Company in pioneering the multidivisional corporation. After World War I, DuPont, originally an explosives manufacturer, had diversified into paint and chemicals in order to make peacetime use of the munitions production capacity it had built up during the war. But it turned out that explosives, paint, and chemicals were so different that it was hard to manage them all within one highly centralized company.

In a centralized organization like the one diagrammed in figure 14.1, it was hard to know who was responsible for profits and losses. If the marketing manager failed to sell paint, he might blame the operations department for making inferior paint. And the operations department would fire back, accusing the marketing department of bad salesmanship. How could the CEO know whom to hold accountable?

So Pierre DuPont—one of the greatest managers in business history—had reorganized the firm into a multidivisional company as shown in figure 14.2. This type of organization is often called an "M-form" because, on an organization chart, it looks like a series of M's cascading

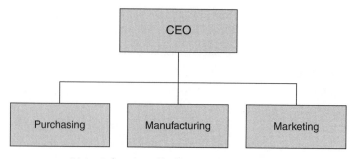

14.1. A functionally departmentalized firm.

downward. One division made and sold explosives, another did the same for chemicals, and a third handled paint. As the chart shows, if the paint division loses money, it is clear whose fault it is: the manager of the paint division is supposed to make money from paint. After all, the division manager has his own purchasing, operations, and marketing departments, all focused on that one product.

The M-form carried with it a long-term danger, a danger unseen at the time. The CEO could use the M-form as an excuse to ignore day-to-day operations of the company, which seemed clearly to be the job of division managers. The CEO was "free" to engage in long-term planning, strategy, and what eventually became known as "visionary leadership." In other words, the M-form increased the risk of unwitting top-tier negligence.

But in the early days, the M-form was the child of America's most talented and thorough managers. The young Alfred Sloan had dreamt up an M-form organizational plan for General Motors. Sloan got his chance to implement it owing to a post–World War I recession that nearly drove GM into bankruptcy. Pierre DuPont had a large investment in GM and rushed in to save it. Recognizing the virtues of Sloan's plan, DuPont put him in charge. Sloan created separate product divisions for GM's inexpensive cars (Chevrolet), mid-price cars (Buick), and luxury brand (Cadillac). The challenges of manufacturing and, especially, marketing such different cars made it sensible to have different product divisions. On the basis of Sloan's M-form, GM surged past Ford and became for decades the largest and most successful industrial corporation in the world.

By 1943 and 1944, when Drucker researched his study of GM, Sloan was a recognized master of management. Sloan generously allowed

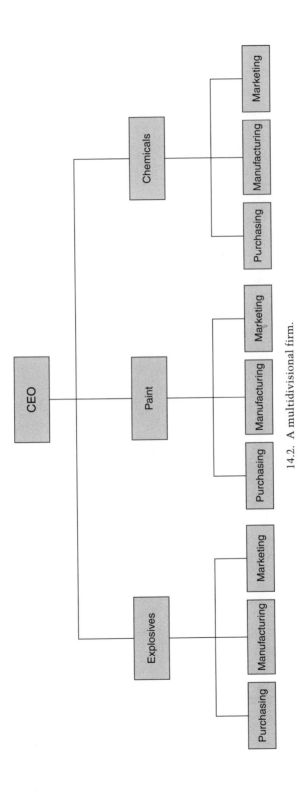

14.2. A multidivisional firm.

Drucker to accompany him to his many meetings and on his long train rides between GM's Detroit and New York offices. Drucker had a remarkable opportunity to study the M-form and one of its main creators. When Drucker's book on GM—*Concept of the Corporation*—was published in 1946, it became an instant classic. Drucker explained the basic principle of the M-form—decentralization into product divisions—more clearly than anyone had to date. Many corporations would begin to build M-forms, and as they did so, they often hired Drucker to advise them. Drucker enjoyed marvelous consulting opportunities for the rest of his life, opportunities from which he continued to learn and on the basis of which he became the preeminent management guru.

At the practical level, no management guru was ever more decent and sensible than Drucker. His 1954 book, *The Practice of Management*, offered the idea of "management by objectives" as a way of liberating subordinates from both the crushing tyranny of scientific management and the psychological manipulation of the human relations movement. When subordinates understood the company's objectives, they did not need to be bossed or manipulated but could act out of "self-control" to help achieve those objectives.[8]

Yet Drucker remained unrealistically optimistic about the moral possibilities of corporate life. In *The Practice of Management* he urged managers to use "private virtue" in the service of "public good" as "the only legitimate basis for leadership."[9] Earlier, in *Concept of the Corporation*, he had asserted that profit should be a third-level priority for GM: "It is first of all the question of a free society and secondly one of full employment."[10] One of the appeals of the M-form to Drucker was the fact that it gave "four or five times as many men" a chance at leadership.[11] Each product division needed its own operations manager, sales manager, and so forth, vastly multiplying the number of managerial positions in corporate America. Seeing the M-form and its decentralization as a sort of jobs program for leaders, Drucker argued in *Concept of the Corporation* that GM's largest and most profitable division, Chevrolet, should be broken up.

GM president Alfred Sloan was probably dismayed at Drucker's airy moralism. Years later, when Sloan wrote his autobiography, he included a chapter titled "Concept of the Organization" as an implicit rebuke to

Drucker's *Concept of the Corporation*. Rejecting Drucker's idea that GM's objective should be to create jobs and train leaders, Sloan said that "the strategic aim of a business [is] to earn a return on capital."[12]

The lesson in realism that Sloan tried to offer Drucker is still relevant today, when so much emphasis is placed on corporate social responsibility. Corporations should be socially responsible, and many are, not just in the sense of obeying the law but in the sense of trying to contribute to society. But it is mistaken to try to place the responsibility for the well-being of society in general on corporations. We have another institution—democratic government—to do that job.

CHAPTER 15

Critics of Managerial Character

BY THE AMERICAN DREAM ERA of the 1950s, not just James Burnham and Peter Drucker but the country at large had awoken to the fact that the United States was a managerial society. Ambitious young people aimed at management jobs. Corporations, with the vast managerial hierarchies of the day, offered inviting career ladders and lots of social status. Thanks to Mayo and his ilk, managers could claim a raison d'être in their leadership ability. Was it possible, however, that managers were not leaders but lemmings, not capitalists but courtiers? Was it possible that managers were mere practitioners of palace intrigue, driven not by a powerful work ethic and the spirit of industry but by company politics and a talent for sucking up?

According to a best-selling book of 1950, alertness to the opinion of others rather than ingrained character had become the main principle of American personality during the corporate era. *The Lonely Crowd*, written by sociologist David Riesman, helped many Americans recognize that they had long since ceased to measure up to their professions of Jeffersonian individualism. Prodded by Riesman's book and other 1950s best sellers—*The Organization Man*, *The Status Seekers*, and *The Man in the Gray Flannel Suit*—many citizens searched their souls about what kind of people the corporate world had made of them. It was an era less of politics than of psychology. The challenge of corporate culture to democratic values went largely ignored. In what may have been psychological denial disguised as self-examination, Americans asked what damage the corporate economy had done, not to the national character but only to their individual characters.

Corporations had not created healthy characters, especially in managers, Riesman said. He claimed that managers were obsessed with "personalizing" or trying to connect with fellow corporate denizens.

Depleting their energy by trying to please others, managers had no resources with which to please themselves. They lacked autonomy. Managers' belief that their ability was exceptional and that their work was important were delusional, according to Riesman. In truth, managers' main talent was the social polish that enabled them to ingratiate. Such Uriah Heeps could easily be replaced from modern society's cornucopia of other-directed people.

Because Riesman saw corporate personalities as psychologically unhealthy, he rejected Mayo's idea that managers should provide therapy for workers. Mayo, Riesman asserted, had been misled by "a fallacy of misplaced participation." Mayo had mistakenly aimed "to personalize, emotionalize, and moralize the factory."[1] Riesman hoped not that the factory could be moralized but that human beings could be liberated from it through automation. Like many 1950s intellectuals, he believed that the gradual displacement of physical labor by automatic machinery held out the possibility of a leisure society, where other-directed people could escape the corporation and find autonomy in play.

The Lonely Crowd touched a nerve. Television talk shows, book clubs, and Sunday sermons were soon exploring the problem of "conformity," which became the popular way of referring to Riesman's idea that corporate Americans had become other-directed. Such popular discussions often missed Riesman's idea that other-directed people could become autonomous in play rather than work. Most of his readers did not look forward to a world of leisure. They looked backward, yearning to recover the inner-directed personalities of the pre-corporate economy. Many Americans could not get their heads around Riesman's idea that they could live meaningful lives outside of work.

They may have been right. Many people approve of work not merely because of convention but because life involves material necessity. The desire to improve the material conditions of life has led to many of humanity's most admirable feats of imagination, invention, and innovation. The element of material necessity in life also makes work better suited than play to satisfy one of the most compelling providers of meaning, the exercise of power. Organized play of course has plenty of scope for the achievement of power. But triumph over material constraint, not to mention survival, seems intuitively more important than play or a leisure society and its promised autonomy. That is why power achieved through work is often accompanied by far greater moral authority than power achieved through play, providing a psychological reward for work that Riesman did not acknowledge is often lacking in playful power.

What it may have come down to for Riesman, with his hope for a future of leisure and play, was that he saw corporate life as tedious and boring. Many commentators from outside the corporate world agreed. One of them, a *Fortune* magazine writer named Daniel Bell, later an eminent professor, offered a fairly popular critique of intellectuals' distaste for managerial work in *The End of Ideology: On the Exhaustion of Political Ideas in the Fifties* (1960). Bell believed that nineteenth- and early-twentieth-century intellectuals had rejected humdrum business values in favor of grand ideologies such as communism and fascism because those intellectual systems seemed to offer a higher, more ambitious, more generous calling than self-interested commerce. But by the 1950s, those ideologies had been revealed as evil, not grand, thanks to their spawning of dictatorial terror, racist genocide, and two world wars. Meanwhile, the tamest of ideologies, classical liberalism, had been co-opted by the business corporation. How sensible, Bell seemed to be saying, but also how boring!

The End of Ideology underestimated the importance of the free-market ideology in 1950s American capitalism. Bell sided with the Harvard economist John Kenneth Galbraith, who dismissed corporate managers' fondness for market ideology as an atavistic fetish. In *American Capitalism* (1952), Galbraith had emphasized that the economy was a mixed system of capitalism and corporate planning, not a pure free market. He believed that labor unions' "countervailing" power offset corporate clout, accomplishing much of the job previously done by free-market competition, the job of preventing monopolistic inefficiency. So Galbraith saw the free-market ideology as outmoded and inaccurate, at least in the simplistic version of it to which some corporate executives felt a deep attachment. To Galbraith, corporate executives seemed too little capable of recognizing how corporate power limited the scope of the market.

Although Bell agreed with Galbraith that corporate managers were naive in their free-market faith, he criticized Galbraith for supposing that it was enough to show managers that their market ideology was unrealistic. The important question, according to Bell, was why managers believed in the free market. To answer that question, he relied on the quarter-century-old idea of Berle and Means that managers had control of corporations even though they did not own them. Precisely because managers' power depended on their positions rather than on their wealth, they suffered from "status anxiety." They sought to secure their social status by clinging to the moral authority that came with "older justifications of capitalism" such as the invisible hand of the market.[2]

In short, Bell, like Galbraith and countless others, did not see that the market ideology was not dying but was being reborn thanks to General Electric and Boulware as well as the men and organizations they had set in motion such as Ronald Reagan and the *National Review*. This incipient new conservatism and its old-fashioned free-market theory perfectly met Bell's definition of ideology as a vast social blueprint that was supposed to solve every problem. The free marketers envisioned no fine-tuning to adapt their ideology to an ever-changing reality. It was only necessary to stick to free-market principles to achieve the best possible society on earth. If this was not a grand ideology, nothing was. Contrary to the title of Bell's book, ideology did not end in the 1950s. It went into business.

Only one major scholar of the 1950s questioned the idea that America was set in a permanently liberal direction. C. Wright Mills, a Texan and a radical social critic who was never quite at home as a sociology professor at Columbia University, cut to some basic truths about corporate conservatism as only an outsider could do. Never acculturated to academic sophistication in the manner of Riesman, Bell, and Galbraith, according to whom nothing could ever be as simple as it seemed, Mills insisted that corporations served the purposes of the rich.

Mills saw, in advance of both Galbraith and Bell, that the free-market ideology poorly suited the needs of the new salaried employees in the lower echelons of corporate America. In *White Collar* (1951), he pointed out that the new middle class, unlike the old middle class, did not assign work but had it assigned to them. Such white-collar corporate employees labored as haplessly in the capitalist maw as did their blue-shirted factory forebears. Mills would have none of the Berle and Means stuff about how the rise of the large corporation, by separating ownership and management, had placed real economic power in the hands of managers, not capitalists. Ownership of property and possession of money still mattered. So he differed from other commentators by refusing to overestimate the power of top managers in relation to stockholders.

Where Bell, following Berle, claimed that managers possessed "independent power in their enterprises,"[3] Mills insisted that "the split of manager and owner . . . have been widely and erroneously taken to mean that a 'managerial revolution' has been and is under way. . . . Power has not been split from property. . . . It cannot be concluded that there is no functional relationship between ownership and control of large corporations."[4]

Almost as if in reply to Mills's *White Collar*, Adolf Berle published a new book, *The 20th Century Capitalist Revolution* (1954). Twenty years earlier, Berle had helped to create the idea that managers, not owners, controlled corporations. He did not back down in this new book. Pointing out that retained earnings enabled managers to replenish capital without help from shareholders, Berle said that "the waning figure in capitalism is the capitalist."[5] In other words, he still believed that managers were in control. Berle claimed that managers, guided by public opinion and corporate conscience, would use their power for good ends. He admitted that corporations' top managers were "tiny self-perpetuating oligarchies."[6] Yet Berle believed that these undemocratic oligarchies would develop a "philosophy" or "conscience" devoted to public good. As evidence, he cited Peter Drucker's idealistic portrait of General Motors as a pioneering social institution in *Concept of the Corporation*.[7]

Mills replied to Berle in what would become a famous and much-loved book among radical youth in the 1960s, *The Power Elite* (1956). Berle, Mills said, had "an odd view of the conscience of the powerful."[8] Given that Berle had earlier argued that managers could not be counted on by shareholders, it seemed strange to Mills for Berle to claim now that managers would somehow attempt to serve the public at large. In fact, Mills argued, executives aspired to become shareholders themselves. They saw, rightly, that "no one can become rich or stay rich in America today without becoming involved . . . in the world of the corporate rich."[9]

Mills raged against the success of the "privately incorporated economy" and its undemocratic culture. Managers had replaced the "reasoned debate of political ideas" with the corporate arts of public relations and psychological manipulation of subordinates.[10] Although ability counted in the lower managerial echelons, there was, according to Mills, no real test of "competence" for top managers other than winning the internecine competition for promotion through the ability to "fit in."[11] As a result, he believed that Americans had fallen into the hands of "crackpot realists" who "in the name of practicality . . . have projected a utopian image of capitalism."[12] To charges that he was unfairly impugning the integrity of corporate America's top managers, Mills replied that senior executives were too phlegmatic to be corrupt. Corporate chiefs were people of principle and "sound as a dollar." Their sin was not lack of integrity but lack of imagination.

Over the next half century the behavior of corporate managers as well as financiers, speculators, and raiders would suggest that Mills saw the meaning of the so-called managerial revolution more clearly than Burnham, Bell, Riesman, and Galbraith. Ownership of corporate property still mattered. Where management was ineffective and the stock price low, corporate raiders mounted hostile takeovers. Once in control, the raiders replaced managers and raised return on invested capital. Or else they broke up the newly acquired company and sold off the parts for more than they had paid for the whole. Either way, it was owners and financiers, not managers, who won out in the long run.

Mills's rhetorical power leant force to his anger and helped radicalize readers who flocked to his books in the 1960s. Today, one winces a bit at his rhetoric, which showed insensitivity to, or perhaps just ignorance of, the element of creativity in many of the people who succeed in corporate life. Yes, the platitudinous windbag remains all too common a corporate creature. But there are more admirable corporate personalities as well.

At least Mills never slipped into naïveté about managerial power and its dangers. It was corporate managers he had mostly in mind when he said that America "appears now before the world a naked and arbitrary power" commanded by men who are not "representative," whose "high position is not a result of moral virtue" but only of "the terrible fact clumsily accomplished."[13] If that was a stereotype, it nevertheless pointed to real dangers of character that occur too often in corporate life. In the years following Mills's untimely death in 1962, Americans would learn he was right to warn that managerial arrogance endangers democracy.

CHAPTER 16

JFK's Pyrrhic Victory over U.S. Steel

"MY FATHER ALWAYS TOLD ME that all businessmen were sons-of-bitches," said President John F. Kennedy on April 10, 1962.[1] Kennedy's angry reflection on corporate character was provoked by Roger M. Blough, head of U.S. Steel. Blough had just left the White House after informing the president that his company would be raising the price of steel by six dollars per ton.

Since taking office a year earlier, Kennedy had made a priority of preventing inflation. He tried to take a balanced approach to unions and corporations, asking both sides to cooperate in holding down wages and prices. U.S. Steel's price increase amounted to a rejection of his bid to fight inflation by serving as an honest broker between labor unions and business corporations. Kennedy's attempt to manage wages and prices from the White House was the closest any post–World War II president came to more or less officially recognizing the corporate basis of the American Dream. If businesses did not raise prices and if unions only asked for pay raises in proportion to productivity increases, inflation could be checked, corporate profits could be maintained, and the standard of living could rise. The president, of course, had no official power over CEOs, but Kennedy thought that as head of state he was entitled to call corporate executives' attention to what he insisted were their "public responsibilities."[2]

Kennedy may not have realized that he was opening an old wound by injecting himself into corporations' pricing policy. He was threatening the "right to manage," the preservation of which had been the mission of American business in the post–World War II era. Whether he knew it or not, Kennedy was resuming the battle that Walter Reuther and the United Auto Workers had lost in their failed 1946 strike against

General Motors. Chapter 10 explains how Reuther and the UAW had tried to force Alfred Sloan and GM to hold the line on prices while raising workers' pay. But Sloan and GM had won that battle. Since then, corporations had been confident that the prices they charged were none of the unions' business, still less the government's. Kennedy, by trying to involve himself in the pricing policies of steel companies, was treading on the corporate equivalent of sacred ground.

Kennedy's policy was the brainchild of his secretary of labor, Arthur Goldberg, a former lawyer for the steelworkers' union. Like Reuther in 1946, Goldberg in 1962 aimed to ensure that pay increases provided real gains in workers' purchasing power. The only difference was that it was the government, not the UAW, that would try to prevent corporate price hikes. Two of Kennedy's economic advisers, Walter Heller and John Kenneth Galbraith, had ideas fairly similar to Goldberg's. They wanted to fight "cost-push" inflation or, as conservatives called it, the "wage-price spiral." Galbraith called it the "wage-price-profit" spiral to emphasize his view that corporate profits were the ultimate driver of inflation. If that were indeed so, it was naive to expect corporations to cooperate in holding down prices. Yet that was the policy to which the Kennedy administration committed itself.

Kennedy's desire to coordinate corporate-labor relations had been intensified by the 1960 presidential campaign, during which he had criticized his predecessor, Dwight Eisenhower, for allowing a 1959 steel strike to drag on for months, threatening to throw the economy into recession. So in 1962, when the steelworkers' contract expired, Kennedy was especially eager to avoid another strike. In January of that year he had invited Blough, head of U.S. Steel, and David McDonald, head of the United Steelworkers, to an Oval Office meeting. At that meeting Kennedy proposed that Blough and McDonald settle on a new contract for steelworkers giving them a wage increase between 2.5 and 3 percent more than the current contract. Such a small increase would be in keeping with productivity gains. Therefore, the steel companies, Kennedy believed, could afford the pay raise while holding the line on prices.

McDonald, speaking for the workers, agreed to Kennedy's proposal.[3] But Blough told the president that U.S. Steel needed a price increase to make up for past wage gains that had outstripped improvements in worker productivity.[4] Blough did not add the fact that he subscribed to the anti-union approach that Boulware had pioneered at General Electric and that had resulted in the defeat of the electrical workers in their 1960 strike. The truth was, though Blough left it unstated, that he did not want to work with the union. He wanted to get the union out of U.S. Steel's way, as Boulware had done at GE.

Kennedy should have seen that he would get no cooperation from Blough. Months earlier he had written to the steel executive that he wanted to avoid an "increase in prices" while preserving "good profits" for the steel companies.[5] Blough had replied that the steel companies needed to raise prices so they could invest in new equipment needed for international competitiveness, a point disputed by Kennedy's economic advisers.[6] Blough concluded by promising Kennedy that he would do what was in the national interest, but the earlier part of his letter had made clear his belief that higher steel prices were in the national interest. Blough's equivocal statements left Kennedy and his advisers little excuse for being fooled, but fooled they were. Most critics hold Blough responsible for the sensational battle with the government that followed, and he surely was duplicitous. But Kennedy and his advisers bore some responsibility for their willingness to be deceived; they wanted to believe that they had an understanding with U.S. Steel when, clearly, they were being played.

Blough held his tongue on prices during the contract negotiations with the steelworkers that followed, and Kennedy dutifully pressed them for wage restraint. In early April 1962, the steelworkers agreed to a 2.5 percent increase in their contract, all of it to be paid in the form of higher benefits, not higher wages. Steelworkers' pay would be held flat, and so too, the public believed, would prices. Kennedy enjoyed great press coverage for a few days as Americans congratulated themselves on a breakthrough, anti-inflationary deal in labor relations. The steel contract was expected to be imitated in other industries and therefore to break the inflationary cycle.

Then, on April 10, U.S. Steel's board of directors voted to raise prices by six dollars per ton. Blough, as a "courtesy" to the president, flew to Washington that afternoon to give him the news in person, in the Oval Office. Kennedy responded, "You've made a terrible mistake." After Blough left, Kennedy declared to his aides that "this is war," adding his soon-to-be-famous remark that opens this chapter.[7] The next day Bethlehem Steel and six other producers followed U.S. Steel's lead, raising their prices six dollars per ton. Only a handful of smaller firms such as Lukens Steel had not yet acted. Kennedy and his advisers were soon phoning Lukens and other small producers, urging them to hold the line on prices.

Kennedy's actions in the next few days were so strong and effective as to obscure the fact that the victory he soon won was only pyrrhic. The president would force U.S. Steel to roll back prices, but his naive policy of coordinating relations between business corporations and the labor unions by appealing to executives' sense of "public responsibility" was wrecked. Kennedy won the short-term public relations victory, but business corporations won a long-term increase in power vis-à-vis government.

On Wednesday, April 11, just a day after U.S. Steel announced its price hike, Kennedy held a memorable press conference. He denounced the actions of U.S. Steel, Bethlehem Steel, and the other producers as "a wholly unjustifiable and irresponsible defiance of the public interest." Attacking the companies' executives personally, the president accused them of pursuing "private power and profit," of ignoring the "interests of 185 million Americans," and of acting "in ruthless disregard of their public responsibilities."[8]

That was just the beginning. Kennedy announced that he had directed the Justice Department, headed by his brother Robert Kennedy, to investigate whether the steel companies had broken antitrust laws in their identical and near simultaneous price hikes. Robert Kennedy ordered an FBI investigation. The FBI learned that at a Bethlehem stockholder's meeting a few days before, a company vice-president had said there would be no price increase. That suggested to the Justice Department that Bethlehem's price increase had been a sudden change of mind, possibly the result of illegal collusion with U.S. Steel. The FBI tracked down newspaper reporters who had been at the Bethlehem shareholders' meeting, woke them in the middle of the night, and interviewed them to learn exactly what company officials had said.

To howls of "Gestapo" tactics by business interests, Kennedy replied by increasing the pressure still more. Bethlehem Steel's main product was armor plate for naval vessels. The Pentagon announced that a multimillion-dollar contract for armor plate was being diverted from the big producers to Lukens Steel and other small firms that had not raised prices. That was more pressure than Bethlehem could stand. On Friday, April 13, Bethlehem rescinded its price increase. At just that moment Blough was meeting with a Kennedy adviser named Clark Clifford who reported that the steel executive turned "pale and shaken" when word arrived of Bethlehem's capitulation.[9] Clifford turned up the heat on Blough, explaining that the administration planned to subject him to a daily salvo of negative publicity during the following week.

Blough caved. Late Friday afternoon, U.S. Steel announced it was rolling back prices in order to improve "relations between government and business."[10] In just four days the U.S. president had forced one of the country's largest industrial corporations into a humiliating surrender. Kennedy, alluding to Grant's generosity to Lee at Appomattox, joked that he had let Blough's men "keep their horses for the spring planting."[11]

Yet Kennedy's seemingly total victory had cost him enormous effort. The president could scarcely fire off such a barrage every time a company raised prices. His battle with U.S. Steel had not shown, as many said at the time, that he had extraordinary power. It only showed that it took extraordinary effort for the president to affect a corporate decision. Blough saw that Kennedy had expended all his ammo. Over the next eighteen months, U.S. Steel quietly instituted its price hikes in piecemeal fashion. Kennedy uttered not a word of protest.

The old cycle of high profits, high pay raises, and high price increases would resume. In 1970, for example, after a sixty-seven-day strike by the United Auto Workers, General Motors signed a contract for a 30 percent wage increase, far outstripping workers' productivity gains. The UAW justified the wage increase as necessary to keep up with earlier outsize price increases by corporations, just as Blough of U.S. Steel had justified price hikes as necessary to keep up with earlier outsize wage increases. Inflation soared during the 1970s, the decade when U.S. automakers were first challenged by high-quality, low-priced cars from abroad.

And there was little that the government could do. No subsequent administration would imitate Kennedy's failed attempt to manage corporate wage and price policy. Fiscal and monetary policy were still set in Washington, but in other respects the American economy was steered with a corporate rudder, or more accurately, many corporate rudders and many union rudders as well. Kennedy's strong-arm tactics against U.S. Steel, even if justified by Blough's duplicity, had alienated corporate leaders from government yet further than before. Kennedy later tried to patch things up with a friendly speech at a U.S. Chamber of Commerce meeting. But the speaker who followed him to the podium compared him to "dictators in other lands."[12]

That ugly statement pointed to a difference not only of economic policy but of cultural style between Kennedy and the corporate chiefs. Corporate life can develop even worse rhetorical habits in CEOs than public life does in politicians. Portentous overstatement and lack of historical perspective are part of the corruption bred by power. Shortly after Kennedy's assassination the following year, one of his advisers reflected on the steel crisis and on the late president's relationship with American business. Kennedy "was outside the business ethos" and "did not consider successful businessmen as the best brains or the most enjoyable company . . . and . . . did not like to have them around in the evening."[13] Kennedy's attitude reflected that of an increasingly large share of the population who, even if they could not control the corporate chiefs, did not have to like them.

PART V

The Corporation in the Wilderness Again

CHAPTER 17

McNamara and the Staffers

LONG BEFORE THE MODERN BUSINESS corporation existed, armies distinguished between "line" and "staff" positions. Authority over military operations flowed down the line from generals to colonels to sergeants to corporals. But a staff officer, say a quartermaster whose job was to procure blankets and boots, guns and ammunition, had no authority in military operations, no matter how high his rank. The quartermaster could require a line officer to submit a requisition form for new weapons. But the quartermaster had no authority over how the line officer used the weapons to fight the enemy.

When business corporations became large organizations in the nineteenth century, they adopted the military distinction between line and staff positions. A line position carried operational authority; a staff job did not. A railroad conductor, for example, could order a train to start or stop but a maintenance manager could not. As far as train operations went, a conductor had a line job whereas the maintenance manager only had a staff function.

As railroads and then manufacturers became complex organizations, they began to chart the relationships among their officers, including the distinction between line and staff positions. Operating authority, as shown in figure 17.1, flowed from the top down, along solid lines. Managers with operating responsibility were "on the line." On the other hand, a staff member such as a chief accountant might report to the railroad president but was connected to the functional departments by a dotted line showing that he had no operating authority.

One weakness of organization charts is that they depict only formal structure and ignore informal relationships in which staff, despite their official lack of authority, often have considerable power. If there had been (or maybe there was) an organization chart for the Continental

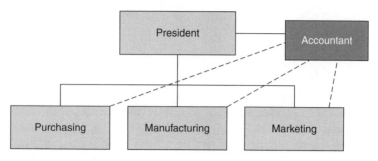

17.1. A line-and-staff organization.

Army during the American Revolution, it might have suggested that Colonel Alexander Hamilton, a member of General George Washington's staff, had little power. But Hamilton was one of Washington's most influential advisers, a position that he parlayed into a brilliant career. This flaw of organization charts, which focus solely on formal authority, was recognized in the twentieth century. As the corporate leadership ideology rose, the distinction between line and staff became less fashionable. Everyone was supposed to throw themselves enthusiastically into the organization's work. Inspirational leadership was supposedly more important than line authority.

But although modern managerial ideology put the distinction between line and staff into disfavor, organizational reality created ever more staff positions. The rise of the M-form (described in chapter 14) with its CEO loftily presiding over decentralized operating divisions opened the way for a large, top-level staff. To measure the short-run performance of division managers while also planning the firm's long-term strategy, the CEO might need the help of expert staff in finance, accounting, legal affairs, human relations, research and development, and many other specialties.

Corporate America's early- and mid-twentieth-century surge in staff positions gave young people opportunities for quick success. The fastest way to get to the top of a corporation was to start there, as a staff member for senior management. An able staff member at corporate headquarters could get noticed quickly and be moved into a high-level line position. On the other hand, to start at the bottom, in operations, could make for a hard climb to the top. By the 1950s, some large business corporations were being run by managers who had started on the staff.

The practice of recruiting top managers from staff positions exacerbated the risk of bad management. Over time, a business corporation could develop a senior management with little knowledge of the company's core operations. A steel company might be run by a finance whiz, a department store by a human relations specialist. By "freeing" the CEO from operations, the M-form had increased the risk of top-level negligence, the risk that the CEO might not stick to his or her knitting. Now, the recruitment of senior management from staff increased the risk of top-level incompetence, the risk that the CEO might not know how to knit.

The new prestige of management and the age-old problem of relations between line and staff were symbolized by the Republican administration of President Dwight Eisenhower (1953–1961). Eisenhower was a fairly active president but, true to his military background, managed through his staff. Access to the president was closely guarded by his chief of staff, a New Hampshire businessman and politician named Sherman Adams. A popular joke at the time had one Democrat saying to another, "Wouldn't it be terrible if Eisenhower died and Vice President Nixon became president?" The other Democrat replied, "Wouldn't it be terrible if Sherman Adams died and Eisenhower became president?"

Only cabinet members were permitted to see President Eisenhower without Adams's approval. Cabinet members served the president much as if they were quasi-independent division managers in a decentralized, M-form corporation. And in fact, Eisenhower's secretary of defense was none other than GM's "Engine Charlie" Wilson. Engine Charlie had given the public a taste of his ingrained managerial arrogance at his Senate confirmation hearings. He told the Senate committee that he saw no conflict of interest in owning a large bloc of General Motors stock while, as secretary of defense, he would be one of the company's largest customers. The hearings were closed to the press, so Wilson's exact words are not known. But it was leaked to reporters that Wilson had said something to the effect that "what's good for General Motors is good for the country." The statement became part of American folklore, an example of unwitting corporate contempt for democracy.

Another auto executive, Robert McNamara, served as secretary of defense in the next two administrations, those of Democratic Presidents John F. Kennedy (1961–1963) and Lyndon Johnson (1963–1969). There,

McNamara provided the era's ultimate example of the danger of recruiting senior managers from staff positions. Before World War II, McNamara
had been a young accounting professor at the Harvard Business School.
He had loved academic life, and both he and the country would have
been better off if he had stayed at Harvard. The entrance of the United
States into World War II lifted McNamara out of the university and put
him on the path to the Pentagon. Tex Thornton, a brash young officer
in the Army Air Force, proposed that the Harvard Business School train
military personnel to manage logistics. So McNamara joined Thornton's
military unit as a commissioned staff officer. Together with Thornton's
other recruits, McNamara coordinated Army Air Force logistics and created the management discipline of systems analysis or statistical control.
The term *systems analysis* is a bit pretentious, suggesting mastery of
esoteric mysteries. All it really meant was that if you were building five
thousand bombers a month, they were not going to help you win the
war if you were not also training five thousand pilots a month. In other
words, a system has interrelated needs that cannot be considered in
isolation if the system is to be effective.

Although McNamara possessed undeniable brilliance and made
important contributions to the war effort, there were other keys to his
success. He had sharp elbows with which he maneuvered to collect data
and to deliver his interpretation of it to people with the authority and
will to use it. It was later said that McNamara's arrogance originated in
his emotionless faith in numbers, but in fact he was highly emotional.
His self-righteousness may have stemmed from his need to justify the
violence he did to others and to himself.

After the war, Tex Thornton, the man who had brought McNamara
into the military, took the brilliant young staffer to Detroit. Thornton,
in a bold act of salesmanship, convinced the Ford automobile company
to hire not only himself but also nine of his Air Force associates, including McNamara, to impose order at the beleaguered company. If there
was ever a business organization that needed systems analysis, it was the
Ford company at the end of World War II. For the preceding twenty
years, Henry Ford had managed his company capriciously while losing
money and market share to General Motors. Ford was no match for the
M-form and the systematic, rational management of Alfred Sloan and
GM. Henry Ford died at the end of the war, and his grandson, Henry II,

took over. Henry Ford II knew that he needed help and therefore hired Thornton, who believed that he was destined to run the company. But not so fast: Henry Ford II, hedging his bets, also hired some GM executives to teach him the art of the M-form. Ford soon had product divisions for its Ford, Mercury, and Lincoln lines. In the end, Ford gave command of the company to one of those former GM executives and fired Thornton.

The disappointed Thornton found backing to buy a small electronics firm, Litton Industries, and turned it into a conglomerate, a form of organization that, later, was a huge success in the go-go stock market of the early 1960s. Conglomerates were M-form corporations, but they differed from companies such as DuPont and GM, where the M-form had begun. At DuPont and GM, the product divisions, however decentralized, still bore some genetic relationship to one another—chemicals were akin to explosives, Chevrolets were poor cousins of Cadillacs.

But a conglomerate was an M-form with no kinship among the product divisions. Litton Industries manufactured ships, electric typewriters, and microwave ovens. What was supposed to make the whole thing work was CEO Tex Thornton, the former staff man who was now considered a managerial genius. And Thornton was not alone. It was also the era of ITT and Harold Geneen, of Textron and Royal Little, of LTV and "Jimmy Ling, the Merger King." For a time, the conglomerates earned spectacular profits. Thornton's Litton Industries was the most spectacularly successful of all. Speculators bid up Litton's stock price to fantastic levels. The widely admired Thornton borrowed the word *synergy* from biology to support his claim that just as an organism amounted to more than the sum of its parts so did Litton Industries.

Conglomerates often made their money not from good management but from mergers and acquisitions. With their high-flying share prices, they could easily trade their own stock for others, cheaply acquiring new companies while spending no cash. Suppose a conglomerate with a stock price of twenty dollars bought a company with a stock price of ten dollars. Suppose also that the two companies each had the same number of shares and that their annual earnings were each a dollar a share. The conglomerate could use half of its stock to buy all of the other company and, by nothing other than this simple exchange of shares, could double its reported earnings. Investors, at least the naive ones, would credit the putative managerial genius at the top for the earnings increase and bid the stock up further, giving the conglomerate even more buying power for more cheap acquisitions, which would further raise its profits. But the game could go on only as long as the conglomerate's stock price kept soaring while the deals got bigger and bigger. The game came to an end for Litton in 1968, when it reported a drop in earnings. Its stock price tumbled, making it harder to acquire other companies on the cheap. As Litton's share price and profits plummeted, it was obvious that Thornton was no managerial genius after all.

Meanwhile back at Ford, McNamara, the ultimate staff man, had out-lasted the GM managers whom Henry Ford II had brought in. McNamara secured the company presidency in 1960 and then, only weeks later, accepted the offer of newly elected president John F. Kennedy to become secretary of defense. McNamara put his systems analysis to work at the Pentagon and in Vietnam, where he helped lead the United States to its first ever defeat in war.

Just as Thornton's Litton Industries was largely a numbers game so, at least to McNamara, was the Vietnam War. The former accounting professor measured wartime success by the most ghastly of numbers, the "body count." Thursday nights, newscasters reported the number of American troops killed the previous week, as if it were progress when measured against Pentagon claims of vastly higher losses by the enemy. At about the same time that Thornton's and Litton's numbers game was exposed, so was McNamara's and the Pentagon's. In early 1968, Communist Viet Cong troops launched well-coordinated and massive attacks against every major city in South Vietnam. This Tet Offensive, as it became known because it happened on a Vietnamese holiday with that name, revealed that, contrary to the message of McNamara's body counts, the enemy was not being weakened by attrition. Although the Tet Offensive was beaten back in a tactical victory for American troops, it marked the loss of the strategic battle for "hearts and minds," the battle for American and Vietnamese public opinion. The Tet Offensive brought widespread recognition that the United States was headed for defeat in Vietnam, and it started McNamara's formerly admired management by numbers toward national contempt.

Corporate management took a reputational hit from the combined effects of McNamara's loss of the war in Vietnam, the crash of the conglomerates, and the soon-to-be-apparent loss of competitive advantage by the American automobile industry. The collapse of corporate prestige seemed a new dawn to American liberals, a chance to create a new version of the American Dream. They were badly mistaken.

CHAPTER 18

The False Confidence
of the Anticorporatists

"Ben—I just want to say one word to you—just one word . . . Plastics." It became one of the most famous movie lines of all time. The well-off Braddock family is giving a college graduation party for their son, Ben, star of the track team and valedictorian of his class. A family friend has taken Ben aside and gravely advises that there is "a great future in plastics. Think about it. Will you think about it?" Young audiences whooped at this scene from the 1967 film *The Graduate*. The pompous phony dispensing one-word profundities was familiar to the era's college students. He was a dad or an uncle, a salesman or a stockbroker, but above all a corporate fool and flack.

Corporate intellectual pretense was personified by all too many business leaders such as Roger Blough of U.S. Steel, whose 1962 fight with President Kennedy was described in chapter 16. Years before, Blough had given a purportedly distinguished but actually leaden series of lectures at Columbia University's business school. Addressing the subject of "Free Man and the Corporation," Blough praised voluntary cooperation in human groups without a mention of the fact that from the point of view of a worker looking up, a corporation is an undemocratic, top-down power structure.[1]

The contrast between graceless heavies like Blough and a seemingly free-spirited president like Kennedy reinforced a rising conviction in the minds of many 1960s youth that the corporate life was not worth living. A subtle anticorporatism, focused less on economics and politics than on culture and style, flourished among artists and intellectuals. A generation would pass before the business world found a way to present corporate life as adventurous rather than deadening. The prevailing anticorporatism in youth culture and among intellectuals helped to convince liberals in the middle 1960s that all was well with their agenda for an activist government and an enlarged sense of public purpose. America's future, they confidently believed, would inevitably surpass narrow corporate interests and free-market shibboleths. Grief over the 1963 Kennedy assassination had helped fuel the 1964 Civil Rights Act and, in the presidential election of that year, the victory of Kennedy's successor, Lyndon Johnson, over Republican Barry Goldwater. The next year brought the Medicare Act, providing national health insurance to senior citizens, along with a raft of antipoverty legislation under the rubric of the Great Society.

The Great Society was the largest wave of social legislation since the New Deal, but with a difference. New Deal reformers had often aimed their bolts directly at corporations. The Great Society, by contrast, focused not on corporations but on culture, education, and welfare. Was this an implicit victory for corporations? However poorly corporations might have been regarded in 1960s popular culture, social reformers had not made big business part of their program.

The question of why 1960s antipoverty campaigners saw corporate America as neither part of the problem nor part of the solution got no discussion at the time. Liberals, confident that they could fight for social justice through educational and social programs, left the corporation out of politics and economics. Anticorporatism was restricted to cultural discussions. Still, the appetite of university students for movies like *The Graduate* showed that youthful anticorporatism ran deep. The cultural victory and ascendancy in moral authority that the corporations had won over the labor unions after World War II had proved short-lived. A new threat had arisen to the corporations' moral standing from an unexpected quarter—academia.

The baby boomers went to college in the 1960s. The World War II generation provided higher education for its children in record numbers. Often, the parents aimed to school their children for the corporate success that had been so prominent in their own lives and ambitions. Yet by the time the 1960s students got their degrees, they were, to the dismay of business leaders, often contemptuous of the corporate world. The teachings of academics cut from the same cloth as David Riesman or, far worse, C. Wright Mills took hold in the mind of a generation. The young did not want to join the lonely crowd or the power elite.

And from 1965 onward, the Vietnam War also alienated many students from "the Establishment." They reviled corporations such as Monsanto, manufacturer of chemicals that defoliated the Vietnamese countryside, and Dow Chemical, producer of the fiery napalm that maimed and killed innocent civilians. College youth who resisted the draft were unlikely recruits for corporate jobs.

Unfortunately, youthful anticorporatists gave little attention to trying to understand the enemy. The New Left movement that arose on campuses in the late 1960s was fundamentally anti-institutional. Its adherents celebrated the humanism of the young Marx rather than the economic analysis of *Das Kapital*. As a result, the New Left had little interest in developments in economic thought that had come after Marx. Few, maybe none, of the 1960s radicals had even heard of the theory of the firm, which had been one of the most important developments in the 1930s study of economics. For the New Left, the corporation seemed so contemptible that its internal dynamics were unworthy of interest, let alone scholarship.

By default, the study of the corporation and its processes was left to mainstream scholars who could have profited from the New Left's emphasis on power. Some of those mainstream academic economists mistakenly believed that the corporation might be tamed by cultural forces. As evidence, they cited the rejection of corporate life by radical students! No one was more hopeful that youthful anticorporatism marked a new era than the renowned economist John Kenneth Galbraith. A politically connected Harvard professor, Galbraith had served in the Kennedy administration and helped influence it to take a hard line against the steel corporations. Yet his anticorporatism was too mild for radical youth of the late 1960s who viewed him as a voice of the hated Establishment.

I was a graduate student at the University of Wisconsin in 1969 when Galbraith visited to give a lecture. A hostile group of student radicals went on stage and read a statement declaring his irrelevance before allowing him to speak. They would have done better to have listened in the hope of improving upon him. Galbraith offered the 1960s' most penetrating—but ultimately mistaken—critique of business corporations.

Galbraith was already known as an anticorporatist. In 1958 he had published a best-selling book, *The Affluent Society*, which caused a stir by its ironic observations about the imbalance between the private and public sides of the American economy. Galbraith pointed out that the United States spent willingly on useless gadgets and grudgingly on public schools. Loving their cars, Americans resented being taxed for roads. Too seldom was it noticed, according to Galbraith, that it was not the government but the corporation that undid Americans' freedom. With its pay and perks, its advertising and marketing power, the corporation managed many aspects of American life. The corporation far outstripped the government, Galbraith said, in creating "for its own purposes, the organization man."[2]

Corporate marketing raised consumer demand, facilitating full production and serving the cause of full employment. But corporate marketers stimulated demand by arousing Americans' desire for pointless products—electric carving knives and automobile tailfins. As a more worthy way of maintaining full employment, Galbraith proposed public investment in education and research in pure science so that fewer citizens would waste their lives in corporate labs and offices, researching deodorants and dreaming up advertising campaigns for shaving cream.

Having written in the 1950s so anticorporate a book as *The Affluent Society*, Galbraith was more than ready for 1960s college students, whom he initially believed to agree with his views. His 1967 book, *The New Industrial State*, delightedly reported that business schools suffered from "a serious decline in the quality of their applicants. . . . good students, when asked about business, are increasingly adverse. They hold it to be excessively disciplined, damaging to individuality, not worth the high pay, or dull."[3]

To Galbraith, student aversion to corporate life not only gratified his personal pique but confirmed his wariness of what he called the "technostructure." Ever since the 1930s, when Berle and Means had argued that managers, not shareholders, controlled corporations, most students of the subject had assumed that self-aggrandizement and love of money in the executive ranks were the driving forces of big business. But Galbraith believed corporate control was exercised by employees far down into the technical and business staff or, as he called it, the "technostructure."

As opposed to conventional anticorporatists of the time, Galbraith argued that money was not the technostructure's main motivation.

Rather, he believed that technocrats aimed to preserve their group identity, their place of power and prestige, and their intellectual kinship with like-minded others. In short, Galbraith's ideas, critical though they were, bore some resemblance to today's rosy notions of corporate culture and knowledge management in which values and intellectual opportunity are thought to be the main motivators of corporations' more skilled employees.

Why then did corporate executives in the 1960s so strongly emphasize the significance of money as a motivator? Galbraith answered that business leaders wanted to believe themselves proponents of the free market rather than an undemocratic and hierarchical technostructure. Money is the free market's medium of exchange, so executives claimed that financial incentives were an important impetus.

Contrary to the corporate executives, Galbraith asserted that two other forces complement money and may even outweigh it as a motivator of corporate folk. If employees respect a company's goals, they may *identify* with the organization and work ardently for it. Alternatively, they may seek to *adapt* the company to their goals. Either way, employees in the technostructure would value the autonomy of the corporation and work to preserve it from government interference. Such autonomy could only be guaranteed by giving the corporation the appearance of being aligned with broader social goals. In the context of mid-twentieth-century America, that meant that the corporation had to be a force for national defense and full employment.

According to Galbraith, profit was only part of what drove the corporate economy to produce the glittering gewgaws that a right-minded society would have seen as waste. The mass marketing that made people want useless kitsch served the cause of corporate autonomy by serving the cause of full employment. By delivering jobs—albeit in often wasteful work producing unworthy products—corporations gave themselves the appearance of essential institutions with which to tamper was to endanger the general welfare.

The corporate technostructure, as Galbraith saw the matter, protected its autonomy by putting Americans on a giant hamster wheel, doing useless work so they could consume useless goods. The frenzied waste seemed likely to be ended only by the still greater wantonness of nuclear war, for which the production of bombs and planes, missiles and submarines, provided another crucial market and source of influence for the technostructure. The alliance of military and corporate interests had led even a president as moderate as Eisenhower to warn against the "military-industrial complex."

"By what means," asked Galbraith, "is human personality to be saved?"[4] The corporate technostructure created economic prosperity and national defense for its own purposes, not for those of its citizens. How was the hold of the technostructure to be broken? Corporations depended on colleges and universities to produce their educated technocrats. Here, Galbraith believed, was the Achilles heel of the corporate system of licentious production and consumption. "Colleges and universities," he said, "can strongly assert the values and goals of educated men—those that serve not the production of goods and associated planning but the intellectual and artistic development of man. It is hard to believe there is a choice."[5]

Galbraith saw a deep threat to liberty in the corporate, industrial state, a threat that could be seen, he claimed, in the convergence between corporatism and communism. Because the American corporate economy had no inherent control over demand, corporations had acquired influence over the government and especially the military establishment in order to create and ensure markets for its goods. American conservatives had long worried—rightly, Galbraith said—that the country was moving in the direction of a planned economy. But conservatives had guarded the wrong flank, expecting the threat of economic planning to come from the government when it actually came from business corporations.

Galbraith saw not only a danger but an opportunity in the convergence of corporate and communist systems. He was confident that the world was moving—"perhaps in less time than may be imagined"—toward a rejection of both corporatism and communism in favor of a mild socialism.[6] The industrial system, Galbraith wrongly prophesied, "will not long be regarded as something apart from government."[7] Public recognition that industrial corporations should be held to a public purpose would enable the "educational and scientific estate" to assert itself.[8] Colleges and universities, educating citizens to work in the technostructure, could also foster people's critical capacity to resist the desire-inducing power of the corporations. In the book's final sentence

Galbraith hopefully averred that the corporate system "brings into existence, to serve its intellectual and scientific needs, the community that, hopefully, will reject its monopoly of social purpose."[9]

If it had not been for the Vietnam War, Galbraith's *New Industrial State* might have stirred real interest in understanding the corporate economy. But events transpired to drive socially aware youth away from mere skepticism of the corporation and toward radical anti-institutionalism. To them, any understanding of the operation of the corporate system came to seem irrelevant to the creation of a good society. Their lack of interest in corporate operations was a lost opportunity in which Americans forfeited the chance of better understanding their own economic lives. Most of the 1960s generation would end up in the corporate world, as their parents had, and could have profited from Galbraith's book.

Even if Galbraith had gotten some attention from the young, he would scarcely have had the last word. For it was not just radical anti-institutionalists' lack of interest in how corporations really worked that accounted for the defeat of 1960s anticorporatist liberals. As later chapters of this book show, information technology would breathe new life into market forces, transforming them from the atavistic cliché they had seemed to Galbraith and renewing the vitality and creativity of business corporations, even if Galbraith would have sneered at much of what they created.

It was not inevitable that Galbraith's anticorporatist hopes would come to seem as irrelevant as they have. It did not have to be that, two generations after he wrongly predicted corporations would come to be seen as part of government, the business system is regarded more strongly than ever as rightly separate from public purpose. Today's corporate world did not have to come to be staffed—at least not to the present degree—with people of large ability and high but narrow educations who, far from resisting the corporate manufacture of desire, crave not just the new advantages over nature and necessity provided by corporate creativity but also pointless fashion in clothes and cars, in high-tech gadgetry and games.

But for there to have been a different outcome, liberals would have had to acknowledge how dependent their dream of a better America was on a vital corporate sector. Instead of turning up their noses at corporate life, liberals would have had to take on as part of their mission of social criticism the job of understanding and improving the business corporation. They would have had to accept some responsibility for working to keep corporate America competitive. Corporate America's century and a half of world supremacy in organizational and managerial know-how was about to end. The corporate prosperity that liberals had sneeringly supposed would always be there was about to be put in question. Along with the death of America's reputation as the undisputed champion of the corporate world was to die the hopes of 1960s liberals for a new and improved version of the American Dream.

CHAPTER 19

Corporate America Loses
World Supremacy

IF MANY AMERICAN INTELLECTUALS in the late 1960s believed it beneath their dignity to study corporations, their European counterparts believed that American firms were too dangerous to ignore. "Fifteen years from now it is quite possible that the world's third greatest industrial power, just after the United States and Russia, will not be Europe but *American industry in Europe.*"[1] So warned Jean-Jacques Servan-Schreiber in his 1967 jeremiad, *Le défi americain* (*The American Challenge*), which outsold any book, fiction or nonfiction, published in France since World War II. Servan-Schreiber, a famous French intellectual and founder of the news magazine *L'Express*, adopted Galbraith's idea of the corporate technostructure to explain why American businesses were outcompeting French companies in Europe.

American corporations were doing better than European companies at exploiting the new free trade across borders allowed by the Common Market (predecessor of today's European Union). IBM, American Express, Union Carbide, and dozens of other American firms set up headquarters in Brussels or Paris and operated on a continental scale while many French firms remained locked in their own country. Europeans often attributed American success at large-scale operations to American corporations' greater capital resources. But Servan-Schreiber followed Galbraith in positing that marketing skills and the stimulation of consumer demand were the key to American corporate success. American companies' ability to market their goods through advertising and the creation of demand allowed them to make large investments that would have seemed too risky to European companies devoid of marketing skills. "This science of marketing is new in Europe," wrote Servan-Schreiber.[2]

Marketing was only one aspect of a manifold American advantage. American corporations understood the "art of *organization* that is still a mystery" in Europe.[3] French corporations lacked, according to Servan-Schreiber, the "remarkable integrated entity that John Kenneth Galbraith calls a 'technostructure.'"[4] Group spirit reaching far down into the organization explained why corporate America was leaping across national borders and, "in its own special way, unifying Europe."[5]

Servan-Schreiber's French echo of Galbraith produced yet another reverberation in the United States. Quickly translated into English, *The American Challenge* was published in New York with an introduction by Galbraith's close friend, the Harvard historian Arthur Schlesinger Jr. Although Servan-Schreiber had written to warn Europeans that they must become corporate in the American style, Schlesinger read Servan-Schreiber as an anticorporatist, saying that Servan-Schreiber saw "social justice" as the key to economic development.[6] Liberals like Schlesinger in the 1960s believed they had it all figured out. American organizational superiority in the corporate technostructure meant that economic competitiveness was not an issue for the United States and that the nation's only challenges lay in culture and politics, in education and social reform.

Caught up in their trans-Atlantic pas de deux, American liberals and the European intelligentsia missed the impending economic challenge from Japan. The land of the rising sun was extending corporate organizational arts far beyond anything that Galbraith had envisioned in his notion of the technostructure. Whereas Galbraith thought the source of corporate productivity resided not in top management but in the group identity of the business and professional staff, the Japanese were about to show that competitive advantage could be got from better relations with suppliers and with frontline employees. The secret lay in a new approach to quality. Corporate America's idea had been to inspect defects out. The Japanese aimed to build quality in.[7] This seemingly simple difference would transform the industrial world and move supremacy in managerial technique to Japan.

Yet the Japanese approach was born in America or, more specifically, at Bell Labs, the research arm of AT&T, which enjoyed a national telephone monopoly for much of the twentieth century. At Bell Labs in the 1920s, a scientist named Walter Shewhart had faced the problem of variation in the quality of telephone equipment that could leave one customer pleased and another with a piercing earache from echo-back. Shewhart's solution was to focus on the biggest variations in telephone equipment, or what he called "assignable" or large errors. The biggest mistakes in the manufacturing process were those whose causes could most likely be found and fixed, thus narrowing but not eliminating variation in telephone equipment. In other words, Shewhart aimed to make better telephones, not perfect ones. Perfection was a metaphysical fiction unknown in the real world. Shewhart's methods became known as "statistical quality control" and "continuous improvement."

For twenty years Shewhart's system was used only in the telephone industry. Then, during World War II, a government statistician named W. Edwards Deming, a friend and admirer of Shewhart, began to teach his methods to weapons manufacturers. Deming's work in moving statistical quality control to industries other than telephones and, after the war, to Japan would make him one of the most important management teachers in history. Deming's World War II audience consisted mainly of engineers and production managers. Top-level corporate executives paid little attention. Deming made a special effort to interest the top brass at the American automobile companies but had no success. As a result, GM, Ford, Chrysler, and their employees would suffer terribly when, thanks to Deming's teaching, the Japanese won competitive advantage over them in the 1970s and 1980s.

The military and commercial applications of statistical quality control that Deming taught to weapons manufacturers and then to the Japanese owed their origins at least partly to his pre–World War II work for the U.S. Census Bureau. Deming taught clerks there to use statistics to improve their accuracy, just as Japanese workers would later use graph paper to chart quality variations and spot assignable errors that could be found and fixed. Deming's early work for the Census Bureau is a reminder that government's role in economic innovation is vitally important in the corporate economy.

Just as the War Department supported interchangeable parts for musket manufacture in early America, and just as space exploration and defense programs later helped foster computerization and the Internet, the American government provided much of the initial impetus behind the quality movement that revolutionized corporate manufacturing.

Ironically, the American government even gave the Japanese their first introduction to Deming. When the U.S. Army occupied Japan after World War II, it found the country's telephone system inadequate and brought in AT&T experts from whom the Japanese learned of Shewhart and Deming, along with their work on statistical quality control.

Japanese executives recognized their opportunity when they heard that the American occupiers were bringing Deming to Japan in 1950 to work on a census of the country. They invited him to give a series of talks that focused on quality products in general, not just on telephones. Managers from many industries attended. Deming gave the Japanese the same lectures he had given American weapons manufacturers during the war but tweaked them to emphasize export success. Over the next several years he made annual visits to Japan to teach quality control, emphasizing Japan's comparative advantage in its highly educated workforce. Predicting that Japan could achieve a competitive position in quality in five years and dominance in ten, he laid out a vision of Japan as one large manufacturing system.

On visits to Japanese factories, Deming observed wide variations in the quality of their supplies. So he suggested that manufacturers not only adopt statistical quality control themselves but also teach it to their suppliers. Quality, Deming told the Japanese, "must be a prairie fire; all Japanese on fire. Everybody will win."[8] The Japanese had never seen the prairie, but they got the idea. Once Deming had taught Japanese workers to spot assignable errors in order to root out and fix their causes, workers began to take over other jobs previously done by specialists. In American automobile plants it took highly paid machinists a full day to change dies on presses that stamped out body panels. The Japanese invented a process that let workers change the dies themselves in just three minutes.[9]

The Japanese car companies also developed quality relations with their customers. Automobile sales representatives visited clients in their homes. Taking orders in the buyers' living rooms, salesmen offered a fair price that eliminated the painful haggling associated with car buying in America. This close relation with customers not only promoted brand loyalty but facilitated customer research. Salesmen tracked an individual car buyer's needs, the buyer's stage in the life cycle, how many children the buyer had, and how large a car the buyer was likely to purchase next.

All this data on likely future demand made for improved production planning.

Japanese employees were soon focused on product innovation, which in America was still management's job. Meeting not only at work but sometimes after work, in bars or even in their homes, workers thought up improved ways to build and sell cars. In the heady days of the 1970s and 1980s, when Japanese management seemed to have triumphed in the world economy, these "quality circles" spread far beyond automobiles into other industries, such as banking, where workers, not managers, created innovations like automatic paycheck deposits.

Deming had nothing to do with the creation of quality circles or the idea of having workers innovate (a practice largely unknown in America, except in pale versions like the suggestion box). Still, he deserves credit for seeing that the quality movement could make the corporation in postwar Japan a center of valued social harmony. With so much dependence on workers' participation in what had once been considered management functions (and also to reduce some workers' latent militancy), postwar Japanese corporations rewarded employees with good wages and long-term job security.

This Japanese social harmony in turn supported the lean production system.[10] Much depended on employees' good will when workers were empowered to stop the line to prevent defects, or when there was an inventory of only an hour's supply of parts before the next small batch arrived from the supplier. Despite the system's fragility, or rather because of it, the line seldom stopped. Workers and suppliers stayed alert precisely because so much was at stake in their doing so. In American car companies, by contrast, the assembly system might have been described as fat rather than lean. Huge amounts of capital were invested in large inventories meant to keep the line moving. Yet the line often stopped.

Japan's quality system, in which workers took a managerial point of view, turned out to have a cost advantage. Japanese manufacturers could offer not only offer higher quality cars but lower prices. Americans were soon voting with their pocketbooks at the Toyota and Datsun (later called Nissan) dealerships that sprang up across the United States. As Japan began to make significant gains in the American car market in the early 1970s, the U.S. companies initially responded with contempt, thinking of Japanese goods as cheap and shoddy. Who cared, Henry Ford II is reputed to have said, if the Japanese sold a few "shitboxes." But by the end of the decade it was apparent that the Japanese automakers had gained considerable advantage over their American competitors.

Outdone on costs, the American auto companies and their suppliers began workforce reductions that would continue intermittently for forty years and from which the middle-class American Dream has never recovered. Corporate management succeeded in shifting more than a fair share of the blame onto American labor unions and their high wages, ignoring the fact that management, in its ardent defense of the "right to manage," shared responsibility for decades of antagonistic labor relations that had brought high costs and low quality.[11] Japanese executives, who could be authoritarian for sure, nevertheless claimed no "right" to manage that excluded workers. The result was competitive advantage.

Not only Detroit but America as a whole was soon focused on economic competitiveness. The liberals' hope for a loftier American Dream went smash. Galbraith, Schlesinger, the American liberals, and the European Left had got it all wrong, or at least not nearly enough right. Galbraith had believed he had a revolutionary insight—that not top management, as Berle and Means had said, but the technical and professional staff, the technostructure, were the basis of the corporate economy. The Japanese quality movement quickly rendered Galbraith's supposedly revolutionary insight outdated by assigning managerial responsibilities to assembly workers.

American liberals had rested their cultural and political self-confidence on the supposed strength of the corporate life they held in contempt. Thanks to the purported superiority of the United States in corporate organization, Americans were expected to dream less and less of economic success, which was more or less guaranteed, and to turn their reveries instead toward government and the public sphere so that they might realize the liberals' version of the American Dream in higher education, pure science, cultural elevation, civil rights, and social justice. But the middle class, faced with reduced economic opportunity, lost patience with the liberal hope to move the American Dream past corporate concerns. Some of President Johnson's antipoverty Great Society programs struggled on for another decade or two. But many Americans came to scorn those programs and wanted the nation to restore economic competitiveness rather than to dream of a Great Society.

In their hour of economic defeat, American corporations had achieved an ironic cultural victory. The cultural anticorporatism of the liberals would slowly evaporate, its mists lingering mainly in academic ivory towers. For most Americans during the late twentieth and early twenty-first centuries, it would take an occasional economic crisis or bout of corporate corruption, not cultural resentments, to provoke some good old-fashioned, and even then only intermittent, corporation bashing.

But if the business corporation was no longer a routine target of cultural contempt, it still faced large challenges. There was still the old question of whether corporate managers (1) served as agents of shareholders, (2) used their offices to enrich themselves, or (3) both of the above. And could managers be made to feather the nests of the rest of us as well? Could the corporation not only restore the nation's competitiveness but also restore the old American Dream of middle-class incomes for ordinary citizens?

CHAPTER 20

Laying the Groundwork for the Corporation's Cultural Comeback

ON JULY 15, 1979, President Jimmy Carter went on national television and told the American people they were suffering from a "crisis of confidence . . . that strikes at the very heart and soul and spirit of our national will." He was basically saying that the American Dream was waning. Americans were losing their "faith that the days of our children would be better than our own."[1] The 1970s was called the "me decade" at the time, mainly to indicate a shift in people's focus from 1960s social protest and social reform to taking care of their individual prospects. This renewed individualism also reflected the fact that the 1970s was a tough time to believe in the national prospect. The Watergate crisis and defeat in Vietnam had weakened Americans' faith in their government. Energy crises in 1973 and 1979 had driven up gasoline prices, brought long lines at gas pumps, and raised demand for Japanese economy cars. The dollar had fallen in value against other currencies, aiding American exports but also fueling inflation that sapped Americans' purchasing power. The nation's impotence seemed confirmed in November 1979 when Iranian revolutionaries seized the U.S. Embassy in Tehran and, with impunity, held dozens of Americans hostage for more than a year.

Carter's White House predecessors had bequeathed him some of his problems. Johnson (1963–1969) had fueled inflation by refusing to raise taxes to finance his "guns and butter" policy that combined a major war in Vietnam with Great Society spending at home. Nixon (1969–1974) largely ignored inflation except for a brief wage-price freeze. Otherwise, he limited himself to complaining about steelworkers' wages while avoiding the risk Kennedy had taken in challenging the steel companies' prices.

In 1972, Nixon ran a large budget deficit that lifted employment and helped secure his reelection at the cost of yet more inflation. His successor, Gerald Ford (1974–1977), dealt feebly with the price surge by calling on citizens to restrain their individual spending in order to "Whip Inflation Now," or WIN. Humorists were soon wearing their government-issued WIN buttons upside down to read NIM—short, they said, for "Non-stop Inflation Merry-go-round."

Missing from the 1970s inflation debate was any mention of corporate profits and prices, until near the end of the decade when President Carter proposed to deregulate the airline and trucking industries in order to expose them to competition and improve customers' purchasing power. Carter was the first president since Kennedy to engage in a bit of corporate criticism, going after the oil companies for attempting to diversify into other industries during the 1979 energy crisis, when their prices and profits surged. Carter's Federal Reserve chairman, Paul Volcker, finally brought inflation to heel with high interest rates, producing a recession that held down both corporate prices and wage increases. But the recession also brought high unemployment that helped defeat Carter's 1980 bid for reelection and left his successor, Ronald Reagan, to enjoy credit for the economic rebound that Carter's policies helped to produce.

Corporations, in short, had largely free rein during the 1970s, especially before Carter's presidency began in 1977. The American government and its leaders were happy to take credit for any good economic news that came along, but the truth was that they mostly fretted fecklessly about the economy. Decisions about America's economic future were made mainly in corporate board rooms, with the help of management gurus and business school professors who were about to surge to unprecedented influence.

In the absence of important public or political discussion of corporate policy, an esoteric academic paper of the 1970s exercised great influence on corporate behavior for the next quarter century. Or perhaps it would be more accurate to say that the paper only supplied ideological justification for going in a direction that some corporate managers had always longed to go. In the economically troubled and politically vacuous 1970s, corporate chiefs with little interest in national and public good felt more free than in many years to drop any pretense of social concern. "Theory of the Firm: Managerial Behavior, Agency Costs and Ownership Structure" by two University of Rochester professors, Michael Jensen and William Meckling, created or at least provided ideological cover for the movement known as "shareholder value."[2]

The idea of shareholder value was that the fundamental job of corporate managers was to produce maximum economic gains for the company's owners, whether in the form of profits, dividends, or a run-up in share prices. Not a very original idea, one might suppose, but for nearly half a century the conventional opinion, shaped by Berle and Means, had been that owners had lost control. Managers supposedly controlled corporations and ran them for their own interest rather than to maximize shareholder value. Jensen and Meckling disagreed that corporations ignored shareholders. Investors around the world, they pointed out, kept trusting corporate managers to act as their agents, suggesting that shareholders evidently felt they got good returns: "Millions of individuals voluntarily entrust billions of dollars, francs, pesos, etc. of personal wealth to the care of managers. . . . Investors have by and large not been disappointed with the results, despite the agency costs" for managers' services.[3]

Ronald Coase, in his 1937 paper "On the Nature of the Firm" (discussed in chapter 6) had distinguished between the cost of market transactions and the cost of management to explain the origin of business firms. When goods and services could be produced and distributed inside a firm at lower cost than in the market, corporate managers began to make decisions formerly made by the law of supply and demand. According to Coase, only where costs were lower for transactions than for management did economic activity take place outside the firm, in the free market. In many industries, the nineteenth-century advent of capital-intensive machinery had lowered the cost of management more than it lowered the cost of market transactions, leading to a multiplying of large corporations managed by bureaucratic hierarchy.

Jensen and Meckling believed that Coase had distinguished too sharply between the corporation and the market. They called the "private corporation" a *"legal fiction which serves as a nexus for contracting relationships. . . . [I]t makes little sense to try to distinguish those things which are 'inside' the firm . . . from those things that are 'outside' of it. There is in a very real sense only a multitude of complex relationships* (i.e., contracts)," whether they take place in the market or within the legal fiction of the firm.[4] In other words, the firm was not, as Coase had believed, an island of power wielded by managers but a series of freely agreed relationships among owners, managers, and employees. Relations within the firm were voluntary and resembled the firm's external transactions with customers and suppliers. And according to Jensen and Meckling, there are agency costs—that is, costs for getting other people to do our work for us—not only in managerial firms but in all cooperative or voluntary contracts, whether inside or outside a firm.

The thrust of Jensen's and Meckling's paper was that if agency costs are more than offset by the gains to which they lead outside the firm, they should also be able to produce profits inside the firm. Most sports superstars, for example, seem to believe that their agents are worth their high fees. So why shouldn't it be similarly profitable for corporate shareholders to employ managers as their agents in relation with suppliers, customers, and employees?

Jensen and Meckling cited their cooperation in writing their paper as an example of profitable agency costs, an idea that seems strained. Surely it is more accurate to describe the two professors' effort to cooperate with each other in writing their paper not in terms of acting as agents for each other but rather, in Coase's terminology, as a transaction; they were exchanging mutual assistance with each other.

And the idea that the internal life of the firm is only a nexus of voluntary agreements among free agents suggests wishful thinking possible only to ivory tower academics with little experience of working under the arbitrary power of managers. Of course no one holds a gun to an employee's head and forces him or her to go to work for a corporation. But once hired, the employee is, as labor law has it, an "employee at will," subject to the possibility of instant dismissal. Corporate employment is indeed a transaction, but there is often far more freedom and power on the corporate side than on the employee side of the deal.

Strained though it was, the argument of Jensen and Meckling that firms were legal fictions and, in reality, nothing more than networks of free, voluntary relations found a receptive audience in the late 1970s corporate world. American managers were weary of the reputation for incompetence with which they had been saddled both by the loss of supremacy in automobiles and by disaster in Vietnam thanks to the supposed master manager, Robert McNamara. In arguments like Jensen and Meckling's for the freedom of corporate life and the effectiveness of management, there was potential for a return to a time like the 1950s, when corporations and management had enjoyed considerable moral standing.

But there was an important difference between the pro-business 1950s and the soon-to-emerge pro-business 1980s. Boulware and others who had won moral stature for corporate America after World War II had emphasized what corporations did for society. Jensen and Meckling emphasized what management did for the shareholder. They made clear that society was no concern of the corporation's. In the demoralized boardrooms and business schools of the mid 1970s, some CEOs and professors had sought to redeem their reputations by talking up "corporate social responsibility," which had stirred some interest in the public at large. But because Jensen and Meckling viewed the firm "as the nexus of a set of contracting relationships," they found it erroneous to engage in the "personalization of the firm implied by asking questions such as . . . 'does the firm have a social responsibility?' *The firm is not an individual.*"[5]

The conservative economist Milton Friedman—awarded the Nobel Prize in 1976, the year in which Jensen and Meckling published their paper—had made a similar argument against corporate social responsibility in 1970. According to Friedman, it was actually *irresponsible* for corporate managers who were supposed to act as agents for shareholders to give away those shareholders' money in the name of corporate social responsibility. His argument was clear in the title of his article, "The Social Responsibility of Business Is to Increase Its Profits."[6]

Although Friedman's article was probably much more widely read, Jensen and Meckling's may have been more influential. Their paper was often cited as justification for the increasingly common practice of compensating managers through stock options. Because such rewards linked managerial compensation to the price of the company's shares, managers were supposed to be tightly focused on creating shareholder value. But stock options would eventually bring many abuses. They gave managers a chance at huge short-term profits through short-term accounting gimmicks, deceit, and illegality that pushed up reported earnings and raised share prices. Shareowners, employers, and citizens were the losers when dubious accounting, stock options, and fraudulent financial reporting eventually led in the early twenty-first century to massive corporate collapses like that of Enron. But as the 1970s came to a close, disasters of that sort lay hidden in the future.

Managers at the end of the me decade were finally, tentatively, finding a way once again to present corporate life as a worthy adventure. Once again, managerial power was to be downplayed in favor of the American admiration for freedom. Corporations, far from being potentially oppressive and stifling employers, were a series of voluntary relations. Managers, far from acting only in their own interests, were effective builders of shareholder value. The immense fortunes that more than a few CEOs were about to shower upon themselves were made all the sweeter by their newfound ability to claim they had earned them.

Executives in the 1950s had rewarded themselves modestly. Ever since Berle and Means had written their 1932 book on the different interests of managers and owners, CEOs had needed to be careful not to prove too blatantly that their interests were in conflict with those of the shareholders. Managers had to forbear claiming as their own rewards the financial gains that shareholders might think came from capital they had invested in the firm. Now that corporations were properly understood not as instruments of capital but as spheres of freedom, with managers serving as agents of owners and raising shareholder value, what fair-minded person could begrudge executives a good-size share of the wealth they so ably created? The deal would be sealed by a new understanding of corporate success as based on values. Virtue must have its rewards.

PART VI

Leadership

CHAPTER 21

Managing by Values

THE CORPORATE CULT of moral leadership dates back to the 1930s. Its origins, as outlined in chapter 13, lay in the Harvard Business School and the Hawthorne experiment. Elton Mayo and, especially, Chester Barnard had seen leadership as moral in the sense of "moral courage." Barnard had said that leaders' power is meager when measured against their responsibilities. As Barnard saw it, lack of adequate power is the paradoxical condition of moral leadership. By accepting responsibility without the authority to fulfill that responsibility, leaders demonstrate existential courage that inspires followers to get the job done. "Out of the void," said Barnard, "comes the spirit that shapes the ends of men."[1]

This notion of corporate leadership as a matter of moral courage had a parallel in politics and may have originated there. During the Great Depression, President Franklin Roosevelt had easily persuaded Congress to legislate vast new powers for the executive branch. Roosevelt covered himself with the claim that leadership had nothing to do with power. Rather, his job was to inspire courage in the American people, and he did.

But this idea of leadership as exemplary moral courage grew repellent over time. In its more extreme 1930s and 1940s versions, as represented in Adolf Hitler and Benito Mussolini, self-proclaimed moral courage translated into a supposedly heroic triumph of will. The fascists' defeat in World War II and the revelation of their crimes discredited the idea of moral leadership as willfully courageous. By the time of the Dwight D. Eisenhower presidency in the 1950s, morally courageous leadership had dwindled down to willful upholding of bourgeois values such as family, faith, and free markets. Indeed, little was heard of moral courage in the corporate world. Most CEOs focused on the bottom line and let existential daring care for itself.

Yet Barnard found followers in business schools, which were trying to make management a social science. From the 1940s onward, a brilliant academic named Herbert Simon—eventually a Nobel Prize winner—leant distinction to this camp by emphasizing values in management. For Simon, values transcended managerial rationality. Values were the ultimate desires, needs, and goals that management served.[2] His notion that values were goals, not tools, got lost in the hands of some of his successors. Moreover, Simon was most influential in the rarefied air of academia. It was not brilliant theorizers but real-world political crises that led the popular mind to substitute values for courage as the key to moral leadership.

The precipitating factors in the new values-oriented notion of moral leadership were the Vietnam War and the Watergate scandal. In 1971, a leak of classified Defense Department material seemed to show that the Johnson administration and some of its predecessors had promoted war while dishonestly claiming to seek peace. Sensational and simplistic media discussion of these "Pentagon Papers" failed to consider the moral ambiguities that are often involved in leadership. In the media view, Johnson and his predecessors could not have been at least partly trying to lead public opinion but only trying to deceive it. That presidents' seeming dishonesty had caused a mistaken war and taken the lives of tens of thousands of young Americans, along with the lives of still more Vietnamese, made a deep impression in the popular mind. The question seemed settled as to what made for good leadership: from then on, good leaders would be thought to have good values.

The 1973–1974 Watergate scandal added support to the idea that good values should be the fundamental quality of a moral leader. The scandal rose out of a Republican burglary of Democratic headquarters aimed at gathering intelligence for the 1972 presidential election campaign. The burglars were caught, and President Richard Nixon attempted an illegal cover-up of Republican involvement. Subsequent court cases, a congressional investigation, and the release of Oval Office tape recordings revealed Nixon—a public preacher of eternal verities—to be in private an amoral, foul-mouthed conniver. In 1974, he resigned the presidency before he could be impeached. Nixon's vice president, Gerald Ford, moved into the White House only to be defeated in the election of 1976 by Jimmy Carter, who promised the American people that "I will never lie to you."

Revelations that recent presidents had been untruthful led to humorous and sententious declarations that America faced a crisis of leadership. A journalist quipped that if a Martian landed and said, "Take me to your leader," people would have no idea where to direct him. Warren Bennis, soon to be a prominent management guru, declared in 1974 that "many of us don't have the faintest idea of what leadership is all about. Leading does not mean managing."[3] So what did leadership mean?

The question of leadership's meaning was tackled by the eminent political scientist James MacGregor Burns in a superb book. *Leadership* (1978) aimed to replace courage with values as the mark of a leader. Although Burns drew his examples from political history, his book exerted great influence in the business world and especially in business schools. Political scientists had focused too much, Burns said, on the exercise of hard power. In the early twentieth century the *Machtpolitik* of Adolf Hitler and Joseph Stalin had been defeated in war but not in the imagination. Americans had conceived of the Cold War and the Vietnam War in terms of force, focusing on "throw weight" in missiles, "body count" in battles, and "kill ratios" in war. Burns's post-Vietnam goal was to win recognition for intangible values as vital elements in leadership.

By inserting values into the leadership equation, Burns unintentionally provided a tool with which the corporate world could interpret the fading American Dream to its own advantage. The economic failures of the late 1960s and 1970s—inflation, low growth, rising unemployment, and loss of industrial supremacy—would focus public attention in the 1980s on restoring the old American Dream of material prosperity, not the liberal dream of education and humanism, science and social justice. That shift gave corporate managers an opportunity to reclaim what they thought was a morally central role in society and, thanks to their misreading of Burns, to justify their restored eminence by claiming they were "managing by values."

Corporate leaders were probably far from Burns's mind when he wrote his book emphasizing the connection of values to leadership. More likely, he was influenced by John Gardner, an architect of President Lyndon Johnson's Great Society programs who had resigned his cabinet position in protest of the Vietnam War. Burns quoted Gardner's call for leaders to "express the values that hold society together" and

added that "leadership has—quite rightly in my view—the connotation
of leading people upward, to some higher values."[4]

From the time of Burns's book, corporate gurus would relentlessly
repeat the mantra of "values-based leadership," "values-driven leadership," and the like. Unfortunately, most of the gurus missed his point.
Burns did not see values as a base or a driver. He did not even see values
as something that, in the common expression, human beings somehow
"hold." Values are actions, habits, and goals. And it is not just leaders'
values but those of their followers, according to Burns, that are the key
to leadership. Leaders induce followers to act in behalf of "the values . . .
of *both leaders and followers*."[5] Leaders help followers achieve their deeply
felt needs and wants—the goals they value.

But the management gurus who came after Burns often gave scant
attention to followers' values, at least until the moment when corporate
leaders supposedly instill new values in their followers. In much corporate discussion today, it is assumed that values-based leadership means
announcing values and getting followers to adopt them. Once the values
are adopted by the rank and file, leadership can be distributed among
them. Employees, driven by their newly adopted values, can be leaders
themselves, pushing management goals. This all-too-common corporate
notion of values-based leadership rests on a dubious notion of human
nature and human behavior. Can companies really instill new values at
will in employees? Or is it more realistic to work with the values that
employees already have?

What about managerial power? For Burns, leaders had to exercise
power as the "means" to achieve values. Leaders help followers understand the implications of their values for the use of power in "political
action and governmental organization."[6] Effective business leaders of
course do something similar, clearly linking employee and shareholder
goals such as pay and profit to managerial issues such as strategy and
organization.

But many gurus lost sight of the idea that values are achieved at least
partly through power. They tried to substitute values for power in order
to claim the high ground of moral leadership. They made values into
tools rather than goals, into means rather than ends. So began the idea of
using values to manage. All too many leadership gurus, often not realiz-
ing the moral danger of their ideas, taught managers to try to change

followers' values in order to manipulate them. Many managers who could probably profit from genuine understanding of values-oriented leadership get no real knowledge of it from those who supposedly teach it.

Burns also helped to pioneer the concept of what he called "transforming leadership" and what has come to be known as "transformational leadership." Here, too, he kept his focus on followers' values. Leaders transform followers not by giving them new values but by helping them to achieve goals that they already value. Even during periods of revolutionary change, Burns says, it is not the leader so much as the new situation that transforms followers' values. The leader does not impose or instill new values. The leader helps followers see that the revolutionary situation calls for them to value new goals because it has created new wants and needs.

It is easy enough to surmise why Burns's superb explanation of the relationship between values and leadership dissolved into simplistic notions of "values-*based* leadership." Managers want tools with which to work. So if values are the key to leadership, managers will instinctively see values as tools. Burns's essential idea of leading *for* values therefore got mangled into the idea of managing *by* values. Of course, only foolish managers actually try to manage by values. Good executives, when they get down to the practice of management as opposed to its theory, know they have to communicate with employees, not manipulate them. But even such sensible managers may be charmed by management gurus into believing they are managing *by* values when they are actually managing *for* values. Some of these sages were susceptible to the same self-deception. Genuinely effective counselors do not teach corporate managers to use values to lead. They may believe that is what they are teaching, but really, they teach good communication and effective use of power to get the job done.

This pot of mistaken theory and sound practice percolated along for a couple of decades. Then, in 1997, two leadership gurus named Ken Blanchard and Michael O'Connor captured the essence of the brew. They wrote a simplistic but successful little book called, naturally enough, *Managing by Values*. Presented as a fictional account of a serendipitous run-in between a leadership expert and a desperate executive, the volume gives some idea of what was going on in motivationally oriented management consulting practices during this period. The central questions for managers to ask themselves were, "By what values do you want to be known? How do you want your customers and your employees to feel toward the company?" These values should then be made the "real 'boss.'"[7]

Burns's notion of followers' valued goals as deeply felt "wants and needs" was lost in "managing by values." Managers met in retreats where consultants presented them with long lists of possible values from which they might pluck a few such as "integrity," "service," and in supposedly distant third place, "profit." The next step was for the company to "adopt" these values, usually with some "participation" by the lower echelons. "Gaps" between employee performance and the new "values" were then eliminated through an "alignment" process.[8] But of course it was power, not values, that made employees get in line.

Corporate workshops in which executives and employees decide to adopt values are not useless exercises. Quite the opposite; they afford opportunity for communication. What is communicated, however, is usually unrelated to values, unrelated to employees' deeply felt needs and wants. Rather, management directives are communicated. Managing by values is not about values but about rules. Yet managing by rules is often a good thing, especially if the rules are clearly communicated. It helps, too, if employees have some input in making the rules. So the managing-by-values gurus, with their emphasis on employee empowerment and participation, often succeeded in fattening the bottom line.

If managing by values got good results, where was the harm in its being based on an illusion? Did it matter that it was falsely labeled "values" when it was really about rules? The problem was that the illusion of values-based leadership helped foster moral complacency, setting leaders on the road to ruin. Managing by values encouraged the impression that corporations were more ethical and less power-centered than they really were. It played into the ancient desire of the powerful to believe that their followers saw them as their moral superiors. It encouraged the moral arrogance that is one of the great dangers of leadership.

In other words, the managing-by-values movement lost sight of the difficulty of self-knowledge taught by both traditional religion and modern psychology. Managers no longer needed to reflect on their conduct to learn what they truly valued. They just had to announce their values and that was supposed to be that. It would take a couple of decades, but the foolish self-congratulation and moral pretense fostered by the half-baked philosophy of values-based leadership would play into scandals like Enron and ruin more than a few corporate executives.

James MacGregor Burns, in his great book on leadership, had set out to deemphasize power in favor of values. In management gurus he found disciples who succeeded all too well.

CHAPTER 22

Creating the Concept
of Corporate Culture

COGNATE TO THE IDEA of managing by values was the idea of managing by culture. The words *culture* and *value* are both often used to imply normative goals and ends. But *culture* is a broader term, suggesting shared values that help unite a society. Corporate operations, whether with employees, customers, or suppliers, are nothing if not social. So it was easy for the corporate world to become captivated by a mistaken notion of culture at the same time that its leaders were subscribing to a mistaken notion of values. The same business leaders who want to "change the values" are eager to "change the culture."

The concept of culture was first developed by anthropologists and then, in the 1970s, made its way into other academic disciplines. It was probably inevitable that it would eventually become a staple of management theory. But the process was greatly facilitated by the discrediting of rationalistic, number-crunching management, which was widely blamed for 1970s disasters such as the near collapse of the American auto industry and the loss of the war in Vietnam.

As the supposedly sharp ratiocination of managers like Robert McNamara fell into disrepute, the question was what would replace it. Precision dancing had gone out of style. The corporate world was ready for a little soft shoe. Tom Peters, more than any other guru, created the idea of corporate culture. He later became something of a parody of himself, preaching "liberation management" in table-pounding prose. But *In Search of Excellence* (1982), in which he and Robert Waterman expounded their notion of corporate culture, was an understandably appealing book to many managers.

Some corporations do have something like a culture in the anthropological sense of the term. That is, they have something deeper than a pleasant ambience and good morale. They have shared ideas and values that employees have acquired and reinforced by working together, ideas and values that preceded any current employee and which will remain even after those employees have left. Peters and Waterman drew their examples from some of the best-run companies of the time—Proctor and Gamble, Johnson & Johnson, 3M, and others.

In Search of Excellence shared with *Managing by Values* a tendency to downplay power, a tendency that violated the notions of some of the social scientists who had helped to develop the culture concept. Those social scientists had thought of culture as a "resource" to employ in a social "arena" shaped by "arrangements of status, power, and identity."[1] But Peters and Waterman did not aim to connect culture to power. They hoped to substitute culture for power. They argued that American companies were being hindered by their "structures and systems, both of which inhibit action."[2] They wanted to use culture to get around structures and systems, maybe even replace them. Where structures and systems inhibited action, culture would enable it.

As Peters and Waterman told the story, the "conventional wisdom" was to "[g]et the strategic plan down on paper and the right organization structure will pop out with ease, grace, and beauty." But their research taught them that "strategy rarely seemed to dictate unique structural solutions." Rather, "the most crucial problems in strategy were often those of execution and continuous adaptation: getting it done, staying flexible."[3] Culture supposedly bound corporate employees to a common purpose while simultaneously liberating them. "The culture regulates rigorously the few variables that do count, and it provides meaning. But within those qualitative values (and in almost *all* other dimensions), people are encouraged to stick out, to innovate."[4]

In Search of Excellence barely acknowledged that culture is a structure of ideas that may inhibit as well as liberate. For example, Peters and Waterman celebrated the stable culture at IBM. They claimed that "IBM's values remain constant and the attendant stability permits it structurally to shift major hunks of resources to attack a particular problem."[5] But a few years later IBM hit a rough patch and acquired a new CEO, Lou Gerstner, from outside the company. He attacked elements of IBM's culture such as the venerable tradition that everyone wore a dark suit and white shirt. For many employees the dark suit was a deeply embedded cultural value that they were reluctant to see go. That was precisely the reason why Gerstner, trying to shake up an organization that was losing its edge, broadened the palette.

Such problems with culture—the fact that it could be a problem rather than the solution—did not fit the goal of *In Search of Excellence*, which shared the tendency of so much American management theory to overestimate the democratic possibilities of corporate life. Peters and Waterman therefore saw intangible culture mainly as enabling. They mostly missed culture's power to inhibit. The intangible nature of culture gave it an aura of creativity and freedom. But part of what makes culture useful to human beings is its making some behavior routine. Mindless routine, whether embodied in systems or in culture, saves a lot of energy and often makes for efficiency. Inept managers who seek creativity by attacking organizational routine often succeed only in slowing things down. The trick is not to endorse creativity over routine but to get the balance right between them.

Peters and Waterman's goal was to show that a freer corporate life was consistent with improved management. So they ended up treating culture as a managerial tool. They saw no contradiction between claiming that culture allowed for freedom but was also an executive instrument. The essence of their approach was to "remind the world of professional managers that 'soft is hard.'" They told managers that "All that stuff you have been dismissing for so long as the intractable, irrational, intuitive, informal organization *can* be managed. . . . Here are some tools for managing it."[6] Managers eagerly grabbed hold of the idea that they could "change the culture." Culture, like values, was a sort of microchip to be installed in employees' brains, after which the employees would do what they were supposed to do without being told, indeed without knowing that they were being managed.

Much of the culture change that was soon under way throughout corporate America was surely bogus. As with "values," many gurus and managers believed culture could turn on a dime. A little top-down tweaking and, presto, a new culture! But culture takes many years or even decades to establish. The ease and speed with which corporate managers claimed to change the culture was proof that what was going on was mostly about employees figuring out what the boss wanted and heading in that direction. If that meant playing into the boss's notion of "culture change," so be it. The real reason, however, for the success of the culture concept in the business world was that it was congruent with the implicit hope in the American Dream that there was no tension between corporate prosperity and democratic freedom. The culture concept was the latest method for the corporate world to have its cake and eat it too. Managed by culture, corporations would make more money, not less, by abandoning top-down hierarchy.

In Search of Excellence had a great deal to say about Mayo, Barnard, and other theorists who had tried to minimize the role of power in corporate life. But Peters and Waterman treated these predecessors as if they had been forgotten. In reality, the ostensible humanism and existential courage pushed by Mayo and Barnard were well remembered and highly influential. Rather than recovering Mayo and Barnard's ideas, Peters and Waterman were shoving them aside. Where Mayo and others had downplayed power in favor of therapy, *In Search of Excellence* downplayed power in favor of culture. Peters and Waterman were scarcely alone in downplaying power. Other gurus such as Peter Senge, who wrote a bit later, opined that there could be "control without controlling."[7]

But Peters and Waterman succeeded best at linking their managerial vision to old-fashioned Americanism. "There is good news from America," they announced. "Good management practice today is resident not only in Japan. But more important, the good news comes from treating people decently and asking them to shine, and from producing things that work."[8] As with managing by values, managing by culture often worked even if, or rather because, what was really being changed was not culture but the rules.

If "culture" was often unreal in any particular corporation, corporate culture threatened to become all too real in America at large. "Nothing is lost save honor," said Diamond Jim Fisk in the late nineteenth century when Americans were learning to live in a corporate economy that contradicted their espoused values of freedom and personal independence. A hundred years later nothing was lost save self-understanding as twentieth-century Americans bought into the concept of corporate culture. The tension between individual freedom and corporate prosperity was to be further masked by, as the leadership gurus called it, "the soft stuff."

CHAPTER 23

Inventing the Leadership
Development Industry

THE 1970S, OFTEN CALLED the "me" decade, were also
the "becoming" decade. Tom, Dick, and Harry were not automatically
themselves. They had to become their true selves. Nineteen seventies
management gurus helped executives to become leaders by becoming
themselves. This focus on what was called "identity formation" was
largely inspired by Erik Erikson, an eminent psychoanalyst. His *Young
Man Luther* (1958) had won acclaim for its argument that the founder
of Protestantism had needed to pass through a youthful identity crisis—
remaking himself by rebelling against his father—before he could reform
Christianity by rebelling against the pope. Erikson followed up with
an influential 1968 book called *Identity: Youth and Crisis.* And the next
year, in *Gandhi's Truth* (1969), Erikson argued that the sainted Indian
leader had hit upon his tactic of revolutionary nonviolence through his
personal process of identity formation.

Erikson's idea that leaders had to reform themselves as preparation
for reforming the world owed some of its 1970s éclat to the rebellion
of young Americans against the Vietnam War. Many college students
encountered Erikson's ideas in their classes. In their sometimes desperate
wrestling with decisions such as whether or not to resist the draft, they
found consolation in the idea that they were forging new identities that
would prepare them to make a better world.

Business students in particular were influenced, often unawares,
by Erikson's ideas. His teachings were reformulated specifically for
corporate leadership by an influential Harvard Business School professor
named Abraham Zaleznik. According to him, leaders have very different
kinds of personalities than do mere managers. Managers supervise routine
operations, whereas leaders create revolutionary change. In a beautifully

crafted and still influential article titled "Managers and Leaders: Are They Different?" Zaleznik presented the typical manager—the central figure of the corporate saga for the previous half century—as leaden in spirit, something like the Roman Catholic priesthood before Luther touched off the Reformation: "While ensuring competence [and] control . . . managerial leadership unfortunately does not necessarily ensure imagination, creativity, or ethical behavior in guiding corporations."[1]

More clearly than most leadership gurus, Zaleznik noted how unreal was the myth of business as a supposed realm of American freedom, and how unreal was the idea that government is the only source of bureaucratic constraint over Americans' individual liberty. Rather, he said, corporations' managerial ethic "fosters a bureaucratic culture in business, supposedly the last bastion protecting us from the encroachments and controls of bureaucracy in government and education."[2] Zaleznik aimed to liberate the corporate world from its managerial bureaucracy by creating processes for the development of revolutionary leaders.

Whereas managers are mindless masters of corporate routine, leaders are "worthy of the drama of power and politics." Zaleznik saw leadership development—*pace* Erikson's *Young Man Luther*—as a "psychodrama in which a brilliant, lonely person must gain control of himself or herself as a precondition for controlling others." Just as the managing-by-values gurus and the mongers of corporate culture risked forgetting James MacGregor Burns's emphasis on the need for leaders to relate values to power, the personality school of leadership would risk losing sight of the need for leaders to be good managers. Managers and leaders, Zaleznik said, are "very different kinds of people."[3] Managers are personally well integrated into their society and time, but leaders "feel separate from their environment."[4] Such estrangement gives them the compensating ability to see the world in new ways. Leaders are creative and imaginative, able to act instead of react, able to shape ideas instead of being shaped by them. According to Zaleznik, a corporate *manager* responds to a market. A corporate *leader* creates a market.

It is lonely at the top not only because there is no one else around but because leaders are loners at heart. They have passed through fiery psychological trials, have had their old selves melted in a crucible and out of the molten remains have painfully forged a new identity for themselves. As a group label for such psychological Lazaruses, Zaleznik followed Erikson in borrowing the rubric "twice-born" that the great pioneering psychologist William James had coined in his book *Varieties of Religious Experience* (1902). Managers, on the other hand, are once-born. According to Zaleznik, managers become themselves through comfortable relations with their parents and a smooth process of social-ization. At ease with themselves and their surroundings since childhood, managers seek not to remake the world but to conserve it.

Leaders have a much harder time of it early on. They become them-selves through a difficult process of "personal mastery which impels an individual to struggle for psychological and social change." If the process is further complicated by difficult parental relations, there may develop a "sense of being special" that "disrupts the bonds that attach children to parents and other authority figures. . . . A form of self-reliance takes hold . . . and perhaps even the desire to do great works."[5] But even combined with great talent, such self-perceived specialness may come to nothing. "Like artists and other gifted people who often struggle with neuroses," potential leaders may be defeated by inner demons.[6] Society, Zaleznik observed, usually leaves potential leaders to sink or swim.

Was there a way to help these struggling leaders become their true selves? Could a business corporation actively develop its leaders rather than passively wait for the occasional lucky soul who, against the odds, has managed to survive his psychological fires? A new industry was about to be born—"leadership development." To develop leaders would not be easy, according to Zaleznik. Potential leaders often make "indifferent students" owing to their preoccupation with their inner struggles. Their self-absorption must be interrupted by "attachment to a great teacher or other person who understands and has the ability to communicate with the gifted individual."[7]

Zaleznik offered examples of corporations that already had, in effect, leadership development programs. Such firms provided chances for young executives to have one-to-one relationships with senior people: "This apprenticeship acquaints the junior executive firsthand with the use of power and with the important antidotes to the power disease called *hubris*: performance and integrity."[8] Leadership development programs, Zaleznik hoped, would also lessen managerial repression by requiring senior executives to tolerate challenges from gifted subordinates. Or if the subordinate was intolerably aggressive, the senior executive would confront the junior administrator rather than indulge in evasive gamesmanship. Corporations had to provide "the emotional relationships leaders need if they are to survive."[9]

Zaleznik's important and insightful article raised as many issues as it resolved. Could corporations really recognize twice-born comers? Was there an inherent contradiction in attempting to institutionalize the process of developing revolutionary leaders? Might leadership development programs only become new channels for the upward ambitions of once-born drones? With a revolutionary heading the hive, would honey remain the worker bees' goal? Would companies led by self-conceived creators of the future be able to manage themselves well in the here and now? With a visionary CEO could corporate employees focus on the mundane operations that make a profit in the present?

Such questions got lost in the shuffle as leadership development became a growth industry. Legions of consultants, gurus, and business school professors set to work helping leaders become themselves. Corporate folk, with a new self-consciousness about leadership, were ready for a self-help manual. A book by Warren Bennis, *On Becoming a Leader* (1989), popularized Erikson's and Zaleznik's ideas for the corporate audience, watering them down at the same time. "The process of becoming a leader," Bennis said, "is much the same as becoming an integrated human being. . . . [L]ife itself is the career."[10] All it takes to become a leader is to become oneself.

Leaders become themselves by being—Bennis repeated Erikson and Zaleznik—"twice-born." But where Erikson and Zaleznik had used the phrase "twice-born" in the sense of William James, the sense of having passed through the fiery trial of something like a Pauline religious conversion, Bennis said a leader only had to "invent" himself. "Twice-borns . . . feel different, even isolated" in youth but learn to rely on themselves and, as they grow up, become "self-assured."[11] Self-assurance is indeed the common denominator of CEOs, but Bennis's vague notion of self-invention lost sight of Erikson's and Zaleznik's idea that the leader is a revolutionary whose personality has been formed by a collapse and rebuilding of the self. Ordinary, middle-class adolescents often "feel different, even isolated" and then emerge as self-assured adults running corporate enterprises. Would such once-borns be tempted by leadership development programs to see a drama and a teleology in their lives that was not really there?

The danger that could be seen vaguely in Zaleznik manifested itself clearly in Bennis. Could corporate programs for leadership development really assist twice-borns in achieving their potential to revolutionize their organizations? Or would such programs only become channels within which savvy, once-born managers maneuvered their way to the top? Because skillful maneuvering is part of corporate success, did it matter if the maneuvering took place in leadership development programs? Such programs undoubtedly helped the maneuverers smooth over their rough edges, improve their people skills, and work a little better with others. What was the harm in giving once-born men and women on the make the notion that their self-assurance was the mark of twice-born specialness?

The trouble, to put it in the acute language of old-time religion, was that self-assurance slides all too easily into false pride. The difficult balance in leadership is to retain some moral humility while achieving power and the will to use it. It is all too likely that the moral arrogance that led to Enron and other corporate scandals of the early twenty-first century had roots in the becoming-a-leader-by-becoming-oneself movement.

Leadership gurus usually appear to be very nice people. They often write with ease and grace, sometimes even beautifully. Many of them seem like literature professors *manqué*—fond, like Bennis, of allusions to Plato, Shakespeare, and Russian novelists. As hiring in university liberal arts programs has dropped off, some humanities professors have made the transition to teaching management. Social scientists, like humanities professors, often made a similar career change, moving into the wide-open ranks of the business school professoriate. The author of this book—obviously a historian by training—is one of those liberal arts faculty who has become to some degree a teacher or at least a student of management. This influx of humanists and social scientists into business schools would eventually result, in the 1990s, in a useful new movement for "critical management studies" aimed at understanding the intellectual assumptions and bases of management rather than uncritically taking them for granted.[12]

Unfortunately, critical management studies and its sophisticated approach to social theory seems destined to remain on the fringes of business schools while the more superficial and self-serving approach of leadership gurus toward ethics and values, culture and psychology, is safely ensconced in the mainstream. Although many of the leadership mavens tell a good story, too many of their books are just stories. Worse, they are stories told by people of power. Bennis, for example, interviewed dozens of executives for his various books on leadership, then wove their narratives into a pastiche that made the post-Vietnam, post-Watergate point that "*[m]anagers are people who do things right and leaders are people who do the right thing.*"[13]

The possibility that these morality tales told by CEOs and other people of power might be self-serving does not seem to occur to leadership gurus. I have read dozens of these books, and I cannot recall encountering in one of them a leader who says, "I blew it." Bennis's *On Becoming a Leader* does offer some examples of bad leadership, but usually from the media and politics. The book provides firsthand knowledge of only one failed corporate leader, a man whom Bennis evaluated for a top job and recommended that he not be given it. The man became a CEO elsewhere but would not return Bennis's phone calls, leaving him in the dark as to whether this formerly failed leader had finally undertaken "the arduous job of becoming himself."[14]

There is all too little evidence that many leadership counselors do much field research. They interview the powerful, send questionnaires to the corporate middle ranks, and gain a lot of knowledge through consulting. But they seldom seem to have observed their subjects at work for any extended period of time. Not one of today's leadership experts seems to have had an apprenticeship like Peter Drucker's two-year shadowing of Alfred Sloan in the 1940s. The dearth of field studies may explain why leadership gurus do not seem alert to the risk that their subjects might turn into Frankenstein's monsters. The risk of moral self-delusion in leaders gets lip service, but I have seen no field reports of how easily such persons can use "values" to justify the wrong thing. Perhaps the gurus have no idea of what it is like to report to a self-righteous, self-conscious "leader" who wears his becoming-a-better-person button on his sleeve.

Can the gurus even be counted on to recognize leadership? By 1989, the year that Bennis published *On Becoming a Leader*, the most successful American president in two generations had just completed two terms in office. Near the start of his book, Bennis blasted Ronald Reagan as a false leader.[15] His inability to come to terms with Reagan calls into question the whole concept of "twice-born" leadership. The son of an alcoholic father, Reagan was a marvel of the self-assurance that Bennis had treated as the mark of the twice-born leader. Yet it was obvious that Reagan was not twice-born. However he dealt with the pain of his father's failings, Reagan had never passed through some fiery identity crisis. The once-born Reagan achieved his self-assurance through lifelong positive thinking and perhaps a good measure of successful psychological denial.

Yet Reagan did measure up to one criterion in the gurus' model for leadership. He was no manager. No one more sedulously ignored the corporation than did America's most pro-corporate president.

CHAPTER 24

Reagan Aids Corporations
by Bashing Government

"THE NINE MOST TERRIFYING WORDS in the English language are 'I'm from the government, and I'm here to help.'" So said Ronald Reagan, a self-assured leader who believed that in his 1980 election to the presidency he had won a mandate to undo the New Deal. The government pressure on business that had forced it to help create the corporate American Dream was about to be lifted.

Reagan helped corporations not by boosting them but by bashing government. The question of the degree to which corporations were instruments of managerial power rather than market freedom, the question that had occupied Coase, Berle, Means, and others for half a century, had no meaning for Reagan. The corporation seemed hardly to figure in his Manichean political calculus, where freedom's only foe was government. In other words, it is not clear to what degree Reagan understood that many 1980s Americans lived under two kinds of authority, governmental and corporate. First, there was the elected government they studied in civics classes. And second, there was the arbitrary power of the corporate executives and factory managers for whom they worked.

By reducing the standing and prestige of government, Reagan set Americans up to take a drubbing from their corporate bosses. Ever since the New Deal, the liberal consensus had been organized around countering corporate power with government power. Reagan lowered Americans' esteem for government, making them less likely to use it to defend themselves against corporations, while distracting attention from the danger that corporate power might pose to freedom.

Vietnam, Watergate, and the seeming ineptness of the Carter administration had of course prepared the way and made it easier for Reagan to turn Americans' hope and confidence away from government. But if antigovernment ideology was to some degree justified, so was anti-corporate ideology, which would be in short supply for the next thirty years. That made it much easier for corporations to increase their centrality in American society while staying out of most popular political discussion. This was partly facilitated by the fact that Reagan shared something of the liberals' weakness when it came to understanding the social role of corporations. Galbraith and his like had based their hope for a liberal future on a corporate economy they held in contempt. Reagan based his hope for a prosperous American future on a corporate economy of whose existence he scarcely seemed aware.

Whatever the shortfall in his understanding of how the American economic system really worked, there is no doubt that Reagan had a superb practical understanding of leadership and its relation to values. The orthodox economic critique of Reagan is that he stubbornly refused to recognize the incompatibility of his economic program's three major points—lower taxes, higher defense spending, and a balanced budget. But Reagan's refusal to balance the budget by altering his plans for lower taxes and higher defense spending reflected his consistent commitment to the primary value for which he led—freedom.

More than any president since Franklin Roosevelt, Reagan offered a practical demonstration of James MacGregor Burns's point that leaders manage *for* values, not *by* them. By lowering taxes Reagan managed *for* freedom by enhancing Americans' independence from government. By raising defense spending he again managed *for* freedom, meaning to secure Americans against communist tyranny during the Cold War. If these measures promoting freedom—the valued goal *for* which Reagan managed—could not be reconciled with a balanced budget, then a balanced budget be damned!

Still, reducing the deficit was at least a secondary goal for Reagan. If he could not reconcile a balanced budget with freedom-promoting defense spending, he could at least aim to reduce non-defense spending. The question was what spending to cut. "Americans are conservative," observed the columnist George Will at the start of the Reagan administration. "What they want to conserve is the New Deal."[1] Or perhaps it would be more accurate to say they wanted to preserve the part of the New Deal that benefited not just the poor but, rather, rich and poor alike—Social Security, along with the Medicare program that had been added to Social Security later. Reagan, an ideologue but not a fool, kept his hands off these popular programs, which served all Americans, including the rich and powerful.

Reagan cut programs aimed at helping the poor. School lunches, subsidized housing, and welfare programs all took a trimming. Families at the bottom end of the social order lost 8 percent of their federal aid while families at the top saw no change in the massive government programs that benefited them—Social Security, Medicare, and the tax deduction for mortgage interest.[2] The rise in poverty and homelessness under Reagan was widely discussed and lamented, even by those who enthusiastically supported the measures that caused it. Meanwhile, far less attention went to the good fortune that Reagan brought to business corporations, especially in the extractive industries. His secretary of the interior promised to "mine more, drill more, cut more timber."[3] Only stiff opposition from environmentalists fended off the worst of the administration's plans to allow aggressive despoiling of public lands.

Emphasis on deregulation and market discipline opened up many possibilities for corporate profit under Reagan. In one sense he was continuing the work of the Carter administration, which, working with liberal legislators, had deregulated airlines and trucking so that consumers could benefit from increased competition in travel and transportation. Yet Carter had refused to deregulate banking and financial services, where he believed that free-market policies would injure rather than help the American people.

Reagan, far less pragmatic and far more ideological than Carter, tended more often to assume that the results of deregulation would automatically be good. Where Carter had drawn the line at deregulating financial institutions, Reagan steamed ahead. Lifting restrictions on leverage by the savings and loan industry, he raised their profits but also their risk. After he left office, a wave of bankruptcies in the industry forced his successor, George H. W. Bush, to ask Congress for a bailout in order to avoid deepening the 1990–1991 recession. At that time, it was the biggest government-funded bailout in American history.

Reagan had ridiculed the Occupational Health and Safety Administration (OSHA) in his 1980 presidential campaign. As president, he and an aide named David Stockman eased many of the OSHA regulations to which business corporations objected. Many OSHA regulations were unnecessarily costly and hurtful to business, injuring the economic well-being not just of corporations but of all Americans. But those who mocked OSHA altogether can never have done manual labor and seen the risks to which many working Americans are daily exposed. Other agencies seemed to have received the message and proceeded with zany deregulation that probably even Reagan would have disapproved if he had gotten wind of it before the media did. His administration delayed the requirement of life-saving seat belts in all cars. And only a lawsuit by a public interest group prevented removal of a regulation requiring aspirin manufacturers to warn on their labels that their product could cause Reyes syndrome in children.

Corporate executives were probably less dangerous deregulators than were free-market pundits and ideologues in the media. They at least recognized a need to prevent their competitors from taking advantage of dangerous practices. Ideologues, however, asserted that "little deregulation" had happened under Reagan.[4] In a sense, that may have been true, compared with the economic deregulation that Carter and the liberals had undertaken just a few years earlier. But the idea that Carter was a greater deregulator than Reagan leaves out Reagan's most important deregulation of all, his deregulation of the labor market. His administration profoundly shifted the balance of power between unions and corporations by appointing a majority of pro-management members to the National Labor Relations Board (NLRB). The NLRB had been created by the 1935 Wagner Act, the key measure of the Second New Deal. As explained in chapter 8, the Second New Deal had created a balance of power between big business and big labor, with government serving as mediator.

Under Reagan in the 1980s, the NLRB consistently ruled in favor of corporations and against labor unions. One of the best scholarly accounts of Reagan's NLRB explains that it "ended employers' statutory obligation to bargain about many major management decisions, substantially deregulated representation election campaigns, increased management's authority to discipline employees for engaging in activity previously protected . . . , and in many other ways elevated management's authority."[5]

The American Dream was about to be whipsawed between the Reagan administration's NLRB on the one hand and international competition on the other. As the quality of foreign manufacturing rose, industries in which America had led the way moved overseas. By the

1980s, for example, televisions were no longer manufactured in the United States. The Reagan NLRB used this rise in international competition to justify deregulation of the labor markets. Regulation, the argument went, raised costs and reduced American competitiveness. But whose competitiveness was in question?

It was not just American corporations that were competing with foreign corporations. American workers were competing with foreign workers. Reduction in union power left workers with little voice in the process of adjusting to the rise of international competition. As Reagan's NLRB tilted toward corporations, union membership fell. At its height in the 1950s, union membership had been 35 percent of the nonagricultural workforce. By the end of Reagan's presidency, it was at 18 percent, well on the way to today's 7 percent, which is about the same as 1932, before the New Deal. General Electric's Boulware, the subtle union buster who played so large a role in creating Reagan and his voters, had won out in the long run.

But it was Reagan himself who struck the single most decisive blow for corporations and against labor. During the first summer of his presidency, in 1981, foolhardy leaders of the Professional Air Traffic Controllers Organization (PATCO) called a strike. The controllers directed airplanes in their flight paths and in takeoffs and landings, preventing collisions and serving a vital public function. As employees of the federal government, they were forbidden by law from striking. Reagan, with typically effective political communication—"I take no joy from this"[6]—gave the air traffic controllers two days to return to work and then fired the eleven thousand who did not. The fired workers constituted 80 percent of PATCO's membership. The union was finished.

The symbolic significance of Reagan's firing of the PATCO strikers at the outset of his presidency can scarcely be overestimated. It was the sort of action of which Boulware could scarcely have dreamed. In one day, the president of the United States had demolished an entire national union. Labor unions and the New Deal policies that supported them had helped many Americans achieve their dreams. Yet ever since the great strike wave of 1946, public distrust of unions had been strong. Now, in the 1980s, it suddenly seemed possible that, as I heard some declare, "we" might "get the unions." The inspiriting effect of the PATCO firings on corporate leadership was no less strong. Surely, corporate executives owed the president their best efforts in crushing, with resolution equal to his, the union power they faced. At long last, corporate executives could secure what they had long believed the unions threatened, their "right to manage."

Reagan's firing of the PATCO strikers cemented his reputation as a decisive leader who sided with the people against the special interests. Thus was continued the post–World War II tendency to think of unions as special interests. The aid that Reagan's anti-labor policies provided to corporations went largely unremarked because of managers' success in identifying themselves with the free-enterprise system. Corporations evidently did not count as special interests. The public of course recognized egregious corporate criminals. But the corporation as a general social institution never received opprobrium of the kind that Reagan succeeded in heaping on government and that corporations often heaped on unions. Did Reagan know what he was doing? Did he intentionally pay minimal attention to corporations, the better to maximize what he could do for them by attacking government? Or did he really believe, as his rhetoric suggested, in a simplistic free market that needed to be safeguarded only against the intrusion of governmental but not corporate power?

There was only one instance when Reagan discussed the corporation in a general sense as a social institution. In January 1983, prefacing his remark with "I'll probably kick myself," he offhandedly suggested that the corporate income tax ought to be abolished "instead of sticking with what is literally a myth about corporations."[7] He did not specify the myth, but he was likely referring to the legal doctrine that corporations are persons. According to the line of thinking that Reagan probably meant to invoke, corporations are not persons and therefore should not have to pay taxes. But the public objected strongly to the idea of not taxing corporations. Reagan recovered from the gaffe with typical ease: "I said that I would kick myself for saying it. I did."[8] The public might not have been able to articulate its objection, but the heart of it surely related to the idea that in a democratic society corporate power ought to answer to the people in some way, if only by paying taxes.

Reagan's idea that the legal personality of corporations was "literally a myth" might be interpreted to suggest that he supported the Jensen-Meckling theory that the "internal" relations constituting firms are no less voluntary than their external market relations with customers and suppliers. But it is more likely that, just as he said, Reagan based his economic program on simple faith in free markets. Either way, he missed the reality of managerial and corporate power.

Reagan was scarcely unprecedented as a president who poorly understood the corporation. After all, Franklin Roosevelt, some of whose work Reagan undid, had not known what he was doing either when he jury rigged the Second New Deal. Oliver Wendell Holmes's assessment of Roosevelt could be applied equally well to Reagan: a "first-rate temperament" and a "second-rate intellect." Niccolo Machiavelli in his unsurpassed, five-hundred-year-old book on leadership, *The Prince*, observed that fortune favors the bold for the simple reason that times change. A leader who cautiously stands pat will almost certainly fall behind the spirit of the age. Bold action at least gives the prince a shot at keeping up with change, even if he does not know what he is doing.

In corporate life as elsewhere, no leader can perfectly master the moment. Economic change, like any other, will always outstrip contemporary human intelligence and leave us partly at the mercy of the gods. But in managing the corporate economy it would still be good to rely a little less on fortune and boldness than did the two presidents most significant for this book. Roosevelt and Reagan both enjoyed Machiavellian luck. But Roosevelt was the more fortunate. The era that Reagan began lasted for twenty-five years and best served the privileged. Roosevelt launched a half-century in which the corporate economy worked better than otherwise for the ordinary citizen.

Still, Reagan's bold advocacy of the free market opened the way for the good luck that put him, like Roosevelt, on the side of historical change that he did not fully understand. Reagan's presidency coincided with the rise of information technology that breathed new life into the free market. As the next and last part of this book shows, information technology would shrink the size of firms in some industries, open new possibilities for entrepreneurs, and make some large corporations less bureaucratic and more innovative than they had been for most of the twentieth century.

Many Americans, however, did not share in Reagan's good fortune. Technological change favoring his free-market ideology made him, somewhat accidentally, a historically important leader. For many ordinary citizens, these same changes threatened to create a corporate American nightmare.

PART VII

Entrepreneurship

CHAPTER 25

Supply-Siders versus the Big Corporation

A MARKET ECONOMY has two sides, a supply side and a demand side. Economists long believed that any imbalance between supply and demand would correct itself. Any rise in supply, for example, would be met by a rise in demand, an idea called Say's Law, after the early-nineteenth-century French economist Jean-Baptiste Say. According to Say, producers protect themselves against a decline in the value of their products by quickly exchanging them for cash. Then they protect themselves against inflation by getting rid of their cash. That is, they buy someone else's products, which increases demand. Supply, therefore, can never outstrip demand. Say's Law was supposed to apply to all commodities, including labor. A rise in the supply of labor would lead to a rise in demand. As with all commodities, the price of labor might fall. But according to Say, there would always be jobs for those willing to work for market wages.

The Great Depression of the 1930s posed a considerable challenge to the idea that there would always be work for those who wanted it. The English economist John Maynard Keynes attempted to correct Say by arguing for the idea of "price stickiness." Sometimes producers may refuse to lower their prices even though it is in their economic interest to get less money rather than none at all. If producers refuse to sell their products, they cannot get money with which to buy other people's products, so demand does not keep pace with supply. Keynes argued that the classical economists had been wrong; the economy could get stuck in a more or less permanent state of depressed demand. He proposed that the government raise demand through deficit spending, low interest rates, and an expanding money supply. The coincidence of Keynes's ideas with the actual policies into which the Roosevelt administration was pushed in the 1930s seemed to prove Keynes right. For forty years, the United States followed his advice. The government aimed to prevent or at least reduce unemployment by increasing its spending during business downturns.

But in the 1970s, employment fell and prices rose. This "stagflation"—stagnation and inflation—brought critiques of Keynes and a resurgence of supply-side economic theory. Because government attempts to manage the demand side of the economy did not seem to be working, perhaps it was time to stimulate the supply side—that is, try to raise the supply of goods in the hope of provoking a rise in demand. Hence the rise of interest in entrepreneurship from the late 1970s down to the present day. Entrepreneurs add to the supply of goods in the market place at, they hope, a price that yields a profit. According to the supply-siders, a rise in entrepreneurial activity would raise both demand and employment, benefiting rich and poor alike. The way to stimulate entrepreneurship, they said, was to cut taxes.

Their focus not just on cutting taxes but on doing so in order to promote growth explains why leading 1970s supply-side thinkers were not initially in Ronald Reagan's corner. Right-wing social critic George Gilder, Republican congressman Jack Kemp, economics professor Arthur Laffer, and *Wall Street Journal* editorialist Jude Wanniski of course saw that Reagan was a tax cutter. But according to the supply-siders, he wanted to cut taxes simply because he saw it as the fair thing to do, not because lower taxes would raise supply and promote growth. As supply-siders tell the story, Reagan failed to win the 1976 Republican presidential nomination because he had no broad economic rationale to justify the tax cuts he proposed. And he won the presidency in 1980, they contend, thanks to his conversion to their ideas. That is, between 1976 and 1980 they converted Reagan to a pro-growth candidate who understood Say's Law and who wanted to cut taxes in order to fuel a virtual cycle of entrepreneurship, rising supply, rising demand, and rising employment.[1]

The supply-siders provided most of the intellectual excitement in the politics of the late 1970s and early 1980s. For the first time in half a century, the Republicans were not the party of "no." Rather than running against Democratic ideas, they had a positive program of their own. They stood for entrepreneurship and economic growth. According to the supply-siders, the Democrats during their near half-century of political dominance had been redistributing wealth rather than creating it. The Democrats taxed and borrowed in order to spend money on Great Society programs aimed at educating poor people, equipping them with the accoutrements of middle-class culture so they could get corporate jobs. In other words, the Democrats just assumed that corporations would have the wealth to absorb the poor once they were prepared for corporate life.

But supply-siders believed that the growth of the corporate sector was not automatic. They pointed out, correctly, that most new jobs were created by small, entrepreneurial businesses. It had been many years since big corporations had been net creators of significant numbers of new jobs. "[F]rom the point of view of overall economic growth and technological innovation," said George Gilder, "these leviathans are of little importance."[2] New economic growth to redeem the poor would come not from the corporate establishment but from entrepreneurs.

Yet the U.S. government, the supply-siders claimed, had been discouraging entrepreneurs for half a century by taxing capital gains at a high rate. The entrepreneur who starts a business not only derives an income from it but also profits from its increasing value. Suppose a "serial entrepreneur" would like to sell one business in order to start another. But selling the first business exposes its owner to the capital gains tax, leaving less capital with which to fund the second. The higher the capital gains tax, the more discouraged the entrepreneur. Instead of taking capital from one business and moving it to another with higher growth potential, the erstwhile entrepreneur will sit pat. All the rest of us are the poorer because of the owner's unfulfilled potential to raise the supply of goods.

Ever since the New Deal, both Democratic and Republican liberals (yes, there once were Republican liberals) had pushed up the capital gains tax until, under Gerald Ford in 1976, it reached 38 percent. That was still lower than the highest tax rates on personal income, which points to one of the reasons the capital gains tax kept rising. Liberals were trying to establish some fairness in the tax code, which, thanks to the capital gains tax and other anomalies, often resulted in lower effective tax rates for the rich than for middle-class and even low-income Americans.

The supply-siders believed that the liberals' eagerness to raise taxes on the rich in the interest of fairness was short-sighted. Congressman Jack Kemp, the leading supply-side politician of the 1970s, quoted Democratic President John F. Kennedy, who in the early 1960s had justified a business tax credit by insisting that "[a] rising tide lifts all boats."[3] Yes, a lower tax on capital gains would further enrich the plutocracy, but it would also improve the lot of the poor, thanks to new jobs created by entrepreneurs.

In 1978, for the first time in two generations, the capital gains tax was cut rather than raised. William Steiger, a talented young Republican congressman from Wisconsin who died later that year, led a legislative battle that lowered the capital gains rate to 28 percent. The supply-siders, who at that time thought of themselves as prophets in the wilderness, believed that Steiger's work, as a *Wall Street Journal* editorial put it, was "not one tax provision among many, but the cutting edge of an important intellectual and financial breakthrough."[4]

Jude Wanniski, the author of that editorial, also popularized "the Laffer curve." Wanniski had accompanied Arthur Laffer, then a University of Chicago professor, to a 1974 White House meeting with President Ford's chief of staff, Donald Rumsfeld, and with Rumsfeld's assistant, Richard Cheney. Laffer told Rumsfeld and Cheney that "[t]here are always two tax rates that yield the same revenues."[5] When Rumsfeld and Cheney asked for an explanation, the brash young economist grabbed a cocktail napkin and drew the letter U, toppled over on its left side (fig. 25.1). The bottom left end represented a tax rate of 0 percent, which would obviously yield no government revenue. The upper left

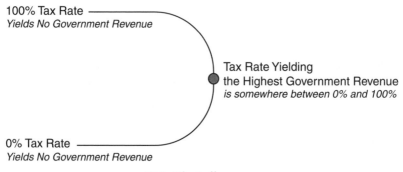

100% Tax Rate
Yields No Government Revenue

Tax Rate Yielding
the Highest Government Revenue
is somewhere between 0% and 100%

0% Tax Rate
Yields No Government Revenue

25.1. The Laffer curve.

end represented a tax rate of 100 percent, which would also yield no revenue, as no one would work if earnings were completely taxed away. Over on the right side, at the furthest extent of the U's curve, was the tax rate that would produce the highest government revenue. There was an obvious problem in that Laffer could not attach a specific number to this point; he could not specify the rate at which government revenues would be highest. Beyond the true but useless statement that a tax rate somewhere between 0 percent and 100 percent would yield the highest amount of government revenue, Laffer had nothing to offer. He could only assert as an article of faith that 1970s tax rates were so high that they lowered overall tax receipts.

Wanniski gave the name "Laffer curve" to what became one of the justifications of the 1981 Reagan tax cuts. Although the supply-siders' real goal was to lower taxes in order to spur growth, they used the Laffer curve to sell tax cuts to deficit hawks. Lower government revenue from lower tax rates would supposedly be more than offset by higher government revenue from economic growth. Laffer turned out to be wrong, of course. Reagan's 1981 tax cuts—including a reduction in the capital gains tax to 20 percent—created huge long-term federal deficits. Even Reagan, in 1986, agreed that a tax increase was needed to reduce the deficit, with the result that the capital gains rate moved back up to 28 percent.

Liberals mistakenly believed that the failure of the Reagan tax cuts to increase government revenues proved the supply-siders wrong in general. As Wanniski had pointed out in his 1979 book, *The Way the World Works*, the supply-siders' real focus was on growth, not deficit reduction. If Laffer was wrong on tax rates, he was surely right that taxes are a social "wedge" that drive people apart and make business transactions more difficult (Laffer did not add that taxes may have an offsetting justification in the public services for which they pay).[6] Despite the failure of the 1981 tax cuts to increase government revenues, they lowered the social "wedge" and probably contributed to the mid-1980s economic surge.

The supply-siders saw earlier than did their liberal critics that a major growth engine of the late twentieth century would be the entrepreneurs of California's Silicon Valley, of Boston's Route 128, and of other clusters of small high-tech enterprises. George Gilder's influential book *Wealth and Poverty* (1981) used these high-tech companies to attack John Kenneth Galbraith's *New Industrial State* (1967) and its idea that the corporate world's bureaucratic "technostructure" pointed inevitably toward socialism: "While the professor chatted . . . about the doings at Ford and GM, imagining himself to be right at the futuristic center of things . . . , a real industrial revolution was, in fact, massively erupting behind his back."[7]

Gleefully calling attention to what he aptly characterized as liberals' "dolorous and surely false reflections on the computer's threat to individuality" and to employment, Gilder insisted that the "entire history of economic progress" showed that high technology would empower people and multiply jobs. Intel, he pointed out, had a staff of twelve in 1971 when it invented the microprocessor. Five years later Intel had eight thousand employees.[8] Big, established corporations were meanwhile failing to add jobs and therefore, according to the supply-siders, were largely irrelevant to social and economic improvement. During the 1970s, entrepreneurial firms in high tech had increased their payrolls at a rate of 40 percent a year while Fortune 1,000 firms showed almost no employment growth. Entrepreneurial firms like Intel, Gilder wrote, were the source of most new jobs and thus were "fighting America's only serious war against poverty."[9]

Gilder's *Wealth and Poverty* served as an inspiration to business school faculty who in the late 1970s and early 1980s were beginning to create entrepreneurship majors for their students. One such national leader in entrepreneurial education taught at the same institution at which I teach, and I remember him taking great encouragement from Gilder's book. Previously, entrepreneurial aptitude had been considered a matter of personality—a taste for risk—and that was all there was to it. Now the idea arose, as was surely correct, that entrepreneurial thought and action could be taught.

The supply-siders and their emphasis on entrepreneurship served as a useful critique of previous economic, intellectual, and political ideology. But did the large business corporation count for as little as Gilder and the other supply-siders said? After all, the successful entrepreneur of today is tomorrow's corporatist. Skillful though Gilder and his comrades may have been in deflating liberal balloons, did they see the future or, for that matter, the past any more clearly than the liberals? Even if the corporate sector was not destined to be a source of vast numbers of new jobs, it was certain to remain in place. A great mass of Americans would continue to work for big corporations, whether hoary goliaths like General Electric or handsome young titans like Intel. Corporations like these, regulated by government and tamed by unions, had been the basis of the mid-twentieth-century American Dream.

The supply-siders, like the liberals, failed to foresee the hollowing out of the American middle class. The very title of Gilder's book, *Wealth and Poverty*, with its focus on entrepreneurs and the impoverished, its hope that the rising rich would lift the poor, betrayed an absence of interest in the economic lives of ordinary, mainstream Americans. As entrepreneurial enterprises matured into big businesses, they ensured that large corporations would continue to dominate the lives of the great mass of working people. Moreover, Gilder and the other supply-siders underestimated the degree to which big corporations could become entrepreneurial. The likes of General Electric, IBM, and Walmart would soon demonstrate entrepreneurial creativity that vastly raised the level of wealth in American society. But these entrepreneurial giants fell short of the supply-siders' promise that entrepreneurship would lift the poor. Instead, they began to leave behind some of the middle class.

CHAPTER 26

Reengineering the Corporation

WHEREAS PRESIDENT GEORGE H. W. BUSH (1989–1993) had been a computer troglodyte, President Bill Clinton (1993–2001) relentlessly talked up "the new economy." Clinton frequently used the 1990s term *information superhighway* for the Internet. The "Infobahn," it was widely believed, would revolutionize the corporate world. And it did, though not quite in the way expected. Late-twentieth-century business cognoscenti believed that the revolution in information technology would (and in this they were right) create many small entrepreneurial companies. Some of those same illuminati erred, however, by supposing that information technology would of necessity put large corporations at a competitive disadvantage. Whether big or small business had the most to gain from information technology turned out to be no easy calculation.

As the cost of communication fell thanks to information technology, so did the cost of business transactions. And it was the fact that transactions cost more than management that, according to Nobel laureate Ronald Coase, had caused the rise of the large, managerial corporation. During the second industrial revolution, capital-intensive technology had lowered the cost of transactions but had lowered the cost of management even more. In the 1990s, technological change seemed to have reversed the forces to which Coase had attributed the rise of the giant corporation. Information technology was lowering transaction costs, giving the market a new efficiency. Many concluded that big corporations were wasting money on managers whose work of coordinating operations within large firms could be done more cheaply by market transactions among small companies. Small firms were supposedly the wave of the future.

In the late 1990s, a rash of Internet start-ups attracted enormous investor enthusiasm—the "dot-com" boom. Often on the basis of nothing more than some vague idea for turning a "bricks and mortar" operation into an Internet "virtual business," these companies soared in market value. Speculators bid worthless stocks up to fantastic levels before the inevitable crash in 2000. Still, such mania often accompanies important technological and organizational change.[1] As with the merger movement of the 1890s, discussed in chapter 4, important change was happening in the 1990s despite the enormous number of dot-com failures. Entrepreneurial successes such as Amazon, Google, and eBay offered important new business models.

But some CEOs of large, long-established corporations defied the conventional wisdom that the information age would witness the triumph of the small, entrepreneurial firm. These leaders believed that the Internet would help big companies become more entrepreneurial than small ones. For just as had been the case with capital-intensive heavy machinery a century earlier, information technology lowered the cost of management as well as the cost of transactions. If information technology reduced the cost of management more than it cut the cost of transactions, the large corporation might not only survive but thrive. Such thinking was supported by *Reengineering the Corporation* (1993), probably the most influential business book of the 1990s. According to authors Michael Hammer and James Champy, information technology would transform management. The traditional corporation, with its rigid structure of functional departments and product divisions, had become outmoded.

The call for reengineering appeared under the democratic facade that was typical of appeals for management revolutions. W. Edwards Deming's quality movement (discussed in chapter 19) had repatriated itself from Japan to America in the 1980s and fueled a lot of optimism about the possibility of workplace freedom. Others optimistically believed that radical change lay ahead "for managers and workers (even if we bother maintaining that distinction)."[2] The reengineers, led by Hammer, agreed that the distinction between managers and workers was senseless and that "neither of these terms has much meaning anymore."[3] Teamwork, bottom-up empowerment, and a democratic spirit would supposedly characterize the firm of the future.

Hammer and Champy believed that corporations could tear down the walls between departments and rid themselves of their "functional silos, or stovepipes, vertical structures built on narrow pieces of a process."[4] Consider order fulfillment, a vital process in many companies. The customer service department had to record the order and hand it off to the finance department to check the customer's credit. Then the order went to the warehouse, which checked to see if the goods were on hand or had to be back-ordered. If the goods were on hand, they were pulled off the shelves, boxed, and sent to the shipping department for assignment to a carrier. With the coming of information technology, it was possible to eliminate all these handoffs between functional departments. One person at a computer could record the order, check customer credit, monitor inventory, and assign a carrier. That same employee could even signal robotic machinery in the warehouse to take the goods off the shelf and put them on a belt to the shipping department. In manufacturing, too, reengineering could deliver immense savings. As early as 1974, in a Japanese plant assembling ultrasound machines, "[w]hen the machines were finished, a worker unbuttoned his shirt, dabbed some gel on his chest, and ran the ultrasound probes over his body for a quick quality test. The same guy then wrapped up the product, put it in a box, attached a shipping label, and got it on the loading dock."[5]

But if America were to achieve such process integration, its corporate bureaucracies would have to be ruthlessly shrunk. Bureaucrats were certain to resist fiercely the tearing down of their "silos." Rather than acting democratically, CEOs would have to govern with an iron fist to get the full benefit of reengineering. Contrary to the reengineers' claims about workplace freedom, command and control were not about to go away in corporate America. The 1990s was the decade of the "superstar CEO." One could scarcely turn on a TV set in that era without encountering a corporate advertisement starring a tough, take-charge CEO eager not just to run the company but to serve as its external face. The most super of them all was Jack Welch of General Electric. Although he seemed charmless and appeared in no television ads, or at least none that I saw, he became a celebrity. Business magazines put him on their covers and fawningly celebrated him as the "change master."

The feisty Welch had gone to work for GE as a young man and had hated the company's rigid bureaucracy. When he took over as CEO in 1981, there were twelve layers of management between him and the factory floor. He devoted his twenty years running GE to getting "the damned bureaucracy out of the way" by hammering it down and flattening it.[6] "Soft stuff won't work if it doesn't follow demonstrated toughness,"[7] he said. Shifting his managers' incentives from bonuses to stock options, Welch then focused not just on their individual performances but on the performance of the entire corporation, which of course was the measure of how well he did.

Welch led GE toward greater diversification, something that was not supposed to happen according to the prevailing wisdom about the effect of information technology. Many other 1990s CEOs, believing that small was better, sold off what they saw as extraneous operations in order to focus on their companies' "core competencies." Welch, by contrast, took on any extraneous operation where he could see a profit: "One thing I never fell for was the popular line 'old versus new economy.'"[8] Diversifying away from manufacturing, Welch converted GE Capital from a financier of customer purchases into a major commercial lender. He acquired RCA in order to get the television network NBC. He considered buying food and drug companies but reluctantly concluded that their stock prices were too high for GE to acquire them profitably.

Welch believed he could diversify GE *and* achieve greater efficiency because information technology made it easier for a company to transfer managerial innovations from one industry to another. Whereas 1960s conglomerates like Tex Thornton's Litton Industries had relied on illusory "synergy," Welch believed information technology made possible genuinely "boundaryless" management. By "boundaryless" he meant more than the sort of process integration about which Hammer and Champy wrote.

Thanks to information technology, new ideas and managerial innovations were to be integrated and shared across diverse business units. There would be no intellectual boundaries within the company. Managers, rather than keeping their best ideas to themselves in order to compete with other managers, were to share their knowledge. By spreading managerial knowledge from one unit to another, GE could maximize performance in its many different kinds of businesses and could aim to be first or second in any industry in which it was involved.

While Welch was pushing GE to new financial heights in the early 1990s, another big corporation, IBM, narrowly averted disaster. IBM had clumsily missed a great opportunity in the early 1980s when it went into the personal computer business and signed a contract with a young entrepreneur named Bill Gates to provide an operating system for its PCs. IBM used Gates's operating system while making the crucial error of allowing him to retain the system's ownership. As a result, Microsoft, not IBM, came to dominate the personal computer industry by the 1990s.

Gates's firm earned great acclaim and was an enormously profitable company, but its software was glitch-ridden and remains unnecessarily difficult to use. Microsoft does not hold great interest for business history or for this book. After its initial success, Microsoft acted the part less of innovator than monopolist and was convicted in court for its anticompetitive practices. Although Gates by the end of the 1990s was often listed as the richest man in the world, IBM spent that decade developing a new corporate strategy and proved in the end to be a far more innovative company than Microsoft.

Like GE, IBM would eventually use information technology to make itself more entrepreneurial. And it taught other big companies to do the same. IBM adopted a business strategy of selling a full line of integrated computer services, a plan that saved the company from its impending collapse and set it on the road, once again, to long-term growth. By the early 1990s, IBM had been living too long on its mainframe computer business, which had declined as customers moved to distributed computing and desktop machines. Probably influenced by the conventional wisdom that information technology gave the advantage to small organizations, IBM then adopted a mistaken, short-lived plan to "disaggregate" the company into a group of more or less independent operating divisions or "Baby Blues." This plan failed to work, and the company's cash reserves spiraled downward, making bankruptcy a strong possibility.

IBM's board sacked the CEO who had dreamt up "disaggregation" and recruited Louis Gerstner to attempt to save the company. Gerstner had run the Travel Services Division at American Express and then headed RJR Nabisco. Not only was he not a techie, he was IBM's first CEO to have been recruited from outside the company. Gerstner came up with the full-service strategy that not only saved IBM but put it on a path to long-term success. He made a bet a little like the one that Alfred Sloan had made seventy years earlier at General Motors, gambling that

IBM's strategy should be built on innovations in marketing and organization more than on innovations in technology. As the 1980s fixation on software upgrades and ever-higher chip speeds faded, IBM won out over small entrepreneurs by offering a full line of computer services that helped other large firms better manage their businesses.

Previously, IBM's service business had been mostly a matter of maintaining and programming the big machines it leased and sold. Now it began to provide consulting services, advising other companies how to use information technology to improve their businesses. At one end, IBM could write code for customers' computers and, at the other, help them think through what improvements in business strategy were possible thanks to information technology. By resisting the idea that small was better, by keeping IBM together rather than disaggregating, Gerstner forged a successful corporate strategy, the creation of a full-service computer company.

Not a media personality like Welch, Gerstner provided few colorful stories for the news outlets or for this book. Yet like Welch in his refusal to believe in a "new economy," Gerstner never "bought into the value of information democratization extended to the extreme."[9] Interoperability of information systems required a big, integrative organization like IBM. Again, like Welch, Gerstner used his power aggressively, getting rid of resistant subordinates and linking his managers' compensation to the company's fate via stock options. He gave the title *Who Says Elephants Can't Dance?* to his excellent memoir of his IBM years, and he was not slow to use the elephant handler's traditional tool, the clout. It takes some pummeling to get a pachyderm to prance.

If Welch's GE and Gerstner's IBM proved the supply-siders wrong that big corporations did not count when it came to entrepreneurial action, they seemed to prove the supply-siders right that the corporate establishment could not be counted on as a source of new jobs. Gerstner broke IBM's "no-layoff tradition," which had offered lifetime employment to its workers. Welch earned the title "neutron Jack" for thinning GE's ranks. When Gerstner and Welch finished their tours of duty, IBM and GE each employed something like one hundred thousand fewer people. Where did those people go? Or more important, where did all the new jobs come from in the 1990s? Millions of new jobs were created during Bill Clinton's presidency, as he never tired of saying.

One place the new jobs did not come from was General Motors, which in the 1980s had seemed bent on proving that some elephants have four left feet. Whereas IBM and Gerstner in the 1990s followed in the tradition of Alfred Sloan by focusing on marketing and organization, GM in the 1980s had spent massively on technology for "lights-out" factories, whose operation would supposedly rely on robotic sensors rather than the human eye. Unable to integrate its expensive technology, GM by the 1990s had shifted from the lowest-cost to highest-cost American auto manufacturer.

Although GM had once enjoyed the reputation, created by Sloan, as America's best-managed company, it now became a laughingstock and the occasion for the emergence of a major new cinematic and satiric talent. Michael Moore's *Roger and Me* (1989) mocked the CEO, Roger Smith, who oversaw GM's foolish technology investments and who, in nearly wrecking the company, also impoverished many citizens of Moore's once prosperous hometown, Flint, Michigan. Moore's understanding of economics and politics was often naive, simplistic, or simply wrong, but there was no questioning his creativity. In a splendid outpouring— *Downsize This!* (1997), *Bowling for Columbine* (2002), *Fahrenheit 9/11* (2004), *Sicko* (2007), and *Capitalism: A Love Story* (2009)—Moore offered Americans a desperately needed anticorporate aesthetic.

Chrysler and Ford had done better, the former saved from bankruptcy by a federal bailout and then, under its colorful CEO Lee Iacocca, introducing innovative products like the minivan. Ford made a turnaround on quality and replaced GM as the best-managed of the American car companies. But if the auto companies were saved for the time being, they were finished as the source of significant numbers of new, high-wage, American Dream jobs.

Many of the new 1990s jobs arose in entrepreneurial firms, especially in information technology, just as the supply-siders had predicted. And many Americans found new, well-paying jobs in financial services, an industry benefiting hugely from information technology. But there was also a tremendous growth in unskilled service jobs, flipping burgers at McDonald's or ringing up sales at Walmart. Walmart was one more example of how high technology sometimes gave the advantage to the big entrepreneur rather than the small one. Originating in the Ozarks and coming in under the radar of small-town mom-and-pops, Walmart emptied the storefronts of main street America and also drove into bankruptcy some of its bigger competitors, including Kmart. It made huge investments in information technology, but as with GE and IBM, Walmart's business success was built by remembering that technology had to serve innovations in management and marketing, not vice versa.

By the early twenty-first century, nearly one and a half million Americans worked at Walmart, making it the country's largest employer and also a harsh one. Fiercely and successfully resisting unionization, it paid its employees only a little better than minimum wage and pioneered human resource strategies that helped undo the American Dream. For example, Walmart offered health insurance, vacation time, and sick leave to full-time employees, then hired large numbers of part-time workers who did not qualify for those benefits.[10] Many who did qualify for health insurance did not take it because Walmart set employee premiums so high.

In the 1980s, Walmart had proudly supported "buy American" programs. But in the 1990s, as its market power grew stronger and as, thanks to information technology, its supply chain management grew ever more sophisticated, the massive retailer turned to China for manufactured goods. China, all but officially abandoning its Marxist ideology, had opened itself to corporate capitalism and used its low-cost labor to make the Pearl River delta "the workshop of the world." Via its overseas purchasing, Walmart became one of this nation's main outsourcers of the high-paid manufacturing jobs on which the American Dream had been built.

But Walmart had the assistance of American manufacturers in diminishing the dream. For example, Nike, which had its origins in the 1960s as an importer of Japanese athletic shoes, had become an innovative manufacturer in the 1970s, only to return to the import game with the opening of China in the 1980s. Thanks to the rapid communication and low transaction costs made possible by information technology, Nike was able to obtain (and continues to obtain) from its low-cost Asian suppliers the never-ending stream of new styles and fashions that American consumers demand. Nike became a "virtual" company, largely abandoning manufacturing in favor of marketing and brand management.

Americans who lost high-paying manufacturing jobs could find work at Walmart, but the new, low-wage, part-time retail jobs would not support a middle-class lifestyle. "Yes," went the late-1990s joke, the American economy had created millions of new jobs, "and I've got three of them." As the twenty-first century dawned, the United States was increasingly divided into a two-tier society of haves and have-nots, with the latter working ever-harder for an ever-smaller piece of the economic pie. It was a time for entrepreneurial leadership in politics and government, but America got the same old corporate fluff.

CHAPTER 27

George W. Bush, Enron, and the Great Recession

IN THE PRESIDENTIAL ELECTION OF 2000, Democratic candidate Al Gore won the popular vote. But Republican George W. Bush triumphed in the electoral college, thanks in part to a badly designed ballot that confused some voters in a key Florida county. It was a fluke, but Americans had elected their first president with a master's degree in business administration. Bush had received his MBA from the Harvard Business School in 1975. Educated in 1970s corporate culture, he became a national exemplar of the moral conceit implicit in the notion of values-based leadership. Not because he had a weak character but because he had a strong or at least a stubborn one, the bad ideas Bush had absorbed about leadership in the corporate world undid him in the White House.

Acculturated to manage by values, Bush saw the vile atrocities of September 11, 2001, as requiring a response in the form of moral leadership, which, in his practice of it, amounted to moral arrogance. Self-deceptive moral pretense is bad enough in a corporate executive suite, but it brought still more disastrous results in the Oval Office—an unconstitutional and counterproductive war on terror along with an unnecessary and horribly wasteful war in Iraq.[1] The Bush presidency made plain the threat that management values posed to democratic values, as well as the danger of allowing corporate culture to become mainstream American culture.

Corporate speak had become part of common American parlance during the 1990s. All too many hospital managers, educational administrators, and elected officials thought they showed a new spirit of service, not ignorance and arrogance, when they substituted the generic word *customer* for the irreplaceable rubrics *patient*, *student*, and *citizen*. School committees, charities, and even churches wrote "mission statements" reflecting less a gnostic spirit than their members' workaday management techniques.

So the membership of the Bush administration marked a logical conclusion to the ubiquitous spread of the corporate mindset. Vice President Richard Cheney had been CEO of Halliburton, a construction and oil services company. Defense Secretary Donald Rumsfeld had run one pharmaceutical company, G. D. Searle; had chaired the board of another, Gilead Sciences; and had also been CEO of General Instrument, a high-tech communication firm. Bush himself had been CEO of a couple of small Texas oil companies and had served on the board of another, Harken Energy.[2]

Bush prided himself on corporate-style "transformational leadership," a phrase that suffused his administration. Defense Secretary Rumsfeld, aiming to make the military leaner and meaner, able to fight wars for a dime instead of a dollar, named his Pentagon program "Transformation." Condoleezza Rice, secretary of state in Bush's second term, was an academic, not a business executive, but she propounded "transformational diplomacy." But whereas James MacGregor Burns had seen an intimate relationship between transformational leadership and managerial skill, Bush seemed to follow too many corporate executives by supposing he could practice moral leadership without hands-on management.

Nowhere was Bush's lack of practical management skills more evident than in his response to the Enron scandal of 2001. So shattering was 9/11 that it is easy to forget that in the following twelve months Bush also had to deal with what was, until then, the largest challenge to the moral standing of corporate capitalism since the Great Depression. Scandals at Enron, WorldCom, Global Crossing, Qwest, Tyco, Adelphia, and other companies put in question the financial statements of every publicly held corporation in America.

Enron, a high-flying energy company, symbolized late-twentieth-century confidence that information technology made possible a new surge of entrepreneurship. Originally a pipeline company distributing natural gas, Enron had become a trader of commodities ranging from water to broadband. The notion that entrepreneurial action had to be fast and loose may have played a role in the Enron board's decision—despite a corporate ethics code forbidding such arrangements—to allow

Chief Financial Officer Andrew Fastow to serve also as an officer of supposedly independent companies or "special purpose entities" (SPEs).

As an officer of both the SPEs and of Enron, Fastow was able to loot the Enron treasury. For example, at the end of 1999, Enron sold low-yielding certificates in a trust called Yosemite to a Fastow SPE, enabling Enron to record millions of dollars of profit on the sale. Then Fastow's SPE sold the Yosemite certificates back to another Enron trading operation.[3] In other words, the SPEs were a device for hiding the fact that Enron was, in effect, selling things to itself and reporting a profit by doing so. And because Fastow's SPEs charged high fees for managing the transactions, Enron was actually losing money in these supposedly profitable trades. Over time, Fastow's special purpose entities, headed by his family and friends, took hundreds of millions of dollars from Enron, the losses kept off the books and masked from shareholders thanks to the supposed independence of the SPEs.

The unraveling came in the fall of 2001 as Wall Street analysts began to demand information on the mysterious SPEs, which, though their operations were unreported, were named in the footnotes of Enron's financial statements thanks to executives' vain hope that doing so had somehow kept the company on the right side of the law. As the pressure mounted, Enron executives' tempers flared. During a widely followed conference call with financial analysts, Enron CEO Jeff Skilling called one skeptic an "asshole." Investors began to sell off their stock, and company officers unwound their Enron positions as well. But the company kept ordinary employees locked into Enron stock in the retirement accounts it managed for them. Enron employees watched helplessly as the company's share price fell from over ninety dollars to pennies and then nothing.

Enron's was the largest bankruptcy in history until then, though soon to be outdone by the collapse of WorldCom, another company so enthralled by the witch's brew of morally pretentious leadership that it neglected mundane operations and hid its corruption from itself as it slipped into fraud. Other deceitful high-flyers such as Tyco, Adelphia, Qwest, and Global Crossing went down like dominoes. As employees lost their jobs, as investors lost their shirts, as the economy lost momentum, public anger surged. The outrage was further fueled by the emergence of more details about the Enron fraud. It was soon proved, as some had believed at the time, that in the summer of 2000, Enron traders in electricity futures had illicitly induced managers of some California power plants to go off-line for "repairs." The resulting blackouts and price spikes had cheated consumers while creating huge profits for Enron.

The Enron scandal spilled over into reputational and/or financial ruin for other companies. J. P. Morgan had helped Enron mask bank loans as cash from operations. The venerable accounting firm Arthur Andersen, formerly renowned for its integrity, had earned high fees by consulting on Enron's accounting practices while serving as its auditor and wrongly assuring investors that the books had not been cooked. Sued by angry investors, Arthur Andersen followed Enron into bankruptcy, throwing yet more thousands out of work.

As the public lost faith in corporate leadership, the 1990s cult of the superstar CEO faded, confirming for some Americans their long-held belief that top corporate officers were vastly overpaid. Half a century earlier, CEOs had made thirty or forty times as much as frontline employees. Now CEOs made hundreds, and in some cases thousands, as times as much as their workers. Much executive compensation came in stock options. CEOs like Jack Welch, Lou Gerstner, and many others had used options to bind the fate of themselves and their managers to changes in shareholder value. But Enron and other scandals showed that stock options could induce executives to report fraudulent earnings in order to push the stock price upward and put their options in the money.

Yet another problem with stock options was that they were "off the books." Companies did not report options as a current expense at the time they were awarded. Only years later, when the executives exercised their option to buy stock from the company at an old, lower price would shareholders know how much of their purported profits had actually gone to management. Some defenders of stock options said, rightly, that no estimate of the present value of a future option could be accurate. But it was still less accurate to give the impression that options were cost-free by keeping them off the books. Inaccurate though an estimate had to be, it was better than no estimate at all.

Underlying the popular skepticism about executive compensation was the public's growing awareness that the corporate world's cult of moral leadership was a fraud and, worse, as journalist Kurt Eichenwald said of Enron, a "conspiracy of fools." When Enron's CEO Kenneth Lay had gone around talking up Enron's "core values," lavishing money on community projects such as a new baseball stadium in Houston called Enron Field, awarding Nelson Mandela the "Enron Prize," and so forth, was he deceiving others or himself? The flatulent Enron verbiage about values, ethics codes, and moral leadership helped the company's top managers hide their incompetence from themselves. That Lay's deceit had included self-deceit was shown by the fact that only when it was explained to him during a court deposition did he finally understand that Fastow's SPEs did not provide an actual economic hedge for Enron.[4]

While the public was fast being disabused of executives' claims to moral leadership, President George W. Bush clung to the idea of managing by values. Joining the olfactorily challenged CEOs who could sniff nothing rotten in Denmark, Bush insisted that the rash of business scandals was a matter of a "few bad apples."[5] He tried to deal with the crisis by substituting moral leadership for hands-on management, just as Kenneth Lay had done at Enron. This caused him to fail in his goal of preventing significant new regulation. He could have best achieved that goal by supporting the recommendation of Treasury Secretary Paul O'Neill to make CEOs legally responsible for not just *reckless* financial reporting (as they then were) but also for *negligent* reporting. In effect, O'Neill was proposing that CEOs focus less on leading and more on hands-on management.

CEOs angrily objected, and Bush gave into them, abandoning O'Neill's proposal and suggesting instead that corporate chiefs sign their companies' financial statements, with the mild penalty of salary forfeiture his proposed punishment for misrepresentation. Bush did sensibly ask Congress to bar accounting firms from conflicts of interest between their auditing and consulting businesses. On stock options, he made no proposals at all.

Like many CEOs, Bush missed the big lesson of the Enron scandal, the danger of self-righteousness in the corporate cult of managing by values. Trying to deal with the crisis through moral leadership himself, Bush made a trip to Wall Street and lavished on an audience of CEOs the sort of flattery to which they were long accustomed: "Leaders in this room help give the free enterprise system an ethical compass. And the nation respects you for that."[6] Actually, the nation was having none of it. Congress, feeling the heat from angry voters, ignored Bush's appeal to handle the crisis through moral leadership. Less than a week after Bush spoke his platitudes on Wall Street, Congress passed by huge margins, including a unanimous vote in the Senate, a tough new regulatory measure, the Sarbanes-Oxley Act.

Sarbanes-Oxley did not rely on CEOs' moral leadership but, rather, required them to do some real management. They had to set up expensive new control and accounting systems to ensure the accuracy of their financial statements. The law also created a new federal accounting board, which would soon require the expensing of stock options. CEOs have bitterly complained ever since that the cost of administering Sarbanes-Oxley hurts their international competitiveness. Sales managers were soon spending their wee hours providing minutiae required by their companies' accounting departments. The corporate world would have been a lot better off if Bush had supported O'Neill's proposal to toughen general legal standards. Hardest hit of all by Sarbanes-Oxley were the small entrepreneurial firms that Bush had wanted to champion. It was disproportionately expensive for small firms to set up the new accounting systems. To avoid Sarbanes-Oxley, some entrepreneurs avoided going public, depriving themselves of access to the capital markets.

Nor was Sarbanes-Oxley the end of the misfortunes that Bush's supposedly moral leadership cast on the American economy. Bush advocated the creation of an "ownership society" in which all Americans would have skin in the game. He thought that if tangible assets were more widely owned, Everyman would support pro-growth economic policies. This notion underlay his failed effort in 2005 to privatize the Social Security system. Although Bush was unable to dismantle Social Security, he succeeded in another part of his program for an "ownership society": the expansion of home ownership. Government policy has long supported home ownership as part of the middle-class American Dream. But Bush wanted to go farther and make home ownership available to low-income citizens. He got Congress to subsidize down payments so that low-income Americans could, in effect, buy houses for nothing down. At the same time, he reduced regulations on banks and urged them to make mortgage payments affordable for low-income citizens. "Corporate America," he said, "has a responsibility to work to make America a compassionate place."[7]

Corporate America compassionately responded with introductory teaser rates on interest-only, adjustable-rate mortgages that lured low-income buyers into homes whose future payments they were unlikely to be able to afford. But for a few years it all seemed to work. Thanks to soaring house prices, low-income owners soon had an equity stake in properties that had cost them little or nothing. Part of what made banks not just willing but eager to participate in these "subprime" loans was the illusion that they could be made virtually risk-free thanks to "derivative" financial instruments such as mortgage-backed securities. Mortgages from many different banks might back a single security, which, once issued, would be sold to numerous other financial institutions, supposedly reducing the risk exposure of any single firm. Banks believed they could further lower their risks by buying the "credit default swaps" sold by investment houses and insurance companies, notably American International Group (AIG). Promising to indemnify the banks in the case of mortgage defaults, AIG believed the danger of such defaults was small and remote. Eager for easy money, AIG therefore sold many times the number of credit default swaps it could possibly honor should a crisis arrive.

And the crisis came. By 2006, a saturation point was reached in the housing market, with not enough new buyers to keep house prices soaring. As prices fell, many low-income owners lost what equity the formerly surging market had given them in the homes that, thanks to Bush, they had purchased with no down payment. Most of the low-income mortgagees were not financial geniuses. But it did not take a genius to see that it did not make economic sense to struggle to make a mortgage payment on a house that was declining in value and in which there was no equity to preserve. Banks were soon on the receiving end of "jingle mail," as mortgagees mailed in the keys to their houses and moved into rental property.

As mortgagees failed to make their monthly payments, financial institutions that had gorged themselves on supposedly low-risk mortgage-backed securities faced liquidity crises. In March 2008, the Wall Street firm Bear Stearns effectively failed despite an emergency loan from the Federal Reserve. Only the company's sale to J. P. Morgan at a bargain basement price, thanks to intervention by Bush's Treasury Department, kept Bear Stearns out of bankruptcy. The administration's intercession in this crisis brought fierce warnings of "moral hazard." Government protection of one reckless firm created the hazard that other investment houses, believing the government saw them as "too big to fail," would feel free to act even more recklessly. The laissez-faire ideologues deserve credit for their consistency in demanding that Wall Street face its free-market music.

Six months later, therefore, the Bush administration stood by and allowed the Wall Street firm of Lehman Brothers to perish without succor, poisoned like Bear Stearns by overindulgence in mortgage-backed securities. (It had probably not helped Lehman Brothers that Henry Paulson, Bush's secretary of the treasury, had been CEO of a rival firm, Goldman Sachs.) The day of the Lehman collapse—September 15, 2008—saw a near freeze-up of the financial system as investors, frightened that the government would allow other firms to suffer the consequences of their recklessness, withdrew billions of dollars from money market accounts, threatening illiquidity at sound institutions as well as unsound. The Treasury Department staunched the bleeding later that week by taking the unprecedented step of guaranteeing money market accounts.

So the day after the Lehman Brothers collapse, September 16, 2008, when AIG indicated that it was in trouble, no peep of "moral hazard" was heard, or at least none was heeded. The Bush administration quickly launched a bailout that made Uncle Sam the majority shareholder of AIG in return for taxpayer funds eventually totaling more than $180 billion. The next month, to forestall further such crises, Bush asked for and received from Congress $700 billion to buy banks' "troubled assets"—that is, mortgage-backed securities.

The Great Recession—the largest economic downturn since the Great Depression—was under way. Fearful of losing liquidity, banks cut their lending. Corporate executives and small-business owners, seeing no upturn of demand on the horizon, not only refused to hire new employees but thinned their payrolls. Foreclosures on more than a million homes in 2008 led Americans to a sudden respect for the danger of debt, with the result that home equity loans could no longer sustain consumer demand, could no longer make up for the failure of middle-class incomes to rise during the Bush years. As demand fell, unemployment soared from under 5 percent in December 2007 to nearly 10 percent in December 2008. When "discouraged" workers—those who had given up looking for work—were added in, the true unemployment rate was somewhere near 15 percent. In 2008, the number of American children living in poverty reached 21 percent, more than one in five. The number of Americans receiving food stamps surpassed forty million.

The recession, as economists measure such things, ended in June 2009 in the sense that economic growth had begun anew. But that growth was so feeble that it could not return Americans to work in significant numbers. The Great Recession as a time of enormous misery for millions and millions of people seemed destined to linger.

At the start of 2011 the situation was hardly better than at the start of 2009, with unemployment at just under 10 percent. Whatever slight drop there was in the official unemployment rate arose less from new jobs being created than from discouraged workers dropping out of the labor force. The officially unemployed, the drop-outs, and the under-employed part-timers who wanted full-time jobs totaled nearly thirty million people. In early 2009, Congress had passed an $800 billion stimulus bill that prevented the Great Recession from becoming a second Great Depression but that was too small to promote recovery. Beneath the immediate crisis with its terrible human costs lay the question of what a recovery would look like. Would recovery mean a return to the Clinton-Bush years with an ever-thinning middle class and ever-greater inequality of income between haves and have-nots? Or could one imagine a recovery of the American Dream? If so, would it be the old, corporate American Dream or some new entrepreneurial dream?

CHAPTER 28

Can the Corporate American Dream Be Saved?

As part II has shown, the business corporation's failure during the Great Depression to deliver a decent life to a large number of Americans brought the government response that created the corporate American Dream of half a century ago. The Great Recession that began with the financial crisis of 2007–2008 has raised again the issue of how a democratic society can make a corporate economy work for all of its citizens. The kind of actions that created the corporate American Dream—for example, laying the foundation for a strong labor movement with the Wagner Act—would not work now in a global economy.

It will require creative new policies and attitudes to restore the American Dream. The hollowing out of the American middle class and the development of a two-tier society was well under way before the Great Recession began. Measures that return the economy to its state before the Great Recession will not alone be enough to restore the American Dream. Only a change in worldview will make possible the new policies needed to save the dream. The popular ideological model that pits freedom and prosperity against government must also place the business corporation in the mix. From the East India Company down to the present, corporations have shown themselves capable of massive incompetence and worse. Yet the business corporation is also capable of great social achievements when balanced by democratic government, by nongovernmental organizations, and above all by citizens and consumers. Just as Ronald Reagan raised the prestige of the business corporation by his antigovernment ideology, Americans now need a moderate anti-corporatism that recognizes that democratic action is needed to restore prosperity. Such moderate anticorporatism will show that the actions we need are less radical than some would have us believe.

Consider health care reform, an issue second only to the general state of the economy in the 2008 electoral campaign of President Barack Obama. Health care reform meant many things to many people—universal coverage, cost reduction, and no exclusion for preexisting conditions. In this mélange of good causes, the fact that the failure of the health care system was a corporate failure fell out of focus. Obama should have called instead for corporate health insurance reform. American medicine is a largely corporate affair, and its history represents the best and the worst of the business corporation. In the late nineteenth century, when business corporations had only just begun their dominance of the American economy, physicians were for the most part poorly trained; techniques such as anesthesia and antisepsis were in their infancy; patients who survived the shock of major surgery might succumb to infection; and the benefits of American medicine, such as they were, were relatively affordable and broadly available.

Since then, American medical care has risen dramatically in quality and even more dramatically in cost. Those high medical costs can be attributed in significant measure to the fact that in the United States health insurance became a product to be sold by corporations rather than a service to be provided by society. The health insurance companies sell, in effect, life itself—a market where Say's Law is surely right, a market where demand will always keep pace with supply. In 2008, 16 percent of U.S. gross domestic product went to health care. That was half again as much as in any other developed nation, including those with single-payer health insurance or what opponents called "socialized medicine." It seemed likely that by 2020 Americans would be spending one out of every five dollars they earned on health care.[1]

Even though Americans spent far more for it, they got worse care than citizens of many other nations. A 2007 study by the widely respected Commonwealth Fund comparing the American health care system to those of Australia, Canada, Germany, England, and New Zealand placed the United States "last on dimensions of access, patient safety, efficiency, and equity."[2] On traditional measures of national health such as life expectancy and infant mortality, the United States lags several dozen countries.[3]

Why did Americans pay so much for such poor health care? Their insurance premiums went to corporate bureaucracies whose job was to make sure that their companies did *not* sell insurance to bad risks, that is, to those who most needed insurance. By leaving many Americans uninsured, the corporate health insurance system encouraged them to defer medical care until they had to visit hospital emergency rooms, where costs were high. Those high costs were then passed along either to those who did have insurance or to the taxpayer.

The corporate health insurance system caused extraordinary financial insecurity. In other developed nations, personal financial ruin because of medical costs is unknown. But in the United States in 2007, 62 percent of all personal bankruptcies were caused by medical bills. The victims included not only the uninsured poor but the underinsured middle class.[4] Corporate insurance executives, being human, wanted to see virtue in this system from which they greatly profited. The real danger, they said, was big government's threat to the free enterprise system and to the freedom of ordinary Americans to choose their own doctor. As President Obama sought congressional approval for universal health insurance, or at least something close to it, the insurance corporations had six registered lobbyists in Washington for every member of Congress.[5]

The corporate lobbyists aimed above all to prevent a "public option" under which uninsured individuals and small businesses would have bought insurance from government managed cooperatives, whose purchasing power might have driven down costs. Although the public option would not have been available to most people, the insurance corporations feared that it would eventually expand. Better to kill it in the first place, which they did. The health care reform that Congress finally passed in 2010 forced previously uninsured Americans to buy insurance from corporations. The intellectual poverty of a corporate society without anticorporatism was shown in the ability of right-wing politicians to demagogue "Obamacare" as socialism or at least as a manifestation of big government. Actually, it was insurance corporations that were destined to swell in size, with between forty million and fifty million new customers required to purchase health insurance from them. Without an anticorporatist framework within which to view the issues, Americans were supposedly threatened by government, not corporations.

What got left out of the discussion was the threat posed by the corporate health insurance system to Americans' economic well-being and to their entrepreneurial freedom. More than a few Americans who would have liked to start small businesses hung on to corporate jobs because they could not take the risk of personal bankruptcy that Americans, alone among peoples of developed nations, faced if they gave up a corporate job with health insurance. If the 2010 health care reform act survives court challenges, it will at least extend health insurance to millions of people. And because those who already have insurance will not lose it if they leave their jobs, there will be a significant gain in Americans' opportunity to practice entrepreneurship.

Anticorporatism could improve Americans' entrepreneurial freedom in other ways as well, because of its potentially broad appeal. There is a latent anticorporatism in the motivation of many young entrepreneurs. Many youth are not so much pulled to entrepreneurship as they are pushed to it by their eagerness to escape the harsh conditions of the corporate world. Corporate life has long since lost the appeal it held during the mid-twentieth-century American Dream era. Management sometimes still speaks the quaint argot of family and community, but countless employees have worked long hours for many years, only to be dismissed by corporate cost cutters.

The rise of information technology provides more opportunities for entrepreneurship than were available to anticorporate youth of the late 1960s and early 1970s. The early-twenty-first-century loss of youthful enthusiasm for corporate life is probably a good thing in itself in a democracy. But in addition, there are surely economic benefits for all Americans in the entrepreneurial zeal of the young.

What other measures in addition to health insurance reform would encourage entrepreneurship? The Obama administration sees entrepreneurship as an instrument of foreign policy, a way of spreading democracy. In April 2010, the White House held an Entrepreneurship Summit on business and social enterprise in the Middle East. But are we doing all that we can to encourage entrepreneurship and democracy at home? One business school that I know well is doing more than its part to "democratize entrepreneurship" at home and abroad, as well as to encourage "entrepreneurial thought and action." But does the United States have in place the public policies needed to support entrepreneurial freedom?

It would be wise to decouple the phrase "American Dream" from the home ownership that it often connotes. Home ownership is a tie that binds. Entrepreneurs need mobility. The central role of home mortgages in the financial crisis that brought the Great Recession showed the danger of the Bush administration's "ownership society," the danger of pushing people into home ownership when they could not afford it. When the American Dream rested on middle-class wages for factory workers, it was good public policy to encourage home ownership. Deductibility of mortgage interest from income tax made sense in the 1950s. In today's more entrepreneurial economy, government policies that provide support for a plentiful rental market make more sense.

The Social Security system should be strengthened and used to encourage entrepreneurship by low-wage earners. Entrepreneurship is not democratic if it simply means "job creation" so that working people always end up on someone else's payroll. Entrepreneurship is democratic only when it means a chance at self-employment for people who would otherwise work in low-wage jobs. Too strong a social safety net may discourage entrepreneurship. But too weak a one will give a low-wage job for a big corporation the appearance of a safe rock, because it offers health insurance and allows a worker to accumulate Social Security credits.

So how could Social Security be used to encourage entrepreneurship by low-wage earners? Here's a suggestion. Exempt the first $30,000 of self-employment income from Social Security taxes but allow that $30,000 of income to earn credit toward future Social Security benefits, just as if one were working the cash register in a big-box retailer. This program could be paid for by removing the income ceiling on Social Security taxes, allowing successful people, including entrepreneurs, to pay society back for the social opportunities from which they have benefited.

As they say in the corporate world, "What gets measured gets done." The government could generate more interest in entrepreneurship simply by measuring it and making the measure one of the ways we judge the health of the economy. Consider the term *unemployment rate*, which implicitly suggests that work is not something people create for themselves but something given to them by an employer. Why not balance this underlying idea by making room in our economic statistics for the *self-employment rate*?

Our present emphasis on job training programs should be complemented with self-employment training programs. Entrepreneurial teaching should not remain the nearly exclusive province of higher education—of business schools—with, again, the implication that others, and especially working people, should wait for entrepreneurs to create jobs for them. Working people able to create their own employment would also find themselves in a stronger position vis-à-vis potential corporate employers. To paraphrase Jefferson on the yeoman farmer, those who are capable of employing themselves are the chosen people of God. Coaching in marketing and operations could be provided by local government, community centers, nonprofits, and others. Many self-employed Americans make middle-class incomes, or come close to it, by doing home repairs and providing other useful services. The market may contain many new possibilities.

Corporate life, of course, is here to stay for the foreseeable future. Even if all the potential entrepreneurial energy in the world were properly harnessed and used, corporate power might not be much diminished; it might even be augmented. As General Electric, IBM, and Walmart showed in the 1990s, big business can be entrepreneurial and, in many spheres, can outdo the small entrepreneur. Important as entrepreneurship is, it will not alone replace the now lost contributions that corporations—forced into doing so by government and labor unions—once made to the American Dream. The global economy makes it much harder for government and labor to exert such force now.

One of the results of corporate outsourcing to Asia in the 1990s was a resurgence of interest in corporate social responsibility (CSR). Some companies such as Nike had mistakenly thought that the transactions that legally separated them from overseas suppliers also separated them from responsibility for child labor and other harsh working conditions there. Such corporate thinking was soon corrected by consumer boycotts. Nike and others adopted a different attitude when sales fell and the reputation of their brands declined. As a result, CSR programs and audits of working conditions in Asian factories became part of the standard operating procedure of many big western brands.

American companies also launched CSR programs in their domestic operations. For companies whose activities had implications for climate change, CSR became nearly obligatory. Outsiders, watchdog groups, nongovernmental organizations (NGOs), and the like kept up the pressure. The new CSR movement met with criticism from those who thought that social responsibility was not a proper corporate concern and also from those who thought that social responsibility should be strictly a government concern. The liberal Robert Reich, who had been secretary of labor in the Clinton administration, saw CSR as a stratagem for preventing government regulation.[6] Conservatives, following the reasoning of Milton Friedman's 1970 article opposing CSR, said that corporations helped society most by focusing on profits.[7]

Michael Porter, a brilliant academic who more or less single-handedly created the field of corporate strategy, and a coauthor, Mark Kramer, wrote a *Harvard Business Review* article offering another approach to CSR. Because "corporations need a healthy society" and "a healthy society needs successful companies," Porter and Kramer proposed that CSR should be part of corporate strategy and focused on the point where the company's and society's interests coincided. "A well-run business," they said, "can have a greater impact on social good than any other institution or philanthropic organization."[8]

This idea of focusing CSR on strategy leads, however, to yet another school of thought, which holds that companies should attempt to improve society only when it is in the company's self-interest to do so. The idea here is to resist outside pressure for CSR, because a corporation "accountable to all is in effect accountable to none."[9] In other words, companies should resist the sort of outside pressure that caused the CSR movement in the first place. According to this theory, companies can be "bullied into doing the wrong thing. When multinationals bow to pressure from campaigners against 'sweatshops' and sever links with suppliers in poor countries, the workers who previously stitched shoes for export may end up scavenging from rubbish heaps."[10]

"Rubbish!" might be a fair response. Such unbalanced ideological posturing is all too typical of opposition to CSR. No doubt there have been cases where outside pressure has led companies to do the wrong thing. But it is thanks to campaigners against sweatshops that there *are* some well-run overseas shoe factories where workers assemble shoes without glues that emit poisonous fumes and with safeguards on machines so that a moment's inattention is not punished with a lost finger. Thanks to outside pressure from anti-sweatshop groups, I have seen working conditions in some Asian factories that are far superior to the dangerous American steel mills, metal fabricating plants, and food processors in which I had numerous summer and night jobs during my admittedly distant student days of the 1960s. I knew a fair number of workers with missing fingers and with scars from burns, and I witnessed others working in foul air, fumes, and smoke that can only have brought some of them an early death. Improving those conditions would have been possible at little cost. Few, if any, jobs would have been lost. Scavenging from rubbish heaps is not the only alternative to CSR.

The narrowly utilitarian ethics of conventional corporate wisdom needs broadening. That corporations, like individuals, might act on a sense of duty when they have nothing to gain from doing so does not register as a possibility in the minds of far too many corporatist ideologues. The very definition of responsibility is sometimes to act against one's narrow self-interest. There are gains in character to be had—both for corporations and for those they employ—from actions that are not self-interested.

Still, a democratic society should never count on good character in its corporate chiefs any more than it counts on good character in its political leaders. Outside pressure is necessary. It is true that outside pressure, like any human instrument, may be mistaken. But it is also true that without such pressure, many more corporations than is now the case would be violating human rights, buying from suppliers with terrible working conditions, and hastening climate change.

Some responsible corporate executives, far from resisting outside pressure, attend to it. They appreciate the work that consumers, watchdog groups, and NGOs have done in raising the bar for their competitors so that they themselves may manage more responsibly. Partnerships between corporations and such outside groups to accomplish specific social objectives often work well, giving each side a chance to learn from the other what is economically possible and morally important.

A society concerned about corporate responsibility does not need instruction from on high as to some supposed natural law holding that "companies aren't charities."[11] It is precisely because companies are not charities that outside pressure for CSR is necessary. Ideological opponents of CSR need more understanding of the challenge of balancing utilitarian economics and utilitarian ethics on the one hand against, on the other, the ethics of duty and virtue. Because duty and virtue do not come naturally to some companies, we need anticorporatism. Awareness that utilitarian economics and utilitarian ethics are a vital part of the equation should make anticorporatism moderate. The aim of moderate anticorporatists should be to make CSR inviting and obligatory—inviting because of public appreciation for it and obligatory because of consumers' punishment of corporate laggards.

Early-twenty-first-century interest in CSR has transitioned into a new field of "social entrepreneurship." The idea is for entrepreneurs to tackle social issues ranging from underperforming schools to global warming. Social entrepreneurship has won the avid interest of business school students, reflecting the fact that American idealism has not died but is busy getting an MBA. In their business school educations, aspiring social entrepreneurs are certainly gaining useful skills, skills that would have made earlier generations of American social reformers even more effective if they had possessed them. It is to be hoped that these students will not buy one of the popular justifications for social entrepreneurship— "government can't do it." Or at least they should qualify that idea with the corollary that social entrepreneurs can't do it on their own either. Government action will be needed in many cases.

No amount of social entrepreneurship will be able to correct, for example, the fact that America's education system has become fundamentally undemocratic, with many children shut out of a decent education. The fact that living in the wrong school district can deprive a child of educational opportunity is a profound social injustice. Corporations needing an educated workforce may provide useful support for educational reform. Social entrepreneurs can provide useful new models. But the fundamental responsibility has to rest not with corporations and social entrepreneurs but with the public and with government.

Within national borders, democratic government—not always and far from perfectly—is the primary instrument through which people achieve their social goals. Government, for all its problems, accomplishes many social aims more effectively than corporations ever have or ever will. Victims of the Great Recession can testify, as could victims of the Great Depression, that when it comes to creating a good society, corporations can't do it, at least not alone. Still, it is true that in a global economy national governments can't do it alone either. National governments, international institutions, and the United Nations can and often do work together to promote global corporate responsibility. But we will not any time soon have an international equivalent of the Wagner Act, the 1930s law that gave labor unions the strength to challenge corporations and force them to create the mid-twentieth-century American Dream.

Therefore, civil regulation of corporations to create conditions for the rebirth and globalization of the American Dream is a necessity. Just as GE's Boulware went around the union to speak directly to workers, so now anticorporatists must sometimes go around government and deal directly with corporations. Whether they do it through nongovernmental organizations, watchdog groups, consumer action, or other means, they will need all the entrepreneurial thought and action they can muster. Moderate anticorporatists will attempt to recognize genuine economic constraints and utilitarian ethics in order not to do wrong. But they will also invoke the ethics of virtue and duty in order to do right, in order to make real the dream of a corporate prosperity that is more generous and just. In a democratic society, corporate social responsibility is everyone's business.

Notes

Introduction

1. Perry Miller, *The New England Mind: The Seventeenth Century* (Cambridge, Mass.: Harvard University Press, 1953), vii.

Chapter 1   The Corporate American Dream

1. James Truslow Adams, *The Epic of America* (Boston: Little, Brown, 1931), 404.
2. Ibid.
3. Robert Sickels, *The 1940s* (Westport, Conn.: Greenwood, 2004), 21.

Chapter 2   Corporate and National Character

1. This and all subsequent quotations of Thomas Jefferson are from *Notes on the State of Virginia*, ed. William Peden (Chapel Hill: University of North Carolina Press, 1954), 164–165.
2. This and all subsequent quotations of Alexander Hamilton are from "Report on Manufactures," Online Library of Liberty, http://oll.libertyfund.org/?option=com_staticxt&staticfile=show.php%3Ftitle=875&chapter=63882&layout=html&Itemid=27.
3. Robert F. Dalzell Jr., *Enterprising Elite: The Boston Associates and the World They Made* (Cambridge, Mass: Harvard University Press, 1987), 28.
4. Thomas Dublin, *Women at Work: The Transformation of Work and Community in Lowell, Massachusetts, 1826–1860* (New York: Columbia University Press, 1979), 93.

Chapter 3   From Public Purpose to Private Profit

1. Adam Smith, *An Inquiry into the Nature and Causes of the Wealth of Nations* (New York: Modern Library, 1994), 170.
2. Ibid., 692.
3. Quoted in Peter Dobkin Hall, *The Organization of American Culture: Private Institutions, Elites, and the Origins of American Nationality* (New York: New York University Press, 1982), 301.
4. William G. Roy, *Socializing Capital: The Rise of the Large Industrial Corporation in America* (Princeton, N.J.: Princeton University Press, 1997), 49.
5. Quoted in Hall, *Organization of American Culture*, 301.
6. Quoted in John Micklethwait and Adrian Wooldridge, *The Company: A Short History of a Revolutionary Idea* (New York: Modern Library, 2003), 71.

CHAPTER 4   CORPORATIONS AS ENEMIES OF THE FREE MARKET

1. Alfred D. Chandler, *The Visible Hand: The Managerial Revolution in American Business* (Cambridge, Mass.: Harvard University Press, 1977), 138.
2. Ibid., 329–330.
3. Arthur C. Brooks, *The Battle: How the Fight between Free Enterprise and Big Government Will Shape America's Future* (New York: Basic Books, 2010).
4. Ibid., 91.

CHAPTER 5   CORPORATE CRASHES

1. Stephen Thernstrom, *The Other Bostonians: Poverty and Progress in the American Metropolis* (Cambridge, Mass.: Harvard University Press, 1973), 231.
2. Ibid.
3. Ibid.
4. Ibid.
5. Edmund Wilson, *The American Earthquake* (New York: DaCapo, 1958), 441.

CHAPTER 6   MANAGERS VERSUS MARKETS

1. Alfred D. Chandler, *The Visible Hand: The Managerial Revolution in American Business* (Cambridge, Mass.: Harvard University Press, 1977), 25, 35–38.
2. Ibid., 495.
3. Ibid., 496.

CHAPTER 7   CORPORATIONS BLOW THEIR CHANCE TO
END THE DEPRESSION

1. John Kennedy Ohl, *Hugh S. Johnson and the New Deal* (DeKalb: Northern Illinois University Press, 1985), 175.
2. Rexford Tugwell, *Roosevelt's Revolution* (New York: Macmillan, 1977), 108.

CHAPTER 8   ROOSEVELT'S CONFUSED ANTICORPORATISM

1. Quoted in Jordan A. Schwarz, *Liberal: Adolf A. Berle and the Vision of an American Era* (New York: Free Press, 1987), 78.
2. Adolf A. Berle and Gardiner Means, *The Modern Corporation and Private Property* (New York: Harcourt, Brace, 1968), vii–viii.
3. Alfred P. Sloan, *My Years with General Motors*, ed. John McDonald with Catharine Stevens (1963; reprint, Garden City, N.Y.: Doubleday, 1990), 475.
4. Sidney Fine, *Sit-Down: The General Motors Strike of 1936–1937* (Ann Arbor: University of Michigan Press, 1969), 31.
5. Quoted in David Farber, *Sloan Rules: Alfred P. Sloan and the Triumph of General Motors* (Chicago: University of Chicago Press, 2002), 196–197.
6. Ibid., 205.
7. Sloan, *My Years with General Motors*, 461.
8. In Studs Terkel, *Hard Times: An Oral History of the Great Depression* (New York: Pantheon, 1986), 135.
9. Bernard Baruch, *The Public Years* (New York: Holt, Rinehart and Winston, 1960), 253.
10. Ibid., 253–254.

CHAPTER 9   THE RIGHT TO MANAGE

1. Howell John Harris, *The Right to Manage: Industrial Relations Policies of American Business in the 1940s* (Madison: University of Wisconsin Press, 1982), 87.
2. Ibid., 59.
3. Alfred P. Sloan, *My Years with General Motors* ed. John McDonald with Catharine Stevens (1963; reprint, Garden City, N.Y.: Doubleday, 1990), 393.
4. James B. Atleson, *Labor and the Wartime State: Labor Relations and Law during World War II* (Urbana: University of Illinois Press, 1998), 85.
5. Stimson quoted in ibid., 25.
6. Harris, *Right to Manage*, 10.
7. Quoted in Nelson Lichtenstein, *The Most Dangerous Man in Detroit: Walter Reuther and the Fate of American Labor* (New York: Basic Books, 1995), 224.
8. Quoted in David Farber, *Sloan Rules: Alfred P. Sloan and the Triumph of General Motors* (Chicago: University of Chicago Press, 2002), 238.
9. Ibid., 236.

CHAPTER 10   CORPORATIONS RECOVER THEIR
             MORAL AUTHORITY

1. Alfred P. Sloan, *My Years with General Motors* ed. John McDonald with Catharine Stevens (1963; reprint, Garden City, N.Y.: Doubleday, 1990), 385.
2. Nelson Lichtenstein, *The Most Dangerous Man in Detroit: Walter Reuther and the Fate of American Labor* (New York: Basic Books, 1995), 220–226.
3. Reuther quoted in ibid., 235.
4. Quoted in David Farber, *Sloan Rules: Alfred P. Sloan and the Triumph of General Motors* (Chicago: University of Chicago Press, 2002), 239.
5. Sloan, *My Years with General Motors*, 406.

CHAPTER 11   KILLING THE UNIONS SOFTLY

1. Quoted in Howell John Harris, *The Right to Manage: Industrial Relations Policies of American Business in the 1940s* (Madison: University of Wisconsin Press, 1982), 121.
2. James T. Patterson, *Mr. Republican: A Biography of Robert A. Taft* (Boston: Houghton Mifflin, 1972), 353.

CHAPTER 12   CREATING REAGAN AND HIS VOTERS

1. Quoted in Kim Phillips-Fein, *Invisible Hands: The Making of the Conservative Movement from the New Deal to Reagan* (New York: W. W. Norton, 2009), 96.
2. Lemuel R. Boulware, *The Truth about Boulwarism* (Washington, D.C.: Bureau of National Affairs, 1969), 3.
3. Lemuel Boulware, "Salvation Is Not Free," in Thomas W. Evans, *The Education of Ronald Reagan: The General Electric Years and the Untold Story of His Conversion to Conservatism* (New York: Columbia University Press, 2006), 232.
4. Ibid.
5. Ibid., 233.

6. Ibid., 232.
7. Ibid., 231.
8. Ibid., 229.
9. Ibid., 230.
10. Ibid.
11. Ibid., 231.
12. Ibid., 233.
13. Ibid., 237.
14. Boulware quoted in Evans, *Education of Ronald Reagan*, 49.
15. Ibid., 49–50.
16. Boulware, *Truth about Boulwarism*, 51; Evans, *Education of Ronald Reagan*, 51.
17. Evans, *Education of Ronald Reagan,* 51.
18. Boulware, *Truth about Boulwarism*, 56.
19. *Employee Relations Newsletter* quoted in Evans, *Education of Ronald Reagan*, 51–52.
20. Quoted in Lou Cannon, *Governor Reagan: His Rise to Power* (New York: Public Affairs, 2003), 109.
21. Ibid., 110.
22. Herbert R. Northrup, *Boulwarism: The Labor Relations Policies of the General Electric Company* (Ann Arbor, Mich.: Bureau of Industrial Relations, 1964), 86.
23. Phillips-Fein, *Invisible Hands*, 110.
24. Quoted in Evans, *Education of Ronald Reagan*, 145.
25. Evans, *Education of Ronald Reagan*, 104.
26. Boulware, *Truth about Boulwarism*, 39.
27. David Broder and Stephen Hess, *The Republican Establishment: The Present and Future of the GOP* (New York: Harper and Row, 1967), 253–254.
28. Evans, *Education of Ronald Reagan*, 168.
29. Ronald Reagan, "A Time to Choose," in Evans, *Education of Ronald Reagan*, 238.
30. Northrup, *Boulwarism*, 104–105.

CHAPTER 13   MASKING THE ARROGANCE OF POWER

1. James Hoopes, *False Prophets: The Gurus Who Created Modern Management and Why Their Ideas Are Bad for Business Today* (New York: Basic Books, 2003), 48, 57.
2. Barry Karl, *Charles L. Merriam and the Study of Politics* (Chicago: University of Chicago Press, 1974), 86.
3. Hoopes, *False Prophets*, 150; Mayo's unpublished paper, "The Blind Spot in Scientific Management" is in his papers, box 5, folder 9, at the Baker Library, Harvard Business School.
4. Elton Mayo, *Human Problems of an Industrial Civilization* (New York: Macmillan, 1933), 73; F. J. Roethlisberger and William J. Dickson, *Management and the Worker* (Cambridge, Mass.: Harvard University Press, 1939), 561.
5. Hoopes, *False Prophets*, 147. For a detailed description of the Hawthorne experiment, see Richard Gillespie, *Manufacturing Knowledge: A History of the Hawthorne Experiments* (Cambridge: Cambridge University Press, 1991).
6. Chester Barnard, *Organization and Management: Selected Papers* (Cambridge, Mass.: Harvard University Press, 1948), 81.

7. Chester Barnard, *The Functions of the Executive* (Cambridge, Mass.: Harvard University Press, 1938), 150.
8. Ibid., 170–171.

CHAPTER 14   RESPONSIBILITY VERSUS PROFIT
              AT GENERAL MOTORS

1. James Burnham, *The Managerial Revolution: What Is Happening in the World* (New York: John Day, 1941), 89–90.
2. Ibid., 8.
3. Peter Drucker, *Concept of the Corporation* (1946; reprint, New Brunswick, N.J.: Transaction Books, 1993), 9.
4. Peter Drucker, *The End of Economic Man: A Study of the New Totalitarianism* (New York: John Day, 1939), 79.
5. Peter Drucker, *The Future of Industrial Man: A Conservative Approach* (New York: John Day, 1942), 99.
6. Ibid., 294–295.
7. Peter Drucker, *Adventures of a Bystander* (New York: Harper and Row, 1978), 258.
8. Drucker, *Practice of Management* (New York: Harper and Row, 1954), 119.
9. Ibid., 391–392.
10. Drucker, *Concept of the Corporation*, 129.
11. Ibid., 127.
12. Alfred P. Sloan, *My Years with General Motors*, ed. John McDonald with Catharine Stevens (1963; reprint, Garden City, N.Y.: Doubleday, 1990), 49.

CHAPTER 15   CRITICS OF MANAGERIAL CHARACTER

1. David Riesman with Nathan Glazer and Ruel Denney, *The Lonely Crowd: A Study of the Changing American Character* (New Haven, Conn.: Yale University Press, 1961), 271.
2. Ibid., 81.
3. Ibid., 41.
4. C. Wright Mills, *White Collar: The American Middle Classes* (New York: Oxford University Press, 1953), 101.
5. Adolf A. Berle, *The 20th Century Capitalist Revolution* (New York: Harcourt, Brace, 1954), 39.
6. Ibid., 180.
7. Ibid., 173, 179.
8. C. Wright Mills, *The Power Elite* (New York: Oxford University Press, 1956), 125.
9. Ibid., 148.
10. Ibid., 361.
11. Ibid., 141.
12. Ibid., 356.
13. Ibid., 361.

CHAPTER 16   JFK'S PYRRHIC VICTORY OVER U.S. STEEL

1. Quoted in Arthur M. Schlesinger Jr., *A Thousand Days: John F. Kennedy in the White House* (Boston: Houghton Mifflin, 1965), 635.

2. "News Conference 30," John F. Kennedy Presidential Library and Museum, http://www.jfklibrary.org/Research/Ready-Reference/Press-Conferences/News-Conference-30.aspx.
3. David L. Stebenne, *Arthur J. Goldberg: New Deal Liberal* (New York: Oxford University Press, 1996), 292–293.
4. Ibid., 293.
5. Kennedy's letter and Blough's reply are reprinted in Roger M. Blough, *The Washington Embrace of Business* (Pittsburgh: Carnegie-Mellon University, 1975), 121–125.
6. Hobart Rowen, *The Free Enterprisers: Kennedy, Johnson, and the Business Establishment* (New York: Putnam's, 1964), 100.
7. Quoted in ibid., 95.
8. "News Conference 30," John F. Kennedy Presidential Library and Museum, http://www.jfklibrary.org/Research/Ready-Reference/Press-Conferences/News-Conference-30.aspx.
9. Rowen, *Free Enterprisers*, 105.
10. Quoted in ibid., 106.
11. Quoted in Schlesinger, *A Thousand Days*, XXX.
12. Ibid., 115.
13. Quoted in Schlesinger, *A Thousand Days*, 638.

CHAPTER 18   THE FALSE CONFIDENCE OF THE ANTICORPORATISTS

1. Roger M. Blough, *Free Man and the Corporation* (New York: McGraw-Hill, 1959).
2. John Kenneth Galbraith, *The Affluent Society* (Boston: Houghton Mifflin, 1958), 205.
3. John Kenneth Galbraith, *The New Industrial State* (Boston: Houghton Mifflin, 1967), 369.
4. Ibid., 322.
5. Ibid., 376.
6. Ibid., 391.
7. Ibid., 392.
8. Ibid., 380–383.
9. Ibid., 399.

CHAPTER 19   CORPORATE AMERICA LOSES WORLD SUPREMACY

1. Jean-Jacques Servan-Schreiber, *The American Challenge* (New York: Athenaeum, 1968), 3.
2. Ibid., 8.
3. Ibid., 11.
4. Ibid., 28.
5. Ibid., 8.
6. Arthur M. Schlesinger Jr., foreword to Servan-Schreiber, *American Challenge*, x.
7. James Hoopes, *False Prophets: The Gurus Who Created Modern Management and Why Their Ideas Are Bad for Business Today* (New York: Basic Books, 2003); pp. 197–230 are the source for much of the rest of this chapter.
8. Quoted in Cecilia S. Kilian, *The World of W. Edwards Deming* (Knoxville, Tenn.: SPC Press, 1992), 9–10.

9. James P. Womack, Daniel T. Jones, and Daniel Roos, *The Machine That Changed the World: The Story of Lean Production—Toyota's Secret Weapon in the Global Car Wars That Is Revolutionizing World Industry* (1990; reprint, New York: Free Press, 2007), 52.
10. Ibid., 103.
11. Paul Ingrassia, *Crash Course: The American Automobile Industry's Road from Glory to Disaster* (New York: Random House, 2010), 9, 46.

CHAPTER 20   LAYING THE GROUNDWORK FOR
THE CORPORATION'S CULTURAL COMEBACK

1. Jimmy Carter, "Crisis of Confidence" speech, July 15, 1979, Miller Center of Public Affairs, University of Virginia, http://millercenter.org/scripps/archive/speeches/detail/3402.
2. Michael C. Jensen and William H. Meckling, "Theory of the Firm: Managerial Behavior, Agency Costs and Ownership Structure," *Journal of Financial Economics* 3 (1976): 305–360.
3. Ibid., 359.
4. Ibid., 311.
5. Ibid.
6. Milton Friedman, "The Social Responsibility of Business Is to Increase Its Profits," *New York Times Magazine*, September 13, 1970.

CHAPTER 21   MANAGING BY VALUES

1. Chester Barnard, *Functions of the Executive* (Cambridge, Mass.: Harvard University Press, 1938), 284.
2. Herbert A. Simon, *Administrative Behavior: A Study of Decision-Making Processes in Administrative Organizations* (New York: Free Press, 1997), chap. 3.
3. Warren G. Bennis quoted in James MacGregor Burns, *Leadership* (New York: Harper, 1978), 451.
4. Burns, *Leadership*, 452.
5. Ibid., 19.
6. Ibid., 163.
7. Ken Blanchard and Michael O'Connor, *Managing by Values* (San Francisco: Berrett-Koehler, 1997), 44, 54.
8. Ibid., 54.

CHAPTER 22   CREATING THE CONCEPT OF
CORPORATE CULTURE

1. Sidney Mintz quoted in Herbert Gutman, "Work, Culture, and Society in Industrializing America, 1815–1919," *American Historical Review* (June 1973): 542.
2. Thomas J. Peters and Robert H. Waterman Jr., *In Search of Excellence: Lessons from America's Best-Run Companies* (New York: Harper and Row, 1982), 17.
3. Ibid., 4.
4. Ibid., 105.
5. Ibid., 122–124.
6. Ibid., 11.

7. Peter Senge, *The Fifth Discipline: The Art and Practice of the Learning Organization* (New York: Doubleday, 1990), 287.
8. Peters and Waterman, *In Search of Excellence*, xxv.

CHAPTER 23   INVENTING THE LEADERSHIP
            DEVELOPMENT INDUSTRY

1. Abraham Zaleznik, "Managers and Leaders: Are They Different?" *Best of HBR on Leadership* (Cambridge, Mass.: Harvard Business School Press, 2004), 74.
2. Ibid.
3. Ibid., 75.
4. Ibid., 79.
5. Ibid.
6. Ibid.
7. Ibid.
8. Ibid., 81.
9. Ibid.
10. Warren Bennis, *On Becoming a Leader* (Reading, Mass.: Addison-Wesley, 1989), 4.
11. Ibid., 49.
12. For an introduction to the subject, see Christopher Grey and Hugh Willmott, *Critical Management Studies: A Reader* (New York: Oxford University Press, 2005).
13. Bennis, *On Becoming a Leader*, 20.
14. Ibid., 32.
15. Ibid., 43.

CHAPTER 24   REAGAN AIDS CORPORATIONS
            BY BASHING GOVERNMENT

1. Quoted in Lou Cannon, *President Reagan: The Role of a Lifetime* (New York: Simon and Schuster, 1991), 21.
2. Cannon, *President Reagan*, 517.
3. Quoted in Cannon, *President Reagan*, 531.
4. William A. Niskanen, *Reaganomics: An Insider's Account of the Policies and the People* (New York: Oxford University Press, 1988), 315.
5. James A. Gross, *Broken Promise: The Subversion of U.S. Labor Relations Policy, 1947–1994* (Philadelphia: Temple University Press, 1995), 256.
6. Quoted in Cannon, *President Reagan*, 497.
7. Quoted in Francis X. Clines, "Corporate Tax Upsets Reagan," *New York Times*, January 27, 1983.
8. Quoted in John Solomon, *Harvard Crimson*, January 28, 1983, http://www.thecrimson.com/article/1983/1/28/reagan-in-high-tech-hub-sees.

CHAPTER 25   SUPPLY-SIDERS VERSUS THE BIG CORPORATION

1. Jude Wanniski, *The Way the World Works* (1978; Morristown, N.J.: Polyconomics, 1989), 350–351.
2. George Gilder, *Wealth and Poverty* (New York: Basic Books, 1981), 77.
3. Jack Kemp, *An American Renaissance: A Strategy for the 1980s* (Falls Church, Va.: Conservative Press, 1979), 18.

4. "Stupendous Steiger," *Wall Street Journal*, April 26, 1978.
5. Wanniski, *The Way the World Works*, 97.
6. Ibid., 87.
7. Gilder, *Wealth and Poverty*, 79.
8. Ibid., 80–81.
9. Ibid., 83.

CHAPTER 26   REENGINEERING THE CORPORATION

1. Ada Chen, "Successes and Failures in Times of Technological Booms: An Investigation into the Effects of New Technology Adoption," honors thesis, Babson College, 2010.
2. Peter Senge, "Building Learning Organizations," *Journal for Quality and Participation* 15, no. 2 (1992): 32.
3. Michael Hammer, *Beyond Reengineering: How the Process-Centered Organization Is Changing Our Work and Our Lives* (New York: Harper Business, 1996), 61.
4. Michael Hammer and James Champy, *Reengineering the Corporation: A Manifesto for Business Revolution* (New York: Harper Business, 1993), 28.
5. Jack Welch, *Jack: Straight from the Gut* (New York: Warner Books, 2001), 139.
6. Ibid., 92.
7. Ibid., 124–125.
8. Ibid., 342.
9. Louis Gerstner, *Who Says Elephants Can't Dance? Inside IBM's Historic Turnaround* (New York: HarperCollins, 2002), 60.
10. Nelson Lichtenstein, *Retail Revolution: How Wal-Mart Created a Brave New World of Business* (New York: Henry Holt, 2009), 286–287.

CHAPTER 27   GEORGE W. BUSH, ENRON, AND
THE GREAT RECESSION

1. James Hoopes, *Hail to the CEO: The Failure of George W. Bush and the Cult of Moral Leadership* (Westport, Conn.: Praeger, 2008), chap. 7.
2. Bush's actions at Harken Energy, some noble, some unethical, are described in Hoopes, *Hail to the CEO*, chaps. 3 and 4.
3. Kurt Eichenwald, *Conspiracy of Fools: A True Story* (New York: Broadway Books, 2005), 286, 300–301.
4. Ibid., 56–58.
5. Quoted in David E. Sanger, "Who Should Mete Out Punishment?" *New York Times*, July 17, 2002.
6. "Transcript of President's Address Calling for New Era of Corporate Integrity," *New York Times*, July 10, 2002.
7. Quoted in Joe Becker, Sheryl Gay Stolberg, and Stephen Labaton, "Bush Drive for Home Ownership Fueled Housing Bubble," *New York Times*, December 21, 2008.

CHAPTER 28   CAN THE CORPORATE AMERICAN DREAM BE SAVED?

1. "National Health Expenditure Fact Sheet," U.S. Department of Health and Human Services, http://www.cms.gov/NationalHealthExpendData/25_NHE_Fact_Sheet.asp#TopOfPage.

2. Karen Davis et al., "Mirror, Mirror, on the Wall: An International Update on the Comparative Performance of American Health Care," Commonwealth Fund, http://www.commonwealthfund.org/Content/Publications/Fund-Reports/2007/May/Mirror—Mirror-on-the-Wall—An-International-Update-on-the-Comparative-Performance-of-American-Healt.aspx.

3. On infant mortality, see Central Intelligence Agency, *The World Factbook*, https://www.cia.gov/library/publications/the-world-factbook/rankorder/2091rank.html. On life expectancy, see the United Nations report *World Population Prospects: The 2006 Revision*, http://www.un.org/esa/population/publications/wpp2006/WPP2006_Highlights_rev.pdf.

4. David U. Himmelstein et al., "Medical Bankruptcy in the United States, 2007: Results of a National Study," *American Journal of Medicine* (August 2009): http://www.pnhp.org/new_bankruptcy_study/Bankruptcy-2009.pdf.

5. Jonathan D. Salant and Lizzie O'Leary, "Six Lobbyists per Lawmaker Work to Shape Health Overhaul," August 14, 2009, http://www.bloomberg.com; accessed summer 2010.

6. Robert B. Reich, *Supercapitalism: The Transformation of Government, Business, and Everyday Life* (New York: Knopf, 2007).

7. For the latest such book, though dealing with Africa rather than the United States, see Ann Bernstein, *The Case for Business in Developing Economies* (New York: Penguin, 2010).

8. Michael E. Porter and Mark R. Kramer, "Strategy and Society: The Link between Competitive Advantage and Corporate Social Responsibility," *Harvard Business Review* 84 (December 2006): 7, 13.

9. "Companies Aren't Charities," *Economist*, October 23–29, 2010, 82.

10. Ibid.

11. Ibid.

Index

academia, 123

accounting, 45, 193, 194

Adams, Charles Francis, 25

Adams, James Truslow, 11–12

Adams, Sherman, 117

Adelphia, 190, 191

African Americans, 12

agency costs, 140

agency problem, 23

agriculture, 17–18

airlines, 138, 165

Amazon, 181

American colonies, 3, 23

American Dream: and anti-union legislation, 72; and Burns, 147; and Carter, 137; complexity of, 17; and corporatism and democracy, 15–16; and freedom, 11, 12; as goal, 15; and government control, 9, 32, 35, 38, 56, 179; and inflation, 71; and Japanese competition, 135; and John F. Kennedy, 106; and labor unions, 9–10; and manufacturing, 19; and New Deal labor legislation, 3; and prosperity vs. democratic freedom, 155; revival of, 2; rise of, 1, 9–14; and Sloan, 65–66, 67; and unions, 75; and Wagner Act, 52; and Walmart, 187

American Express, 130

American International Group (AIG), 195, 196

American Revolution, 3

Anthracite Strike (1902), 37–38

anticorporatism: ad hoc, 63; and American colonies, 23; and Boulware, 77; in cultural discussions, 123; and democracy, 2; and economy, 4; and entrepreneurship, 4, 5, 201; and Franklin Roosevelt, 52; of Galbraith, 124–128; and Great Depression, 3; and health care reform, 200; of liberals, 136; moderate, 2, 4, 5, 198–199, 206, 207; modern, 25; of Moore, 186; need for, 205–206; and New Deal, 52; of New Left, 124; post-Revolutionary, 3, 24–25; reactive vs. wise, 4–5; and Reagan era, 163, 164; and Schlesinger, 131; in youth culture and among intellectuals, 122–123

anti-institutionalism, 128

anti-Semitism, 89, 94

antitrust laws, 3, 109. See also Sherman Anti-Trust Act

arrogance, 89, 150, 160, 189; of managers, 3, 105, 117; of McNamara, 118

Arthur Andersen, 192

Asia, factories in, 203, 204

Atomic Energy Commission, 89

AT&T, 131, 133

automation, 101

automobile industry: and anticorporatism, 4–5; and assembly line, 42; Japanese, 4, 133–135, 137;

automobile industry (*continued*)
loss of supremacy in, 3–4, 121, 140;
near collapse of, 152; postwar
potential of, 64, 65; and quality
control, 132; and United Automobile
Workers, 54–56; U.S., 133
Automobile Manufacturers
Association, 62
autonomy, 126

Baltimore & Ohio Railroad, 29
Bank of the United States, First, 19, 24
Bank of the United States, Second,
24–25
bankruptcy, 27, 28, 29, 191
banks/banking, 165; commercial, 45;
corporate charters for, 24; and
Glass-Steagall Act, 45; and Great
Recession, 196; and home
ownership, 194–195; investment,
45; Japanese, 134; and recessions,
38; regulation of, 10, 194
Barnard, Chester, 92, 93, 145, 146,
155; *The Functions of the Executive,* 91
Baruch, Bernard, 46, 47, 48, 56
Bear Stearns, 195, 196
Bell, Daniel, *The End of Ideology,*
102–103, 105
Bell Labs, 131–132
Bennis, Warren, 147; *On Becoming a
Leader,* 159–160, 161–162
Berle, Adolf, 163; *The 20th Century
Capitalist Revolution,* 104; *The
Modern Corporation and Private
Property,* 51–52, 62, 93, 103, 104,
125, 135, 139, 142
Bethlehem Steel, 109–110
big business, 4, 32, 51, 81, 82
Blanchard, Ken, *Managing by Values,*
149–150, 153
Blough, Roger M., 106, 107–108,
110, 111; "Free Man and the
Corporation," 122

Boston, social mobility in, 36
Boston Manufacturing Company,
20, 26
Boulware, Lemuel, 76–81, 82–84,
103, 108, 141, 167, 207
Bowling for Columbine (film), 186
Brains Trust, 45, 47, 51
Brown, Donaldson, 95
Brown, Moses, 19
*Brown v. Board of Education of Topeka,
Kansas,* 13
Bryan, William Jennings, 83
Buckley, William F., 82
Building Trades Council, 47
Burnham, James, 95, 100, 105; *The
Managerial Revolution,* 93–94
Burns, James MacGregor, *Leadership,*
147–149, 150, 151, 157, 164, 190
Bush, George H. W., 165, 180
Bush, George W., 45, 189–190, 193,
195–196

canals, 25, 27
capitalism, 16; and Baruch, 46; and
Bell, 103; and Berle, 104; blame for
injustices of, 87; and Burnham, 93;
and China, 187; Galbraith on, 102;
and George W. Bush, 190; and
Great Depression, 46; industrial, 27;
and Jefferson, 20; and Mayo, 100; as
mercantile phenomenon, 27; and
Mills, 103, 104, 105; and New
Dealers, 93; post-Revolutionary,
19; and Stimson, 64
Capitalism: A Love Story (film), 186
Carlton, C. C., 62
Carnegie, Andrew, 37
cartels, anticompetitive, 29
Carter, Jimmy, 137, 146, 163, 165,
166
Census Bureau, 132
CEOs, 2, 142, 145; and M-form, 95,
96, 116, 117; as overpaid, 192; and

postwar higher education, 11;
superstar, 182, 192; suspicion of, 5
Champy, James, *Reengineering the Corporation*, 181–182, 183
character: development of, 12, 17;
integrated, 15; and Jefferson, 18;
and John F. Kennedy, 106; and
Mills, 105; and self-interest, 205;
and working class, 21
Cheney, Richard, 176, 190
child labor, 38, 47, 203
children, Hamilton on, 19
China, 13, 187
Chrysler, 56, 132, 186
civil rights, 135
Civil Rights Act of 1964, 123
civil rights movement, 13–14
Civil War, 35, 36, 87
Cleveland, Grover, 37
Clifford, Clark, 110
Clinton, William Jefferson, 45,
180, 185
closed shops, 74
coal industry, 38
Coase, Ronald, 163, 180; "On the
Nature of the Firm," 41, 139, 140
Cold War, 13, 147, 164
collective bargaining, 47, 75. *See also*
labor unions
Committee for Industrial
Organization (CIO), 54
Common Market, 130
communication, 41
communications technology, 4.
See also information technology
communism, 12, 13, 102, 127
company, multidivisional, 95–98
competition: capital-intensive, 27, 28,
29; and cooperative codes, 49; and
Great Depression, 46–47, 48;
international, 36, 135, 166–167;
and mass production, 30; and
railroads, 29; and Rockefeller, 30

competitiveness, 108, 135
computerization, 132. *See also*
information technology
computer services, 185
conglomerates, 119–120, 121, 183
Congress, 19, 24, 29, 36, 61,
193–194, 197
conservatism, 103; and corporate vs.
political freedom, 3; and economic
planning, 127; and leader-managers,
89; and Reagan, 81, 82, 84
consulting services, 185
consumer demand, 125, 126, 130
consumer rationing, 65
consumers: and Galbraith, 125; and
Great Depression, 43, 46–47; and
postwar prices, 69; and railroads, 29
consumption, 68
Coolidge, Calvin, 72
Cordiner, Ralph, 82, 83
corporate charter: for banks, 24; for
Boston Manufacturing Company,
26; and economic development,
22–23; and English colonies, 3, 23;
for First Bank of the United States,
19; and Lowell, 20; and public
purpose, 20; for Society for
the Establishment of Useful
Manufactures, 19; suspicion of, 24;
and textile industry, 19
corporate raiders, 105
corporate social responsibility (CSR),
203–204, 205, 206
credit collapse, of 2007, 4
credit default swaps, 195
critical management studies, 160–161
culture, 135, 152–155

Datsun, 134
defense spending, 164
deficit, federal, 177
Delaware, 31
demand, 43, 46, 173, 174

Deming, W. Edwards, 132, 133, 134, 181
democracy: and anticorporatism, 2; and Blough, 122; bottom-up, 15; and Carnegie, 37; and civil rights movement, 14; and corporate charters, 26; and corporate economy, 11, 16, 198; dangers to, 11; and Drucker, 95; and education system, 206; fitness for, 17; and freedom, 155; and George W. Bush, 189; Jefferson on, 18; and leader-managers, 89; and management, 1, 2, 3; and Mills, 104, 105; and moral danger of power, 92; and moral leadership, 2, 91–92; and Peters and Waterman, 154; and suspicion of power, 16; and wariness of government, 5
Democratic Party, 61, 72, 74, 174, 175
Dennison, Henry, 46
depression, of 1890s, 29. *See also* Great Depression
deregulation, 138, 165–166. *See also* government regulation
derivative financial instruments, 195
Dickens, Charles, 19
dot coms, 180, 181
Dow Chemical, 124
Downsize This! (film), 186
Drucker, Peter, 96, 98–99, 100, 161; *The Concept of the Corporation*, 98, 99, 104; *The End of Economic Man*, 94–95; *The Practice of Management*, 98
DuPont, Pierre, 95, 96
DuPont Company, 31, 32, 95, 119
Dutch East India Company, 23

eastern Europe, 13
East India Company, 3, 4, 23, 24, 25, 198

East Indies, 23
eBay, 181
economic forecasting, 43
economies of scale, 51, 67
economy, 9; agricultural, 17–18; and anticorporatism, 4; and Boulware, 78; and Carter, 138; and corporate charters for banks, 24; downturns in, 36; and First New Deal, 45; and Galbraith, 127; global, 203, 206; and Great Depression, 39, 40; growth of, 22, 24, 147; and Hamilton, 19; labor-intensive, 27–28; and luck, 17; peacetime, 68; planned, 127; private and public sides of, 125; as privately incorporated, 104; and Reagan, 164; and Republicans vs. Democrats, 72; and Sloan, 67; and World War II, 61
economy, corporate, 3; acceptance of, 63; and democracy, 15, 16, 17, 38, 198; development of, 35; and downturns, 36; and First New Deal, 45; and Galbraith, 127, 128, 135, 164; and Great Depression, 39, 40, 44; prosperity from, 11; and racial justice, 14; and unemployment, 38
education, 11, 13–14, 125, 127, 135, 147, 206
efficiency, 27, 28, 32, 40, 41, 154, 180, 183
efficiency expert, 87
Eichenwald, Kurt, 192
Eisenhower, Dwight D., 107, 117, 127, 145
electrical workers, 108
Elizabeth I, 23
employment: and consumption, 68; and entrepreneurial firms, 174, 175, 186; factory, 12; and Galbraith, 125, 126; and information technology, 186;

in Japan, 134; and manufacturing, 9; in peacetime, 64; postwar, 68, 70; in service jobs, 186; wartime, 65; and women, 12. *See also* unemployment

energy crisis, 137, 138

engineer-managers, 87, 88, 89, 90

England, 22, 23, 24, 61

English colonization, 3

English monarchy, 3

Enron, 142, 151, 160, 190–193

entrepreneurial firms: and big business, 179; and employment, 174, 175, 186; in high tech, 178; and information technology, 180; and Sarbanes-Oxley Act, 194

entrepreneurship: and anticorporatism, 4, 5, 201; and big business, 4, 185, 203; encouragement of, 202–203; and Enron, 190; and information technology, 181, 201; social, 206; and Social Security, 202; and tax cuts, 174

Entrepreneurship Summit, 201

entry, barriers to, 31

environmentalists, 165

Erie Railroad, 29

Erikson, Erik, 158, 159; *Gandhi's Truth*, 156; *Identity: Youth and Crisis*, 156; *Young Man Luther*, 156

European Left, 135

Europeans, 130, 131

European Union, 130

executives, 45, 48–49, 62

Fahrenheit 9/11 (film), 186

fascism, 102, 145

Fastow, Andrew, 191, 193

FBI, 109

federal accounting board, 194

Federal Reserve, 195

Federal Reserve Act (1913), 38

Filene, Edward, 46

financial services, 165, 186

financial statements, 193, 194

financiers, 87, 88, 94, 105

firms: origins of, 41, 139; and voluntary relationships, 140, 142

Fisk, Diamond Jim, 155

Ford, Gerald, 138, 146, 175, 176

Ford, Henry, 118–119

Ford, Henry, II, 118–119, 120, 134–135

Ford Motor Company: and assembly-line, 42; and McNamara, 118; and quality control, 132, 186; and Sloan, 96; tyranny of, 43, 53, 62; and United Auto Workers, 56

foreclosures, 196

foremen, 62, 74

France, 23, 130

freedom, 32, 75, 142; and American Dream, 11, 12; and character, 12; and corporate economy, 16; corporate protection of, 63; corporate vs. political, 3; and democracy, 155; economic, 5; and Franklin Roosevelt, 51; and Galbraith, 125, 127; as goal, 15; and government, 63, 67, 72, 198; Jefferson on, 18; and managers, 73; not to unionize, 73; and order, 17; political and economic, 11; and prosperity, 11, 13; and Reagan, 163, 164; and separation of powers, 1; and Sloan, 67; surrender of economic, 40–41; and Wagner Act, 53; and wealth, 42

free enterprise, 32; and health insurance, 200; and leader-managers, 89; and postwar labor relations, 69; and Sloan, 67

free market: and Bell, 102–103; and Berle, 52, 52; and Coase, 41, 139; corporation as part of, 3;

free market (*continued*)
and efficiency, 27, 28, 40, 41; and Galbraith, 102, 126; and government, 32, 63; and information technology, 169; interference with, 72; and management, 1, 57; and Mills, 103; and monopolies, 31; and Reagan, 168, 169; and Sloan, 53, 67; and Smith, 28, 32; and World War II, 63
free trade, 36
Friedman, Milton, 204; "The Social Responsibility of Business Is to Increase Its Profits," 141

Galbraith, John Kenneth, 103, 105, 107, 130, 131; *The Affluent Society*, 124–125; *American Capitalism*, 102; anticorporatism of, 124–128; and corporate economy, 127, 128, 135, 164; and freedom, 125, 127; and free market, 102, 126; and government, 125, 126, 127; *The New Industrial State*, 125–128, 178; and values, 127
Gardner, John, 147
gasoline, 137
Gates, Bill, 184
gays and lesbians, 12
G. D. Searle, 190
GE Capital, 183
Geneen, Harold, 119
General Electric: and Boulware, 76, 78, 207; and economic forecasting, 43, 46; Employee Relations Department, 80; *Employee Relations Newsletter*, 82–83; and entrepreneurship, 179, 203; and management innovation, 187; and market ideology, 103; and mergers, 31, 32; and strikes, 76, 80, 82, 83, 108; and Welch, 182–183, 185

General Electric Theater (TV program), 80–81
General Instrument, 190
General Motors, 117; and economic forecasting, 43; and Ford, 118; and M-form, 119; as multidivisional, 95, 96; and postwar prices, 68–69; and quality control, 132; and Smith, 186; and strikes, 66, 107; and unions, 63–64, 65, 70; wages at, 110; and Wagner Act, 53–56
George III, 63
Gerstner, Louis, 153–154, 184, 186, 192; *Who Says Elephants Can't Dance?*, 185
Gilder, George, 174, 175; *Wealth and Poverty*, 177–178
Gilead Sciences, 190
Glass-Steagall Act (1933), 45
Global Crossing, 190, 191
Goldberg, Arthur, 107
Goldman Sachs, 196
Goldwater, Barry, 83, 123
Google, 181
Gore, Albert A., Jr., 189
government, 24; and American Dream, 9, 32, 35, 38, 56, 179; and Baruch, 56; deficit spending by, 173; democratic wariness of, 5; effectiveness of, 35; esteem for, 163; as favoring labor unions, 63–64; and Franklin Roosevelt, 51; and freedom, 63, 67, 72, 198; and free market, 32, 63; and Galbraith, 125, 126, 127; and Great Depression, 44; Hazlitt on, 81; and Jefferson, 4; and managers, 93–94; and prosperity, 198; and quality movement, 132–133; and Reagan, 81, 163–164, 168, 198; and Sloan, 65; and social reform, 206; and spending and unemployment, 173, 174; and support for employers vs. workers, 37–38

government deficits, 10
government regulation, 3, 9, 24, 83, 138, 165–166
Graduate, The (film), 122, 123
Great Depression: and anticorporatism, 3; and corporate cooperation, 49; and corporate economy, 40; and economic forecasting, 43; emergence from, 57, 61; and engineer-managers, 88; as failure of corporate economy, 45–46; feared postwar resumption of, 64–65; and government, 32, 38–39, 198, 206; and Great Recession, 196, 197; and leadership of Franklin Roosevelt, 145; and progressive businessmen, 47; and Social Security, 10; and unemployment, 35, 173
Great Recession, 4, 45, 196, 198, 202, 206
Great Society, 123, 135, 137, 147, 175
group identity, 126, 131

Halliburton, 190
Hamilton, Alexander, 17, 18–19, 24, 116
Hammer, Michael, *Reengineering the Corporation*, 181–182, 183
Haney, Lewis, *How You Really Earn Your Living*, 80
Harken Energy, 190
Harriman, Henry, 46
Hawthorne effect, 90
Hawthorne experiment, 145
Hawthorne Works, 90
Hazlitt, Henry, *Economics in One Lesson*, 80, 81
health care reform, 199–201
health insurance, 10, 57; reform of, 199–201
Heller, Walter, 107
high technology, 177–178, 186–187

Hitler, Adolf, 93, 94, 145, 147
Holmes, Oliver Wendell, 169
home equity loans, 196
homelessness, 165
home mortgages, 202
home ownership, 194–195, 201–202
Homestead Mill, 37
Hoover, Herbert, 88
hostile takeovers, 105
Hudson Bay Company, 23
humanism, 147
human relations movement, 90, 91, 98
human rights, 205

Iacocca, Lee, 186
IBM, 130, 153–154, 179, 183–185, 186, 187, 203
identity crisis, 162
identity formation, 156, 157
immigrants, 21, 36, 37
imperialism, 23
income: disparities of, 35; distribution of, 10. *See also* wages
incorporation, 22
individualism, 51, 137
industrial codes, 46–47, 48
industrialism, 36
industrialization, 26
industry, 9, 35, 67, 127, 147
inflation, 147; and American Dream, 71; and Carter, 137–138; cost-push, 107; and Democratic Party, 72; and John F. Kennedy, 106, 108; in 1970s, 110; and Nixon, 137–138; and Office of Price Administration, 63; postwar, 10, 68, 70; and World War II, 56
information systems, 185
information technology, 128, 169, 180–182; and employment, 186; and Enron, 190;

information technology (*continued*) and entrepreneurship, 201; and IBM, 184; and Nike, 187; and Welch, 183
insurance companies, 199–200
integrity, 15, 17
Intel, 178, 179
interchangeable parts, 132
interest, 27, 28; rates, 10, 138, 173
Internet, 132, 180–181
Interstate Commerce Act (1887), 38
interstate commerce clause, 50
Interstate Commerce Commission (ICC), 29
Iran, 137
Iraq, war in, 189
Irish potato blight, 21
Irish workers, 21
ITT, 119

Jackson, Andrew, 24–25
Jacksonians, 25
James, William, 159; *Varieties of Religious Experience*, 158
Japan, 4, 131, 133, 181, 182
Jefferson, Thomas, 4, 17–18, 19, 20, 203
Jeffersonianism, 24, 35–36, 40, 100
Jensen, Michael, 168; "Theory of the Firm," 139–141
job training programs, 202–203
Johnson, Hugh, 47, 48, 49, 50
Johnson, Lyndon, 117, 123, 135, 137, 146, 147
Johnson & Johnson, 153
Jones, Thomas Roy, 62
J. P. Morgan, 192, 195
justice, 16
Justice Department, 109

Kemp, Jack, 174, 176
Kennedy, John F., 124; assassination of, 123; and business tax credit,

176; and McNamara, 117, 120; and U.S. Steel, 106–111, 122, 137
Kennedy, Joseph, 46
Kennedy, Robert, 109
Keynes, John Maynard, 173–174
Kmart, 187
Korean War, 13
Kramer, Mark, 204

labor: and immigration, 36; laws governing, 3; and supply and demand, 173. *See also* workers
labor arbitration, 63
labor market, deregulation of, 166–167
labor movement, 198; crippling of, 75; and Republican Party, 72; and World War II, 61–62
labor unions, 47, 54, 123; and American Dream, 9–10; and Democratic Party, 72; and foremen, 62, 74; and Franklin Roosevelt, 63–64; Galbraith on, 102; government as favoring, 63–64; industrial, 56, 73; industry-wide, 54; and international competition, 167; and Japanese competition, 135; and John F. Kennedy, 106, 109; membership in, 167; and postwar prosperity, 65; and prices, 71; public distrust of, 167; and Reagan, 166; and right-to-work laws, 75; and Second New Deal, 57; as special interests, 168; and Taft-Hartley Act, 74; as tyrannical, 63, 73; and wages, 10, 11; and Wagner Act, 52–54, 72; and World War II, 61–62
Laffer, Arthur, 174, 176–177; Laffer curve, 176*fig.*
laissez-faire, 27, 40, 44, 67, 196
laws: antipoverty, 123; antitrust, 30, 31, 37, 47, 48; anti-union, 72; business regulation, 3; general

incorporation, 26; labor, 3;
right-to-work, 74–75
Lay, Kenneth, 192–193
leader-managers, 88, 89–90
leaders: estrangement of, 157; and
followers' values, 148–149; and
managers, 156–159; as twice-born,
158, 159, 162
leadership, 17, 88–92; and Barnard,
91; crisis of American, 147;
development of, 4, 158–160; and
Franklin Roosevelt, 145; and
George W. Bush, 189; and
management, 94; moral, 2, 16, 146,
189, 192, 193, 194; and moral
humility vs. power, 160; and moral
influence, 91–92; morally
pretentious, 191; personality school
of, 157; and power, 145; and
Reagan, 164; revolutionary,
156–157, 159; transformational,
149, 190; and values, 2, 146,
147–148, 149, 150, 189
leadership counselors, 161
legal unity, 30, 31
Lehman Brothers, 196
leisure society, 102
Levant Company, 23
liberalism, classical, 102
liberals: and anticorporatism of 1960s,
123; and deregulation, 166; and
Gilder, 178; and government, 163;
and Great Depression, 47; and
Japan, 131; and leader-managers,
88; and Lilienthal, 89; and middle
class, 179; and Mills, 103; and need
for corporate sector, 128–129, 135,
136; philosophy of, 67; in post-
Vietnam era, 121; and Reagan, 164,
177; and Schlesinger, 131; and
taxes, 175, 177
Liberty League, 53
Lilienthal, David, 89

limited liability, 26
Lincoln, Abraham, 36
Ling, Jimmy, 119
Little, Royal, 119
Litton Industries, 119, 120, 183
London, 22
Lowell, Francis Cabot, 20, 26
Lowell, Massachusetts, 20–21
LTV, 119
Lukens Steel, 109, 110

Machiavelli, Niccolo, *The Prince*, 169
machinery, capital-intensive, 139, 181
Madison, James, 1, 5
management: boundaryless, 183;
bureaucracy of, 157; and Coase, 41,
139; cost of, 139, 180, 181; and
democracy, 1, 2, 3; and Drucker,
94; and free market, 1, 41, 57, 139;
Japanese, 135; and Japanese
competition, 135; and John F.
Kennedy, 106; and leadership, 4,
94; and MacNamara, 121; as more
efficient than free market, 41–42;
by objectives, 98; and postwar
higher education, 11; power as
concentrated with, 51–52; power
of, 67; and price controls, 68–69;
and prosperity, 5; rationalistic, 152;
scientific, 87, 89, 98; and Second
New Deal, 57; and values, 146,
148–151; and Wagner Act, 53, 54;
and Walmart, 187
managerial presidency, 88
managerial rationality, 146
managerial society, 94, 100
managers, 40; and agency problem,
23; arrogance of, 3, 105, 117;
and business slumps, 43; and control
vs. ownership, 52, 103, 104, 125,
139; and corporate vs. political
freedom, 3; and foremen, 62; and
freedom, 73; and Gerstner, 185;

managers (*continued*)
in government, 93–94; and Great
Depression, 44; and information
technology, 181; and leadership,
87–92, 100, 116, 156–159; and
line-and-staff organization,
115–117, 116*fig.*; as moral, 93,
94–95; and power, 5, 148;
production, 87; and profit, 136; and
public good, 104; and Riesman,
100–101; scientific, 87; and
shareholders, 62, 93, 104, 125, 136,
139, 141, 142; and status anxiety,
103; stock options for, 141; and
Taft-Hartley Act, 74; and values,
147; and voluntary relationships,
140; and Welch, 183
managing: by culture, 152–155; by
rules, 150; by values, 149–150, 152,
155, 157, 193
manufacturing, 115; in Asia, 203,
204; automation of, 101; and
employment, 9; Hamilton on,
18–19; and information technology,
182; and Jefferson, 17, 18, 20; and
managerial efficiency, 42; and
transaction costs, 41; and World
War II, 61
market, 40, 57
marketing, 126, 130, 131, 185, 187
Marshall Fields, 41–42
Marx, Karl, 19
Massachusetts Bay Company, 3, 23
mass distribution, 29–30
mass marketing, 126
mass production, 9, 29–30
mass transportation, 26
Mayo, Elton, 90–91, 92, 93, 100,
101, 145, 155
McDonald, David, 107
McDonald's, 186
McNamara, Robert, 117–118, 120,
141, 152

Means, Gardiner, *The Modern
Corporation and Private Property*,
51–52, 62, 103, 104, 125, 135, 139,
142, 163
Meckling, William, "Theory of the
Firm," 139–141, 168
Medicare, 10, 164–165
Medicare Act (1965), 123
medicine, 38, 199
mercantilism, 27
merchants, 27, 41
merger movement, of 1890s, 181
mergers, 30, 31
mergers and acquisitions, 119–120
Merriam, Charles, 88
M-form, 95–98 97*fig.*, 116, 117, 118,
119
Microsoft, 184
middle class, 10; and founders, 17;
and higher education, 11;
hollowing out of, 179, 197, 198;
and Japanese competition, 135; and
Mills, 103
middlemen, 41, 42
Midwest, 75
military, 61, 127
Mills, C. Wright, 123; *The Power
Elite*, 104–105; *White Collar*,
103–104
Model T Ford, 42
Moline Implement Company, 48
money market accounts, 196
money supply, 19, 24, 38, 173
monopoly, 25; and East India
Company, 3; and mergers, 31;
and price gouging, 29; and
Rockefeller, 30
Monsanto, 124
Montgomery, Donald, 65
Moore, Michael, 186
moral authority, 16, 56, 63, 66, 71,
72, 73, 75
moral courage, 91, 145

moral failure, 40, 50
moral hazard, 195–196
moral influence, 91
morality, 1; in business, 17; and democracy, 16; and leadership, 2
moral leadership. *See under* leadership
Morgan, J. P., 29
mortgage-backed securities, 195, 196
mortgages, 202; interest, 165, 202
Mott, Charles Stewart, 56
Murphy, Frank, 55, 56
Muscovy Company, 23
Mussolini, Benito, 93, 145

Napoleonic Wars, 20
National Association of Manufacturers, 53, 73, 75
National Cordage Association, 31
national defense, 126, 127, 132
National Industrial Recovery Act (NIRA) (1933), 47–48, 49, 52, 53
National Labor Relations Act. *See* Wagner Act
National Labor Relations Board (NLRB), 52–53, 74, 83, 166–167
National Recovery Administration (NRA), 48–49, 50
National Review, 82, 103
National War Labor Board, 63–64
Nazis, 13, 63, 93, 94, 95
NBC, 183
New Deal, 61, 67, 76, 167, 175; and anticorporatism, 52; and Boulware, 77, 78; Burnham on, 93; First, 3, 44, 45, 49, 56; and leader-managers, 88; and Reagan, 81, 163, 164–165; Second, 3, 51, 53, 56–57, 166, 169; and syndicalism, 93; undoing of, 3
New Jersey, 30, 31
New Jersey Holding Company Act (1889), 30

New Left movement, 124
New York Central Railroad, 29
Nike, 187, 203
Nissan, 134
Nixon, Richard, 137–138, 146
North, 36
Northeast, 75

Obama, Barack, 199, 200
Obama administration, 201
Occupational Health and Safety Administration (OSHA), 165–166
O'Connor, Michael, *Managing by Values,* 149–150, 153
Office of Price Administration, 63
oil industry, 30–31, 138
O'Neill, Paul, 193, 194
operating authority, 115–116
operating costs, 28
opportunity, 35
organization man, 125
outsourcing, 203
owners, 105, 140
ownership society, 194, 202

Packard, Vance, *The Status Seekers,* 100
Paterson, New Jersey, 19
Paulson, Henry, 196
Peek, George, 46
Pennsylvania Railroad, 29
Pentagon Papers, 146
Perkins, Frances, 55
personal computer business, 184
Peters, Tom, *In Search of Excellence,* 152–155
Pinkerton detectives, 37
poor people, 35, 135, 165, 175, 179, 197
Porter, Michael, 204
power loom, 20
price fixing, 28, 29, 31

prices: communications about, 41, 42;
    competition in, 29; cooperative
    codes for, 49; and inflation, 138;
    and John F. Kennedy, 106, 107,
    108, 109, 110; and labor unions, 71;
    and Office of Price Administration,
    63; postwar, 68–69, 70, 71; and
    railroads, 29; and Reuther, 107;
    and Rockefeller, 30; and World
    War II, 64
price stickiness, 173
process integration, 182, 183
Proctor and Gamble, 153
product innovation, 134
productivity, 5, 18, 131
Professional Air Traffic Controllers
    Organization (PATCO), 167–168
profit: and agency costs, 140; and
    centralized organization, 95; and
    Charles Francis Adams, 25; and
    Galbraith, 125–126; and General
    Electric, 79; individual, 22; and
    inflation, 138; and John F.
    Kennedy, 110; and limited liability,
    26; and managers, 136; as
    motivation, 125–126; private, 24,
    26; and Reagan, 165; and
    shareholders, 25; and shareholder
    value, 139; and World War II, 64
Progressive Era, 3
property rights, 52, 53, 62, 68
prosperity, 32, 71, 147; and character,
    12; and consumption, 68; corporate,
    155; and corporate economy, 35;
    and equal employment, 14; and
    First New Deal, 3; and freedom,
    11; and Galbraith, 127; as goal, 15;
    and government, 198; and
    manufacturing, 9; as mark of divine
    favor, 13; and overbearing
    managerial power, 5; and top-down
    corporate power, 15; and wages, 10
public good, 22, 26, 104

public purpose, 20, 23, 25
public utilities, 89
public utility companies, 38
public works, 47
Pullman strike (1894), 37
purchasing power, 10, 48, 49, 52, 65
Pure Food and Drug Act (1906), 38

quality circles, 134
quality control, 131–135
quality movement, 181
Qwest, 190, 191

race, 12
racial integration, 13
racial justice, 13–14
railroad industry, 25–26, 27–29, 35,
    38, 41, 42, 115
RCA, 183
Reagan, Ronald, 80–81, 84, 103; and
    Bennis, 162; and Boulware, 81, 83;
    and conservative movement, 81,
    82, 84; and economy, 138, 174;
    "Encroaching Control," 81–82; and
    Goldwater, 83; and government,
    163–169, 198; and message
    discipline, 82; "Our Eroding
    Freedoms," 82
recession, 38, 138
reengineering, 181–182
regulation. *See* government regulation
Reich, Robert, 204
relations, voluntary, 140, 142
rental market, 202
Republican National Committee, 83
Republican Party, 61, 174–175; and
    conservative movement, 83;
    and labor movement, 72; and
    Lilienthal, 89; and Reagan, 81;
    and Taft-Hartley Act, 74
Reuther, Walter, 65, 68, 69, 70, 71,
    106–107
Rice, Condoleezza, 190

Riesman, David, 103, 105, 123; *The Lonely Crowd*, 100–102
Rockefeller, John D., 30–32
Roger and Me (film), 186
Roosevelt, Franklin, 44, 61, 67; and anticorporatism, 52; and Committee for Industrial Organization, 54; Commonwealth Club speech, 51; election of, 38–39, 44; and First New Deal, 3, 45, 49; and Keynes, 173–174; and labor unions, 63–64; and leadership, 88, 93, 145; managerial presidency of, 88; and National Industrial Recovery Act, 47–48; and National Recovery Administration, 50; and Office of Price Administration, 63; and Reagan, 164, 169; and Second New Deal, 3, 51; and Sloan, 55
Roosevelt, Theodore, 31–32, 38
rope manufacturers, 31
Route 128, 177
Rumsfeld, Donald, 176, 190
Russia, 93, 94

Sarbanes-Oxley Act (2002), 194
savings and loan industry, 165
Say, Jean-Baptiste, 173; Say's Law, 173, 174, 199
Schlesinger, Arthur, Jr., 131, 135
science, 125, 135, 147
Scott, Howard, 88
Screen Actors Guild, 81, 82
Searle, G. D., 190
second industrial revolution, 35, 180
Securities and Exchange Commission (SEC), 45
Securities Exchange Act (1934), 45
securities markets, 45
self-employment, 40, 202–203
self-knowledge, 150
Senge, Peter, 155
September 11, 2001, attacks, 189, 190

Servan-Schreiber, Jean-Jacques, *Le défi americain*, 130–131
shareholders, 22, 24, 26, 45; and agency problem, 23; and managers, 51–52, 62, 93, 104, 125, 136, 139, 141, 142; and price controls, 68
shareholder value, 139, 141, 142
Sherman Anti-Trust Act (1890), 30, 31, 37, 47
Shewhart, Walter, 131–132, 133
Sicko (film), 186
Silicon Valley, 177
Simon, Herbert, 146
Skilling, Jeffrey, 191
Slater, Samuel, 19
slave plantations, 87
Sloan, Alfred, 184, 186; and Drucker, 96, 98–99, 161; and Ford, 118; and multidivisional organization, 96; and postwar economy, 65–66, 67; and postwar prices, 68–69, 70, 71, 107; and unionization, 53–56; and World War II, 63–64
Smith, Adam, 27–28, 32, 67; *The Wealth of Nations*, 23–24
Smith, Roger, 186
socialism, 52, 57, 62, 63, 127, 178, 200
socialized medicine, 199
social justice, 12, 123, 131, 135, 147, 206
social mobility, 11
social protest, 137
social purpose, 22
social reform, 137, 206
social responsibility, 141, 203–204, 205, 206
Social Security, 10, 164–165, 194, 202
Society for the Establishment of Useful Manufactures, 19
South, 75
southeast Asia, 13

Soviet Union, 13, 63
space exploration, 132
Spain, 23
special purpose entities (SPEs), 191, 193
stagflation, 174
Stalin, Joseph, 93, 147
standard of living, 52, 106
Standard Oil of New Jersey, 30, 31, 32
Standard Oil Trust, 30
state government, 24, 25, 26, 27, 75
statistical control, 118
statistical quality control, 132, 133
steel industry, 106–111
Steiger, William, 176
Stimson, Henry, 64
Stockman, David, 165
stock market, 11; and crash of 1929, 39
stock options, 192, 193, 194
strikebreakers, 37
strikes, 37–38, 63; and General Electric, 76, 80, 82, 83, 108; and General Motors, 66, 107; of 1946, 167; postwar, 69–70, 72, 73, 76; Pullman, 37; sit-down, 54–56; and Sloan, 54; and Taft-Hartley Act, 74; and Wagner Act, 53; and World War II, 61
subprime loans, 195
supply and demand, 40, 139, 173
supply side: and corporate growth, 175; and economic theory, 174; and entrepreneurship, 178, 185, 186; and middle class, 179; and tax policy, 176, 177
Supreme Court, 32, 50, 52, 53
Swope, Gerard, 46
synergy, 119, 183
systems analysis, 118

Taft, Robert A., 73–74
Taft-Hartley Act (1947), 74, 77, 83

tariffs, 36
taxes, 24; and Boulware, 78; on capital gains, 175–176, 177; on corporations, 168; and Democratic Party, 175; and entrepreneurship, 174; and mortgage interest, 202; postwar, 10; and Reagan, 164, 177; and self-employment income, 202; and supply side, 176, 177; and World War II, 64
technocrats, 88, 126
technology: and barriers to entry, 31; capital-intensive, 180; Hamilton on, 18–19; information, 36; and managerial efficiency, 41–42
technostructure, 125, 126, 127, 130, 131, 135, 178
telegraph, 29, 41, 42
Tennessee Valley Authority, 88–89
Tet Offensive, 120
textile industry, 19, 20–21, 27
Textron, 119
Thornton, Tex, 118, 119, 120, 183
3M, 153
Toyota, 134
trade: conspiracies in restraint of, 30, 31–32; restraint of, 47
traffic pools, 28–29
transaction costs, 41, 42, 139, 180, 181
transportation, 24, 41
Treasury Department, 195, 196
trucking industry, 138, 165
Truman, Harry S., 68, 72, 73, 74, 89
trusts, 30, 32
turnpikes, 25
Tyco, 190, 191

unemployment, 147; from business slumps, 43; and Carter, 138; and government spending, 173, 174; and Great Depression, 39; and

Great Recession, 196–197; rate of, 202. *See also* employment

unfair trading practices, 45

Union Carbide, 130

union shops, 74

United Auto Workers, 65, 71; and General Motors, 54, 55, 56; and John F. Kennedy, 106–107; and postwar price controls, 68–69; and wages and prices, 68–70, 110; and Wagner Act, 72

United Electrical Workers, 80

United Mine Workers, 38

United Rubber Workers, 72

United Steelworkers, 72, 107–108

urban proletariat, 18

U.S. Chamber of Commerce, 46, 111

U.S. Steel, 56, 106, 107, 108, 109, 110, 111, 122

values, 142; and culture, 153; democratic, 2, 16, 67, 89, 100; and Galbraith, 127; as goals vs. instruments of profit, 17; of leaders and followers, 148–149; and leadership, 2, 147–148; and leadership development, 4; and management, 148–151; and managers, 147; managing by, 149–150, 152, 155, 157, 193; motivation from, 126; and power, 148, 150, 151, 157; and Reagan, 164; and Simon, 146; as tools vs. goals, 148–149

Vietnam War: and faith in government, 137, 163; and managerial arrogance, 3; and managerial incompetence, 140; and McNamara, 120–121; and moral arrogance, 92; and moral leadership, 146, 147; and rationalistic management, 152, 156; and students, 124, 128; Viet Cong, 120

Virginia Company, 3, 23

Virginia Supreme Court, 24

Volcker, Paul, 138

wage earners, 17, 18, 36

wage-price-profit spiral, 107

wage-price spiral, 71, 107

wages, 9; cooperative codes for, 48, 49; and factory workers, 10; and founders, 17; and General Electric, 79; industry-wide standards in, 46–47; in Japan, 134; and Japanese competition, 135; and John F. Kennedy, 106, 107, 108, 110; middle-class, 38; minimum, 38; postwar, 68, 69, 70, 71; and Reuther, 107; and scientific management, 87; and Sloan, 54; and supply and demand, 173; and unions, 10, 11; and Wagner Act, 52, 53; and Walmart, 187; and World War II, 56

Wagner, Robert, 52

Wagner Act (1935), 52–54, 72–73, 74, 75, 166, 198, 207

Walmart, 179, 186–187, 203

Wanniski, Jude, 174, 176; *The Way the World Works*, 177

War Department, 132

War Industries Board, 46, 47, 48

War of 1812, 20

war on terror, 189

Washington, George, 116

Watergate, 92, 137, 146, 163

Waterman, Robert, *In Search of Excellence*, 152–155

wealth: creation of, 2, 4; and freedom, 42

Welch, Jack, 182–183, 185, 192

West, 75

whites, 12

Whyte, William, *The Organization Man*, 100

Will, George, 164

William the Conqueror, 22

Wilson, Charles ("Electric Charlie"), 77

Wilson, Charles ("Engine Charlie"), 69, 77, 117

Wilson, Edmund, 39

Wilson, Sloan, *The Man in the Gray Flannel Suit,* 100

women, 12, 19, 20–21

work: and corporate economy, 35; and meaning, 101–102

workers: assembly-line, 42–43; and Drucker, 94; educated, 206; factory, 10; as fearing responsibility, 91; and foremen, 62; geographic mobility of, 36–37; and Great Depression, 43, 46; and Great Recession, 196; and IBM, 185; and immigration, 36; and information technology, 181; and international competition, 167; Japanese, 134, 135; and managers, 40–41; manipulation of, 149; in mass production, 54; as morally inferior, 56; and

outsourcing, 203; productivity of, 90; and quality movement, 135; and Reagan, 165–168; safety of, 203–205; sympathetic attention to, 90; therapy for, 101; and voluntary relationships, 140; and Walmart, 187. *See also* labor

working class, 20; and higher education, 11; postwar, 10; rising incomes of, 36

working conditions: cooperative codes for, 48; industry-wide standards in, 46–47; and Wagner Act, 53

WorldCom, 190, 191

World War I, 46

World War II, 10, 35, 52, 56, 132, 141; end of, 68; and McNamara, 118; and racial justice, 13

Wuerthner, J. J., 83

yeoman farmer, 36, 203

Yosemite trust, 191

Zaleznik, Abraham, 156–159, 160

About the Author

James Hoopes is Murata Professor of Ethics in Business at Babson College. The author of numerous books and articles on American intellectual and business history, Professor Hoopes lives in Newton, Massachusetts.